# Cooperatives, the State, and Corporate Power in African Export Agriculture



Agriculture is still a major contributor to Africa's GDP, as well as the region's biggest source of employment, and its largest food producer. However, agricultural productivity remains low and buyer-driven global value chains offer few opportunities for small producers to upgrade into higher value-added activities. In recent years, the revival of Africa's cooperatives has been celebrated by governments and international donors as a pathway towards inclusive agricultural development, and this book explores the strengths, but also the issues, which surround these cooperatives.

The book scrutinizes the neoliberal ideal of economic prosperity arising through the operation of liberalized labor markets by illuminating the discriminatory nature of Uganda's informal labor relations. It points to the role of cooperatives as a potential instrument of progressive change in African export agriculture, where large numbers of small producers depend on casual wage work in addition to farming. In contrast to the portrayal, advanced by some governments and rarely questioned by donors, of an unproblematic co-existence of small producers' collective action and big capital interests, the author calls for a re-politicized debate on the Social and Solidarity Economy. As part of this, she highlights the adverse political and economic conditions faced by African cooperatives, including intense international competition in agricultural processing, inadequate access to infrastructure and services, and at times, antagonistic state-cooperative relations.

Supported by wide-ranging interdisciplinary evidence, including new ethnographic, survey, and interview data, this book shows how cooperatives may be co-opted by both the state and corporations in a discourse that ignores structural inequalities in value chains and emphasizes poverty reduction over economic and political empowerment. It provides a critique of New Institutional Economics as a framework for understanding how institutions shape redistribution and develops a political economy approach to explore the conditions for structural change in African export agriculture.

**Karin Wedig** is the Chief Economist for Africa at the German Society for International Cooperation (GIZ). She holds a PhD from the School of Oriental and African Studies (SOAS), University of London and degrees from the London School of Economics and Political Sciences (LSE) and the University of Cambridge. She has worked as an Assistant Professor of International Political Economy at the Josef Korbel School of International Studies, University of Denver; consulted social and economic reform programs in Sub-Sahara Africa and Southeast Asia and spent more than three years living and working in Uganda as an advisor and researcher.

## New Political Economy

General Editor: **Richard McIntyre**, *University of Rhode Island, USA*

**14. Unions and Class Transformation**
The Case of the Broadway Musicians
*Catherine P. Mulder*

**15. Worker Identity, Agency and Economic Development**
Women's Empowerment in the Indian Informal Economy
*Elizabeth Hill*

**16. Seeking Sustainability**
On the prospect of an ecological liberalism
*G.J. Paton*

**17. Class, Gender, and the American Family Farm in the 20th Century**
*Elizabeth Ramey*

**18. Late Neoclassical Economics**
The restoration of theoretical humanism in contemporary economic theory
*Yahya M. Madra*

**19. From Economics to Political Economy**
The problems, promises and solutions of pluralist economics
*Tim B. Thornton*

**20. Cooperatives, the State, and Corporate Power in African Export Agriculture**
The Case of Uganda's Coffee Sector
*Karin Wedig*

For more information about this series, please visit: www.routledge.com/New-Political-Economy/book-series/TFSE00174

# Cooperatives, the State, and Corporate Power in African Export Agriculture

## The Case of Uganda's Coffee Sector

**Karin Wedig**

Routledge
Taylor & Francis Group
LONDON AND NEW YORK

First published 2019
by Routledge
2 Park Square, Milton Park, Abingdon, Oxon OX14 4RN

and by Routledge
52 Vanderbilt Avenue, New York, NY 10017

First issued in paperback 2020

*Routledge is an imprint of the Taylor & Francis Group, an informa business*



*British Library Cataloguing-in-Publication Data*
A catalogue record for this book is available from the British Library

*Library of Congress Cataloging-in-Publication Data*
A catalog record has been requested for this book

ISBN 13: 978-0-367-66054-3 (pbk)
ISBN 13: 978-1-138-07051-6 (hbk)

Typeset in Bembo
by Taylor & Francis Books

To the coffee farmers and coffee workers on the slopes of Mt. Elgon

# Contents

# Illustrations

## Figures



## Tables

# Acknowledgements

I am indebted to the many people in Uganda who generously shared their time and knowledge with me and invited me into their homes and work places on the farms and in the coffee processing factories, field washing stations, workshops, and firms where research for this book was conducted. This book would have not been possible without their hospitality and readiness to allow me to accompany them during work routines, meetings, and labor action. Special thanks go to the Ugandan research team, including Samuel Bbosa, Ruth Sanuba, Martin Masuba, Lydia Khanakwa, Irene Atim, Kia Jacquelyn, and Kityo Saul, who made a huge contribution to data collection. I especially thank Robert Wedig, Christian Reichel, Christopher Cramer, and Aaron Moritz for their comments, invaluable support, and continued interest in discussing the issues covered in this book.

# 1 Africa's cooperative revival

Investing in African agriculture is essential to improve the economic prospects of rural people and revitalize visions of 'Africa rising'[1]. The UN (2018) estimates that by mid-century, slightly more than half of Africa's population will live in cities, but the increase in the urban population will be concentrated in a few mega-cities while in most countries, the proportion of rural dwellers will remain high. Furthermore, urbanization in sub-Saharan Africa ('Africa', henceforth) has not been accompanied by industrialization, but by a significant expansion of the service sector, with an increase of informal and low-skilled jobs at low levels of productivity (Rodrik 2016). As a result, the slow but continuous reduction in agriculture's contribution to Africa's total GDP has not led to an economic transformation through higher productivity and rapid growth driven by the greater demand elasticities for manufactured products in global markets (*ibid.*). Despite the rise in service sector jobs, agriculture is still the biggest employer for African people: based on conservative estimates[2], the sector currently provides 57% of total employment (ILO 2017). In this setting, agriculture remains central to inclusive and sustained economic development.

The importance of smallholder production for achieving inclusive rural development, (and possibly alleviating pressures on growing cities with high poverty rates), has by now been widely recognized (*see*, for example, AGRA 2017). Throughout Africa, small-scale production dominates the agricultural sector: in most countries, well over 80 percent of farms are small, with two or less hectares of land, and family farms (up to 10 ha) produce an estimated 70–80 percent of food consumed in the region (AGRA 2017; Rapsomanikis 2015; Graeub et al. 2016). Furthermore, Africa's major export commodities, including tea, coffee, and cotton, are predominantly grown in small-scale production systems (Rapsomanikis 2015). In addition to the contributions to food self-sufficiency (and often food security) as well as export earnings, small farmers provide ecosystem services that are essential to a climate-smart agriculture: inter-cropping and traditional methods of pest control help to maintain biodiversity, regulate soil and water quality, and sequestrate carbon. Finally, small-scale agriculture

*Figure 1.1* Coffee worker in Mbale, Uganda

remains a major source of income for the majority of rural people in Africa, either as farmers or as on-farm wage workers, or both.

Despite these contributions to food production, incomes, and ecological sustainability, the dominance of small-scale production in African agriculture is often perceived as highly problematic due to its low levels of land, labor, and total agricultural productivity (Benin 2016). Against the background of widespread rural poverty, recurring food insecurity in more than a dozen countries, and an increasing dependence on food imports (Adesina 2017), debates by policy makers, donors, and scholars about agricultural development are increasingly centered around the question of what types of farming systems can drive the fastest increases in yields. While output growth is important, a narrow focus on yields disregards important socioeconomic and social-ecological dimensions of agricultural transformation. For example, support to an extensive expansion of mono-cropping ignores that large numbers of small producers will be pushed out of the sector, with only a limited number of low-skilled jobs created (*see*, for example, Collier and Dercon 2009). The socioeconomic effects of the increased concentration of land ownership, which is associated with large-scale farming systems, as well as the likely intensification of socioecological pressures through increased freshwater use and the reduction in biodiversity, receive limited attention in such scenarios (*see*, for example, Hazell and Rahman 2014). So far, agroecological farming systems and other approaches that center on small farmers' and agricultural wage workers' economic and socioecological needs (*see*, for example, Jayne et al. 2014; Peters 2013) continue to play a marginal role for the design of agricultural policy in Africa.

The prevalence given to yield increases has shifted the focus away from questions about the distribution of benefits from agricultural growth and the political-economic structures that shape these distributional patterns. Agro-industrial development as a driver of development has historical precedents in other world regions and can trigger economic transformation processes that benefit large numbers of people, if it integrates local businesses into value addition and creates significant numbers of local jobs, including higher-skilled employment. However, the dependence on such a development model without a redistribution agenda also creates serious challenges, which are aggravated by the lack of enforcement of social and environmental standards. Wage work in Africa's agricultural processing plants tends to be insecure, unsafe, temporary, and low-paid, with no opportunities for further training. Workers are often physically 'spent' long before reaching old age, and because wages are too low to allow for savings, workers drop back into poverty after a number of years in the industry.

The evidence from Uganda's coffee sector, as discussed in this book, further indicates that many workers in agricultural processing (usually factory jobs) depend on additional on-farm work and/or farming. Due to the low social status of agricultural wage work, these *farmers-cum-wage workers* tend to identify as farmers if they own land, even if their plots are too small to provide a sufficient income base. The identification as farmers and the fragmentation of work lives between the farm and the factory reduces the likelihood of workers to organize. Given the weak presence of trade unions in rural Africa, this is unlikely to change in the near future. In order to function as a development model, agro-industrial processing therefore needs to be accompanied by broader social and political changes to provide a basis for structural transformation processes that can sustainably improve the living standards of large numbers of people.

There is a remarkable lack of internationally-financed programs that focus on improving the economic prospects of agricultural wage workers in Africa. But, a growing number of agricultural development programs that work with value chain concepts cautiously address unequal distributional patterns in African export agriculture. However, the political-economic conditions that reproduce inequalities in buyer-driven value chains are rarely scrutinized in such programs. Most initiatives focus on strengthening small producers' capacities for production and (usually primary-stage) processing. They also often establish public-private dialogues to improve small farmers' operating environment, but pay limited attention to farmers' capacities for political advocacy to defend their interests vis-à-vis stronger economic actors and the state.

Furthermore, such programs rarely call for the creation of state institutions that specifically support functional upgrading efforts by small farmers and local agro-businesses. Instead, there seems to be an expectation that the attraction of investments by large international buyers and processors will provide vertical linkages that enable local producers to acquire the abilities necessary to advance into higher value-added activities. Thus, such programs aim to facilitate local upgrading by offering capacity-building and limited financial services for small farmers and agro-businesses, but generally fail to address the institutional and structural barriers to inclusive development that are posed by a high concentration of corporate power in Africa's agricultural export markets. Small producers' access to financial services remains highly inadequate and private sector investment into the agricultural production infrastructure has not filled the gap that was created by the massive reduction in public spending during neoliberal reforms. Some large buyers act as supply chain service providers by offering credit or saving devices through contract farming schemes, but until today, there have been no indications that such services are sufficient to allow small producers to move into higher value-added activities in large numbers.

In recent years, support to small producer organizations or cooperatives (the two terms will be used interchangeably in this book) has become a widespread instrument used by international donors and African governments to promote rural development. Taking the revival of the African cooperative movement since the early 2000s as a starting point, this book examines the conditions under which cooperatives can contribute to greater economic equality within a heterogenous rural population and within the wider society and economy. Based on an in-depth case study of the Ugandan coffee sector as well as supporting data from Uganda's agricultural and non-agricultural labor markets, this book examines economic organization among small farmers as a lens for understanding the potential for democratic change processes that can interrupt the reproduction of inequality and promote a redistribution of resources from large corporate actors to small producers and farmers-cum-wageworkers. The book offers a people-centered analysis of economic and political change that hopes to trigger a new debate about structural inequality in African export agriculture and the potential role of collective action for transforming existing power asymmetries in buyer-driven agricultural value chains.

## Conceptualizing cooperatives

The rapid and far-reaching neoliberal restructuring of Africa's agricultural markets in the 1980s and early 1990s led to the collapse or near-collapse of most cooperative activities. The structural adjustment programs, which were designed by the international financial institutions and largely supported by international donors at the time, downplayed the importance of non-price factors to stimulate agricultural production and promoted the complete dismantling of inefficient and often corrupt government-run marketing boards and state-subsidized co-operative banks. The refusal to support a reform of Africa's poorly-performing monopolist cooperatives and state institutions that regulated agricultural production, processing, and marketing was legitimized by the neoliberal credo that price controls represented the greatest constraint to agricultural export growth. The underlying assumption was that giving small farmers access to the full international market price for their crops would suffice to overcome non-price production and marketing constraints. According to this view, the expected output growth would allow farmers to protect themselves against price fluctuations. This conveniently overlooked the fact that in the two decades prior to structural adjustment, export crops had performed strongest, followed by other cash crops and trailed by falling per capita production levels for food crops (Jorre et al. 1992).

Less than a decade after the end of monopolistic cooperatives and state-run marketing boards, small producers throughout the region had established new processing and marketing organizations and, in some cases, formerly monopolistic organizations had re-entered business (Develtere et al. 2008; Pollet 2009; Wedig & Wiegratz 2017). This revival of agricultural cooperatives has received widespread support by African governments and international donors, who celebrate small producer organizations as a pathway to inclusive rural development. The underlying logic of this support seems to be that a massive improvement of rural living standards is possible without reversing the substantial inequalities between farmers-cum-wage-workers on the one hand, and transnational corporate buyers and processors of agricultural commodities on the other. Thus, Africa's revitalized cooperative movement has frequently been portrayed as an apolitical instrument for creating a triple-win situation: small producers increase their incomes, international buyers access greater volumes of higher-quality produce, and the country's export revenues increase. In this narrative, neither the presence of dismal working conditions in agricultural processing plants – where international processors employ many of the farmers that supplied the crops being processed – nor the vast power asymmetries between cooperatives and international buyers receives systematic attention.

The narrow conceptualization of cooperatives as an apolitical and uncontroversial instrument for inclusive economic development is advanced by a variety of actors, including transnational corporations, international donors, governments, and some scholars, and it is frequently couched in the terminology of the Social and Solidarity Economy (SSE), which is, in this narrative, used to describe a depoliticized pathway to achieving rural prosperity. This book argues that the dominant discourse of inclusive rural development that is thus created promotes a constricted and incomplete view of cooperatives that emphasizes social entrepreneurship over the collective action and social movement aspects of economic organization. The vision of the SSE that is thus created substitutes a broader understanding of social and economic solidarity and cooperation with a much more limited understanding of organization as an instrument of limited economic, but not political, empowerment.

To be sure, the scholarly SSE literature has called for the creation of an alternative, non-capitalist society (Dacheux and Goujon 2011) and has described the SSE as a 'tool for organizing hope' and a practice that guides concrete action towards the development of new institutions (Dinerstein 2013, p. 5). However, the current debate on the SSE – and on cooperatives as an essential part of it – which is led by policy makers and international donors and taken up by some transnational corporations (TNCs), seems to legitimize the reversal of this pursuit of a radically different society and economy into a protection of the status quo. Thus, instead of addressing the far-reaching redistribution of resources that the development of a transformative SSE would entail, many cooperative development programs focus on improved access to markets, appropriate technologies, training, and financial services, but pay little attention to building the political lobbying capacities and linkages between cooperatives that would allow small producers to better defend their interests vis-à-vis stronger economic actors and the state. The ensuing narrative of inclusive rural development through agricultural cooperatives is over-simplified, because it ignores the structural inequalities that cooperatives face in Africa's buyer-driven value chains.

The new and previously unavailable evidence from Uganda's coffee cooperatives, which is presented in this book, illuminates the extent to which disadvantaged groups can, on the basis of collective action, shape contested relations with more powerful economic actors and the state to their advantage. Despite the political and economic constraints on the growth of permanent organizational structures among farmers in Uganda, significant numbers of cooperatives exist and some of these organizations are not only economically viable, but also contribute to greater equality at the local level. Furthermore, they contribute to the development of institutional structures that allow farmers to represent their interests vis-à-vis the state. By addressing structural inequalities in agricultural value chains through political lobbying, some cooperatives position themselves in conflict to big capital interests in Uganda's agricultural export markets. At the same time, international buyers and processors of agricultural commodities are able to co-opt cooperative ideas through support programs that aim to alleviate rather than change the structural inequalities in Africa's export agricultural markets and the global agricultural value chains that they are part of. These programs de-emphasize the collective action and social movement component of cooperatives and utilize a depoliticized vision of the SSE that obscures the contested political and economic conditions for agricultural cooperatives in Africa today.

## Outline of chapters

Chapter Two sets up the ensuing discussion of cooperatives by raising and then dismissing the neoliberal ideal of economic prosperity arising through the operation of liberalized labor markets. It provides substantial ethnographic data, which I collected among farmers-cum-wageworkers in Eastern Uganda, as well as data from a labor market survey which I conducted separately in rural and semi-urban labor markets throughout Uganda. The ethnographic fieldwork included several months of participatory observation among female agro-processing factory workers who kindly 'adopted' me into their ranks temporarily. The data shows how employers' strategies in Uganda's labor markets utilize culturally legitimized forms of inequality and exploitation to segment the labor market and limit labor organization. The chapter then raises the question: are there alternative working-class organizations that may strengthen the ability of the farmers-cum-wageworkers to defend their interests, either through spill-over effects to labor unions, or through other means?

Chapter Three introduces the SSE concept and contributes to a re-politicized debate on the SSE by analyzing the political conditions that can foster the growth of cooperatives with a redistribution agenda. The chapter provides a literature review on the SSE, before tracing the historical development of agricultural cooperatives and examining their mixed performance in post-independence Africa. It concludes that the widespread failures of monopolistic cooperatives to engender structural change were to a significant extent caused by unfavorable political and economic conditions as well as organizational characteristics that were created as part of large-scale, top-down collectivization efforts. An analysis of cooperative policies in present-day Uganda indicates that state engagement with cooperatives is often top-down, which can undermine the autonomy and democracy principles of the cooperative movement and potentially weaken the position of cooperatives in buyer-driven value chains with high concentrations of corporate power.

Chapter Four provides a theoretical framework for the analysis of cooperatives as an instrument for achieving institutional change that is supportive of a redistribution agenda. The discussion assesses the scope and limitations of different strands of New Institutional Economics (NIE) – which has conceptually supported the work of international donors in the fields of good governance and inclusive economic development – for understanding the development of historically specific institutions. The chapter introduces a political economy approach to explain how relations of power and inequality shape the internal institutional structures of cooperatives as well as the wider institutional structures in which they operate. It concludes by discussing cooperatives as a form of collective action that is potentially more effective as a driver of social and political change processes than the less formalized community-based organizations that are sometimes promoted by international donors as key instruments for inclusive development.

Chapter Five assesses the ability of cooperatives in Uganda's coffee sector to contribute to improved welfare levels of small producers. The socioeconomic effects of cooperatives vary depending on internal organizational characteristics and external political and economic determinants. The chapter focuses on internal factors by exploring the development of democratic organizational structures in different types of cooperatives, their effects on improved economic equality among farmers, and their success in generating output and productivity growth and improved output quality. Particular attention is paid to the role of women in cooperatives, because women remain underrepresented as members, leaders, and landowners, albeit contributing a large share of agricultural labor, production, and marketing know-how.

Chapter Six examines the relations of TNCs with small coffee farmers. Evidence from ethnographic fieldwork in some of the coffee processing plants run by the TNCs that dominate Uganda's coffee value chain, and the analysis of a large donor-funded support program for small coffee producers, which was designed and managed by the foundation of one of the world's largest green coffee traders, illuminate how TNCs mimic cooperative structures and evoke notions of collaboration with producers to secure their supply of crops. In their relations with small farmers, TNCs use a language that is reminiscent of that used by cooperatives and they offer limited services that focus on increased production and improved produce quality. However, they do not provide the organizational functions of a cooperative union.

The chapter concludes that despite the support that some TNCs provide to small farmers, the relations are at best pragmatically progressive. In some cases, TNCs' programs seem to damage existing cooperatives with a social movement character by creating parallel cooperative structures that are essentially non-threatening to corporate power and have no political influence. The book's conclusion draws together the arguments made in the different chapters and reflects on the basic hypothesis of the book: that the potential of cooperatives to generate structural changes towards a redistribution of resources is only partially strengthened by the state and is actively challenged by the dominance of corporate power in agricultural export markets.

## Methodological notes

This section explains the choice of sector and country case studies, outlines the research design, provides an overview of the quantitative and qualitative research methods, and describes the sampling strategies of the coffee sector and labor market surveys that were conducted for this book.

Coffee is one of Africa's most important non-extractive industry export products. In Ethiopia and Burundi, it is the biggest source of export revenues (17% and 27% of total exports), in Rwanda (8.9%) and Kenya (4.3%), it ranks 4th, and in Rwanda and Kenya coffee respectively ranks 2$^{nd}$ and 3$^{rd}$ among the non-extractive export products.[3] As a source of income, coffee is of overwhelming importance in the region's 25 coffee-growing countries. An estimated 53% of the rural population in these countries grow coffee, and 64% of the total population are considered rural (ICO 2015, p. 5). Lastly, out of the approximately 20 million people worldwide who depend on coffee as a source of income, whether as farmers or wage workers or both, more than 10 million are found in Africa (*ibid.*).

The choice of Uganda as a case study follows from the country's history of economically powerful agricultural cooperatives, with a broad member base, but also from its early and far-reaching implementation of neoliberal reforms in the agricultural sector, which caused an almost complete collapse of the cooperative movement. This was followed by a remarkable revival in the early 2000s, especially in the country's coffee sector, which remains the country's most important source of export revenues.[4] While coffee cooperatives across Africa frequently sell their parchment (primary-processed coffee beans) to subsidiaries of foreign buyers, cooperatives in Uganda aim at not only cutting out local traders, but also foreign buyers. The strong drive by Ugandan cooperatives to export secondary-processed coffee (green beans) themselves provides an excellent example of economic organization among small producers that explicitly aims at a redistribution of resources within the value chain. Lastly, relations between the state and cooperatives in Uganda reflect the divergence between official rhetoric of cooperatives as an instrument for inclusive development and a more ambiguous reality in which the government has attacked cooperatives and actively worked to limit their political influence (Wedig & Wiegratz 2017).

The research design was based on between-method triangulation to conduct an in-depth qualitative exploration of potentially conflicting aspects of economic organization, while also explaining larger trends of cooperative and rural labor market development on the basis of quantitative data. The combination of qualitative and quantitative research methods allowed a multi-dimensional perspective on complex social relations of power and inequality (Berg et al. 2007, p. 5). The multiple data-gathering techniques supported the validation of findings based on the repeated cross-checking of preliminary results (Jick 1983; Leedy 2001; Webb et al. 1981).

As suggested by Fielding and Fielding (1986, p. 31), effective triangulation should go beyond the simple combination of data types to include the development of meaningful linkages. Thus, the surveys provided aggregate data on welfare levels, the status quo of cooperatives and labor organization, and the functioning of highly informal labor markets. Subsequently, semi-structured interviews and focus group discussions, as well as participant observation among small producers and casual wage-workers, allowed an exploration of causal linkages between economic organization, access to resources, and relations of inequality at the local level. Some of these linkages had been indicated by the results of the coffee sector survey, but conflicting perspectives on sensitive issues, such as aspects of gender- and class-based inequalities, or patterns of elite capture of resources, could not be examined through questionnaire-based interviews. By using several methods of data collection, the body, or bodies, of knowledge created were expanded to illuminate different aspect of the research topic and realize the "essence of triangulation" (Francfort-Nachmias & Nachmias 2000, p. 206).

The choice of between-method triangulation also entails shortcomings, because the endeavor to combine different methods imposes limitations on individual data sets given the logistical, time, and financial constraints. However, the choice of multiple methods also allowed for the creation of synergy effects. Thus, conducting face-to-face surveys provided preliminary information about the villages, coffee processing factories, and field processing stations throughout the fieldwork area. Because of the paucity of secondary data on coffee production, cooperative activities, and labor relations, this information was useful for the identification of locations for subsequent qualitative work.

The analysis of processes of socioeconomic change and reproduction requires both an examination of distributional patterns on the basis of quantitative methods, and an interpretation of discursive processes to illuminate the reasons for human actions that shape distributional patterns. However, the reductionist tendency of positivist, deductive approaches to the analysis of social phenomena largely fails to reflect the multidimensional reality of human agency (Carey 1989; Denzin & Lincoln 2008; Mills 1959). The value of quantitative analysis depends on its application to a research context in which core research questions can be answered on the basis of predetermined analytical categories and quantifiable units of measurement (Danermark et al. 2002). Surveys, for example, can only be used to investigate social phenomena on which sufficient background knowledge is available to specify in advance all questions necessary to uncover the object of study (Merriam 2001). Also, the respondents must have a clear and comparable understanding of the concepts under investigation in order to make the use of structured interviews meaningful (Berg et al. 2007). For the socially sensitive and less-clearly defined issues of inequality and socioeconomic change, these conditions hardly apply. Therefore, this book rejects a reduction of qualitative analysis to an ancillary instrument of confirmation of quantitative research. Instead, the survey-based examination of cooperatives and labor markets generated gender-specific data with a high comparative value, and qualitative methods were subsequently employed to explore the causal relations that were pointed to by the survey results.

To ensure the relevance of the findings from Uganda beyond a given historically and geographically specific context, the generation of comparable data is essential. Proponents of orthodox economics commonly claim that quantitative methods provide the rigor, objectivity, and precision to ensure generality (Debreu 1991; Krugman 1998). However, objectivity may be compromised by the role of historically specific concepts that influence the selection of analytical categories for quantitative data generation. As has been repeatedly pointed out by feminist economists, a widespread male bias in statistics caused, amongst other things, by the low educational levels of female survey respondents as well as gender inequalities within organizations that generate statistical data, is likely to skew results, possibly masking existing structural inequalities (*see*, for example, Siegmann & Blin 2006; Greenwood 1999; Esim 1997; Akram-Lodhi 2003). During the research for this book, quantitative data proved insufficient to illuminate women's contribution of labor in the coffee sector and their level of participation in decision-making processes within cooperatives. However, semi-structured interviews and discussions of single-sex focus groups revealed significant gender inequalities in the division and remuneration of labor as well as the organizational structures in the coffee sector.

Against this background, this study insists on a twofold methodological approach aimed at exploring the dynamics of socioeconomic change and reproduction not only on the basis of predetermined analytical categories, but also, as much as possible, through the various actors' points of view. By relying on quantitative and qualitative analysis, universally applicable categories of investigation provided a guiding framework for the creation of comparable and generalizable data which were subsequently expanded and cross-checked by processes of interpretative understanding. As McGovern (2011, p. 346) observes:

> This attempt has the positivist objective of fact checking both one's facts and one's categories of analysis, so as to be sure that there is some semblance of fit between the motives, incentives, and rationales attributed to actors and those they may actually be using.

## Data collection

The initial data collection in Uganda took place over the course of 12 months, between 2009 and 2010. In 2012 and 2016 respectively, follow-up interviews were conducted with small producers, wage workers, government representatives, cooperative staff, coffee buyers, and processors, as well as employers' and workers' representatives. The first phase of data collection consisted of semi-structured interviews with government officials at the national and district level and with management and operational staff of domestic and international coffee buyers, cooperatives, and selected NGOs and donors. Secondary data, including government documents and Ugandan National Bureau of Statistics (UBOS) sources were also analyzed during this phase. On this basis, Eastern Uganda emerged as a suitable research area, because the country's largest coffee cooperative, the National Union of Coffee Agribusinesses and Farm Enterprises (NUCAFE), and the umbrella organization Uganda Cooperative Alliance (UCA) are particularly active in this region. Furthermore, Gumutindo, which is one of Uganda's two economically viable, medium-sized coffee cooperatives that directly export their members' coffee to other world regions, is located in Eastern Uganda.[5]

The main objectives of the semi-structured interviews (*see* Table 1.2, all interviews except those with coffee producers) were as follows:

- Understanding the recent development of cooperatives in Uganda's coffee sector;
- Exploring the nature of relations between cooperatives and the state and between the state and labor unions;

- Exploring the nature of relations between international coffee buyers/ processors and small farmers;
- Exploring the nature of donor-funded rural development programs that support agricultural cooperatives.

The second phase of data collection consisted of a face-to-face survey among small producers and rural wage workers in Eastern Uganda's coffee sector. This survey guided the analysis based on predetermined, universally applicable categories, covering four thematic areas of investigation. The first addressed economic well-being, and included data on educational attainment, access to credits, the ability to save, and the estimated size of landholdings. This area of investigation produced data based on the respondent's entire household (including economically dependent or contributing members who live elsewhere), while the remaining investigation areas focused on respondents' personal experiences. The second area covered work and employment, focusing on the nature of income generation strategies and the occurrence of occupational pluralism, while the third addressed the nature and socioeconomic effects of formal economic organization, especially in cooperatives. The fourth investigation area focused on access to skills training and its effects on work and employment.

The main objectives of the coffee sector survey (*see* Survey I, Table 1.1) were as follows:

- Exploring the status quo of formal economic organization among small producers and agricultural wage workers in Eastern Uganda's coffee sector;
- Assessing the conditions for access to formal economic organization, especially cooperatives;
- Gathering information on the socioeconomic effects of formal economic organization, with a special focus on access to skills training;
- Exploring perceptions on the political advocacy capacities of cooperatives and on state-cooperative relations.

The third phase of data collection concentrated on the generation of qualitative data based on semi-structured interviews and focus group discussions with small producers in Eastern Uganda's coffee sector (*see* Table 1.2). The method of focus group discussions was particularly well suited to some of the cultural characteristics of the fieldwork setting. Thus, the cooperative structures are embedded in a predominantly oral tradition, in which group discussions are crucial for the organizational decision-making processes. The focus group discussions were therefore treated, as much as possible, as open-ended conversations to reflect dominant local forms of communication. Because focus group discussions can mask social hierarchies, as disadvantaged individuals may feel inhibited to speak their mind, 12 out of 16 group discussions with cooperative members were single-gender, to reduce potential barriers to an open discussion. Furthermore, two single-gender groups of non-organized small producers were formed to crosscheck for differences in the viewpoints expressed by cooperative members.

Both the interviews and the discussions examined socially and politically sensitive issues, most notably the nature and extent of inequalities in access to resources and power within cooperatives, the challenges encountered by cooperative members and leaders, and the socioeconomic effects of cooperative membership. Focus group interviews, which utilize group interaction as an explicit data-gathering method, were particularly useful to learn about more or less conscious social and cultural processes. Thus, the focus group discussions with female cooperative members produced controversial discussions on access to resources within cooperatives, which exposed widespread gender-based inequalities. The effects of class-based divisions within cooperatives were discussed by male and female cooperative members in both single-gender and mixed-gender focus group discussions, while the group discussions with non-organized producers focused on inequalities in access to cooperatives and the socioeconomic effects of cooperative membership.

The main objectives of semi-structured interviews and focus group discussions with small farmers were:

- Assessing the conditions of access to and the socioeconomic effects of cooperative membership;
- Exploring relations of power and inequality within cooperatives and assessing the development of these relations since the liberalization of the coffee sector;
- Exploring challenges faced by cooperatives in their broader social and political context;
- Exploring relations between small farmers (organized and non-organized) and transnational coffee buyers and processors.

The fourth phase of data collection consisted of participant observation among small coffee farmers as well as agricultural and non-agricultural workers at their working, training, and meeting places, mainly in the form of unstructured interviews (*see* Table 1.2). The method provided insights into first, the social and economic inequalities among and between cooperative members and non-organized producers and second, the nature of informal labor relations in agricultural and non-agricultural labor markets. After establishing friendly relations with the management of Eastern Uganda's largest coffee processing factories, warehouses, and processing field stations, which were run by several transnational coffee buyers and processors, the author was able to move around freely on factory shop floors and in outdoor processing areas. This enabled the generation of in-depth knowledge about the nature of wage labor relations in the coffee sector. The unstructured interviews with non-agricultural workers helped to prepare the non-agricultural labor market survey in the hotel/gastronomy and construction sectors (*see* Survey II, Table 1.1). Conducting these interviews before the start of this survey helped to minimize the attention that this part of the research received by employers. This was necessary to allow the author to talk with casual workers about sensitive issues, such as working conditions.

The fifth phase of data collection consisted of a face-to-face, questionnaire-based survey in non-agricultural labor markets, conducted in Uganda's fast-growing construction and hotel/gastronomy sectors (*see* Survey II, Table 1.1). The sectors were selected due to the large and increasing numbers of low-skilled and skilled jobs they offered in semi-urban and urban areas. This survey was country-wide, covering Eastern, Northern, and Central Uganda, and it provided complementary data about employment quality, labor market regulation, and the quantity and quality of training in informal labor markets. Because organization in trade unions was virtually absent, the survey focused on working conditions and the provision of in-service training. The analysis of working conditions examined contractual agreements, employment status, and payment irregularities, while the provision of in-service training was examined for the determinants of access and quality aspects. Employers' engagement in training was focused on in terms of existing incentives or barriers to invest in training in a highly informal labor market. Similar to the coffee sector survey, the utilization of variables that are widely used in labor market and household surveys ensured that this survey provided data suitable for sub-national and cross-national comparisons. A small number of semi-structured interviews with employers' and workers' representatives complemented the survey results.

The main objectives of the non-agricultural labor market survey (*see* Survey II, Table 1.1) were as follows:

- Gathering comparative information on working conditions for low- and higher-skilled labor in non-agricultural labor markets;
- Examining the quantity and quality of on-the-job training for non-agricultural workers;
- Exploring the nature of labor market regulation in highly informal, non-agricultural labor markets.

*Table 1.1* Overview of quantitative data collected in Uganda

| *Survey I:*<br>Questionnaire-based coffee sector survey<br>*Geographical coverage:*<br>Eastern Uganda's Arabica growing area | *Survey II:*<br>Questionnaire-based survey in the construction and hotel sectors<br>*Geographical coverage:* Country-wide |
|---|---|
| 117 female small producers | 47 employers in the construction sector |
| 136 male small producers | 13 skilled workers in the construction sector |
| 41 female wage workers | 54 employers in the hotel sector |
| 36 male wage workers | 17 skilled workers in the construction sector |
| **Total no. of interviews: 330** | **Total no. of interviews: 131** |

*Table 1.2* Overview of qualitative data collected in Uganda

| *Semi-structured interviews* | *Focus group discussions* | *Unstructured interviews* |
|---|---|---|
| Coffee buyers: Bancafe; Neumann Kaffee Gruppe, Olam; Kawacom; Kyagalanyi; Zigoti; Lakeland; Great Lakes. (11 interviews, incl. 3 follow-ups) | Female members from mixed-gender primary coops (5 groups) | Female small coffee producers (8 interviews, incl. 3 follow-ups) |
| National government: Ministry of Gender, Labor & Social Development; Ministry of Trade, Tourism and Industry; MES; Ministry of Agriculture, Animal Husbandry & Fisheries; Uganda Coffee Development Authority/ UCDA. (8 interviews, incl. 3 follow-ups) | Female members from women's primary coops (2 groups) | Male small coffee producers (8 interviews, incl. 3 follow-ups) |
| Local government: National Agricultural Advisory Services/NAADS; UCDA; Departments of Agricultural Development. (8 interviews, incl. 3 follow-ups) | Male members from mixed-gender primary coops (5 groups) | Female coffee wage workers (8 interviews, incl. 3 follow-ups) |
| Farmers' organizations: Uganda National Farmers Federation/UNFFE; Uganda Cooperative Alliance/UCA; NUCAFE; BCU; Gumutindo; UOCG. (18 interviews, incl. 6 follow-ups) | Male & female members from mixed-gender primary coops (4 groups) | Male coffee wage workers (8 interviews, incl. 3 follow-ups) |
| NGOs and donors: Literary & Adult Basic Education/LABE; LitNet; GIZ; FarmAfrica; EU, WB; Danish Embassy. (9 interviews, incl. 3 follow-ups) | Male & female non-organized small producers. (2 groups) | Hotel/gastronomy workers (4 female, 1 male). (5 interviews, incl. 2 follow-ups) |
| Employers' and workers' organizations: Federation of Uganda Employers/FUE; UG Hotel Owners Association/UHOA; UG Manufacturers Association/UMA; UG National Chamber of Commerce & Industry/UNCCI; National Organization of Trade Unions/ NOTU. (8 interviews, incl. 3 follow-ups) | | Construction workers (5 interviews, incl. 2 follow-ups) |
| Small coffee producers (13 interviews, incl. 5 follow-ups) | | |
| Total: 81 | Total: 18 | Total: 42 |

During the sixth and last phase of data collection, additional semi-structured interviews were conducted, as follow-ups, with government representatives, coffee buyers and processors, cooperatives, international donors and NGOs, employers' and workers' organizations, coffee farmers, and agricultural and non-agricultural workers. The interviews helped to update information and reflect on the research results from the original data collection phases.

### *Sampling strategies*

Due to inadequate census data, the establishment of a complete sample frame of small producers and wage workers in the coffee sector was not possible. Instead of random sampling, the sample was therefore established through snowballing. Thus, sampling was purposive and guided by theory rather than merely statistically random. This allowed an explicit focus on members of active cooperatives, because these cases are most likely to confirm, extend, or contradict theoretical assumptions about the impact of economic organization on the capacities of small producers to defend their interests. Such a deliberate selection of theoretically relevant cases was considered useful because it is more likely to explain why and in what context particular socioeconomic effects occur, rather than testing whether certain effects exist (Deaton 2009). As Deaton (2009, p. 125) argues, following Cartwright (2007, "evidence from randomized controlled trials has no special priority", because randomized evaluations of a specific social structure may provide information on its average effect, but fall short of explaining the underlying reasons to allow a prediction of potentially generalizable mechanisms.

During purposive sampling, the available statistics and the documentation of cooperatives and labor organizations supported the selection of the geographical area of research. Eastern Uganda indicated particularly high membership and activity levels (UCA 2008; NUCAFE 2009). Furthermore, the region provided theoretically meaningful comparative cases of small producers who sell unprocessed coffee cherries to international buyers, as well as relatively large numbers of rural wage workers. Thus, Kyagalanyi, one of Uganda's largest coffee trader and a branch of one of the worldwide largest transnational Corporations (TNCs) that trades coffee, buys significant quantities from Eastern Uganda (UCDA, accessed Dec 05, 2017).[6] At the same time, Kyagalanyi conducts extensive processing in the region, with Uganda's largest functional coffee processing factory outside the capital city Kampala and an increasing number of primary processing field stations.[7] Regarding trade unions, the national statistics show extremely low membership numbers for the agricultural sector throughout the country, and union membership was therefore not a relevant selection indicator.

For the selection of locations within Eastern Uganda, a list of villages with *active* primary cooperatives of UCA, NUCAFE, and Gumutindo was established on the basis of available household data (in particular UBOS 2010a and UCA 2008), interviews with secondary-level staff of cooperatives and staff of the National Agricultural Advisory Services (NAADS), and visits to villages and workplaces. Information on producers, including estimated land holdings and expected output levels were provided by Gumutindo, UCA, and NUCAFE, although complete lists were not available. The identification of a particularly active community-based cooperative was achieved through the conduction of interviews with NAADS fieldworkers and visits to various villages. The list of selected villages and processing stations was subsequently compared with the available data on estimated poverty levels and living standards in mid-Eastern Uganda (UBOS 2010a). Poverty data at district level is restricted, but some information was available that could be used to adjust the selection of villages to ensure that both better-off and particularly poor areas were represented.

Furthermore, the three largest employers of coffee wage-workers in the region (Kyagalanyi, Gumutindo, and BCU, which was operating parts of its processing factory, while the other part of it was rented out to Kyagalanyi), were selected as research sites. UCA and NUCAFE do not employ agricultural wage-workers, because they function as service providers to small producers, rather than processing coffee directly.

The sample was stratified according to two main sub-groups: small producers (main income source), wage-workers (main income source). The producers' sub-group was made up of members of four different case study cooperatives, which were either large, nation-wide operating, medium-sized and regionally specific, or small and community-based. Two control groups of small producers who were not formally organized were included in the sample. The total number of interviews conducted was 333, out of which roughly one quarter consisted of interviews with wage-workers and three quarters with small producers. This number was large enough to ensure that several interviews could be conducted with each sub-group of the sample at each location. Because formal organization among agricultural wage-workers is largely absent, the sample included a larger proportion of small producers.

The gender composition of the sample was managed on the spot at each location during the survey. Due to their responsibilities for domestic, caretaker, and agricultural work, women throughout the fieldwork area presumably shoulder a heavier work burden than men (UBOS 2007b). As a result, potential female respondents have less time for lengthy interviews. Furthermore, men still tend to be over-represented in cooperatives throughout sub-Saharan Africa (Pollet 2009). Therefore, achieving a perfectly equal distribution of gender was challenging, but could nearly be achieved.

The lack of a complete sample frame imposed limitations regarding the statistical significance of the quantitative data that was generated. However, the generation of new data, although not strictly statistically representative of the

*Table 1.3* Gender distribution (%) of coffee sector survey samples

| | *Producers and wage-workers* | *Wage-workers* | *All producers* | *Cooperative members* | *Non-organized producers* |
|---|---|---|---|---|---|
| Female | 47.9 | 53.2 | 46.2 | 44.2 | 57.9 |
| Male | 52.1 | 46.8 | 53.8 | 55.8 | 42.1 |

entire population of small producers and agricultural wage-workers in Eastern Uganda, filled significant gaps within the existing national-level data. The national figures provide no information on the extent of dependence on casual wage-work in rural households. Also, there is a complete lack of statistical data on casual wage-work, because the national statistics divide the working population into formal employees, farmers, and micro entrepreneurs (UBOS 2010a). Thus, casual wage-workers are represented as self-employed, which means the present survey provides previously unavailable statistical data on rural income generation strategies.

Overall, the coffee sector sample is to some extent statistically representative, at least with regard to *active* cooperative members, because the number of small producers who actually sell their coffee through cooperatives is considerably smaller than the existing documentation indicates. Thus, the management staff of all of the large cooperatives in the region confirmed that a significant proportion of registered primary cooperatives are dormant. In addition, even the members of active primary cooperatives are likely to sell some of their coffee to local middlemen or directly to exporting companies. Based on the rough estimations of cooperative field-workers in the region, the total number of active cooperative members, who sell most or all of their coffee through a cooperative, may be around 30,000, which would mean that the sample of over 300 interviews represented roughly 1% of the relevant population.

The sample of the non-agricultural labor market survey included a country-wide selection of small, medium-sized, and large companies in both sectors. Due to the lack of up-to-date business registries, a complete survey frame for random sampling could not be established. Thus, companies were selected through snowballing on the basis of personal communication with employers, with a particular focus on companies with a strong interest or actual engagement in the provision of training. The sample was stratified to approximately represent the ratio of small, medium-sized, and large companies in each sector. Due to the small number of large and medium-sized companies in northern Uganda, only small companies were selected in this region.

While the large majority of respondents of the non-agricultural labor market survey were employers, major aspects of the respondents' statements were cross-checked with workers on the basis of a small number of interviews as well as informal conversations.[8] The construction and hotel sectors were chosen, because both sectors are growing particularly fast with regard to employment figures, while the level of informality remains high for both unskilled and skilled workers (UBOS 2007b, UBOS unpublished data, accessed in March 2009). The survey was carried out in Eastern, Northern, and Central[9] Uganda. The North is a region with particularly high poverty estimates, while the locations chosen in Eastern Uganda present a more average picture, and Central Uganda is particularly prosperous (UBOS 2010a).

The selection of respondents for semi-structured interviews was made by following a purposive sampling strategy that enabled a stronger focus on the perspectives of disadvantaged groups than the survey. Thus, women from particularly poor or single-headed households, widows and male farmers who consider themselves as 'too poor to organize' were prioritized. For the focus group discussions, separate groups of members and leaders were formed to avoid large differences in social hierarchies among group members. Also, single-sex groups were formed to ensure that gender-relevant topics were discussed as openly as possible.

### *Data evaluation*

For the evaluation of both surveys, a statistical software was used to analyze all data sets. The analysis of the qualitative data largely followed a deviant-case strategy. Summaries of the interviews and discussions results were arranged in a number of tabular displays, following priorities and assumptions made during the data design and collection phase. This allowed methodological rigor without unnecessarily reducing interpretation options of the data contents (Berg et al. 2007). The consistent set of thematic priorities for data entry included the challenges encountered regarding access to cooperatives, various aspects of the socioeconomic effects of cooperative membership, the quantity, quality, and socioeconomic effects of training for small producers and wage workers, employment quality, and selected further aspects of labor relations. By examining all entries of the tabular displays, examples that supported or contradicted the previously made assumptions were identified. In addition to tabular displays, short answer sheets were prepared to provide more elaborate summaries of respondents' statements. These answer sheets were equally scrutinized for relevant patterns of supporting or contradicting cases. Furthermore, the perceptions of social phenomena articulated by the different respondents were cross-checked with each other to create a preliminary synthesis, which was in turn compared with survey results.

To evaluate the results of participant observation, no comparative tabular displays were prepared because observations could not be made for all thematic priorities. Instead, recurring observations were identified by producing short summaries of the fieldwork notes and identifying categories of observations, including poverty levels, access to resources, patterns of labor division within the household, the farm and the primary cooperative, and the quality of working conditions in coffee processing field stations and factories.

### *Researcher positionality and ethical issues*

As in any research that is based on the interpretation of social relations through personal interaction, the researcher and her assistants might unwittingly influence respondents' answers. Thus, the selection of the research teams was guided by the requirements of relevant research experience as well as in-depth knowledge about local social structures and cultural concepts to support the building of the research relationship with each community. Furthermore, the research teams' intimate knowledge of fieldwork areas helped with the development of appropriate strategies to negotiate access to the communities with different gatekeepers. Acquiring the consent of respondents was a critical ethical issue for this study. As in other research settings, significant differences in social status between the research team and the respondents may have contributed to or created feelings of obligation to participate. For this reason, the time spent in explaining the voluntary nature of participation to possible respondents was taken very seriously.

The choice of methods to conduct research on people necessarily affects how they will be viewed by producing specific bodies of knowledge about them (Bodgan & Taylor 1975). The qualitative research methods applied in this study allowed for an exploration of multi-dimensional perspectives on social and economic relations. This not only broadened the analytical framework from which answers to the research questions were extracted, but it also ensured a more differentiated representation of the respondents and their life worlds. To ensure confidentiality with regard to individual respondents, the exploration of socially and politically sensitive issues was conducted in as secure an environment as possible. With regard to small producers and wage-workers, all respondents' names were removed from the data records before presenting them. Any of the respondents from NGOs, aid agencies, government institutions, and coffee buying companies whose names were not changed had given their explicit consent.

## Notes

1 The 'Africa rising' narrative was engendered by strong economic growth between 2000 and 2014, but looks less convincing today, due to declining commodity prices and continuously low levels of FDI flows to the region.
2 This figure may be even higher, given that agricultural work tends to be underreported due to the definition of some dependent economic activities as self-employment or unpaid family work in national labor force surveys.
3 Tanzania: $10^{th}$ biggest export product at 2.6%; ($9^{th}$ biggest non-extractive product); Cameroon: $8^{th}$ at 1.4% ($6^{th}$ biggest non-extractive industry product); DRC: 0.3% ($2^{nd}$ biggest non-extractive industry product); Guinea: 1% ($7^{th}$ biggest non-extractive industry product).
4 Coffee made up 19% of total exports in 2015 (OEC, accessed in 2017) http://atlas.media.mit.edu/en/visualize/tree_map/hs92/export/uga/all/show/2015/
5 The other one being 'Good African Coffee', which operates in Western Uganda.
6 Kyagalanyi is the Ugandan branch of the Volcafe Group, the coffee division of ED&F MAN, one of the largest agricultural commodity buyers worldwide.
7 Figures on the scope of processing activities were provided by Kyagalanyi operational managers.
8 Efforts to create secure surroundings for employees to speak about sensitive issues significantly reduced the possible number of interviews. Sensitive issues were

further discussed informally outside the workplace, to minimize possible distress for workers.

9 The term 'central' refers to the Central and Southern regions of Uganda (UBOS 2010a).

## References

ADESINA, A. 2017, 'Why is Africa importing $35bn in food annually? – AfDB boss asks', Africanews, 21 April 2017. Available from <www.africanews.com> [25 April 2017].

AGRA 2017, *Africa Agriculture Status Report: The Business of Smallholder Agriculture in Sub-Saharan Africa*, Issue 5, Alliance for a Green Revolution in Africa (AGRA), Nairobi, Kenya.

AKRAM-LODHI, A. H. 2003. How should feminist economists approach and use data? Reflections on gender statistics and the epistemology of feminist data analysis. IAFFE 2003 Annual Conference, Bridgetown, Barbados.

BENIN, S. 2016, *Agricultural productivity in Africa: Trends, patterns, and determinants*, IFPRI, p. 386.

BERG, B. L., LUNE, H. & LUNE, H. 2007, *Qualitative research methods for the social sciences (6th ed.)*, Pearson Education Inc., Boston, MA.

BODGAN, R. & TAYLOR, S. J. 1975, *Introduction to Qualitative Research Methods*, Wiley, New York.

CAREY, J. W. 1989, *Communication as culture: essays on media and society*, Unwin Hyman, Boston.

COLLIER, P. & DERCON, S. 2009, 'African agriculture in 50 years: smallholders in a rapidly changing world', Proceedings of a technical meeting of experts, FAO, Rome.

DACHEUX, E. & D.GOUJON 2011, 'The Solidarity Economy: An Alternative Development Strategy?' *International Social Sciences Journal*, 62, UNESCO, 205–215.

DANERMARK, B., EKSTROM, M., JAKOBSEN, L. & KARLSSON, J. C. 2002, *Explaining Society: Critical Realism in the Social Sciences*, Routledge, London.

DEATON, A. 2009, 'Instruments of Development: Randomisation in the Tropics, and the Search of the Elusive Keys to Economic Development', Keynes Lecture in Economics, Read at the Academy 9 October 2008, British Academy, 2009.

DEBREU, G. 1991, 'The Mathematization of Economic Theory', *American Economic Review*, 81, 1–7.

DENZIN, N. K. & LINCOLN, Y. S. (eds.) 2008, *The landscape of qualitative research*, SAGE, Thousand Oaks, CA.

DEVELTERE, P., POLLET, I. & WANYAMA, F. 2008, *Cooperating out of poverty: The renaissance of the African cooperative movement*, Geneva, ILO.

DINERSTEIN, A. C.2013, 'The Hidden Side of SSE: Social Movements and the Appropriation and 'Translation' of SSE Policy (in Latin America)', Potential and Limits of Social and Solidarity Economy, Geneva, Switzerland.

ESIM, S. 1997, 'Can Feminist Methodology Reduce Power Hierarchies in Research Settings?', *Feminist Economics*, 3, 137–139.

FIELDING, N. G. & FIELDING, J. L. 1986, *Linking Data: the articulation of qualitative and quantitative methods in social research*, SAGE, Newbury Park, CA.

FRANCFORT-NACHMIAS, C. & NACHMIAS, D. 2000, *Research Methods in Social Science*, W.H. Freeman, New York.

GRAEUB, B., CHAPPELL, J.WITTMAN, H., LEDERMANN, S., KERR, R.B. & GEMMILL-HERREN, B. 2016, 'The State of Family Farms in the World', *World Development*, 87, 1–15.

GREENWOOD, A. M. 1999, 'Gender issues in labour statistics', *International Labour Review*, 138, 273–286.

HAZELL, P. and RAHMAN, A. (eds.) 2014, *New Directions for Smallholder Agriculture*, Oxford University Press.

ILO 2017, ILOSTAT database, International Labour Organization, Geneva, Switzerland, Available from: <www.ilo.org>. [23 November 2017].

JAYNE, T.S., CHAMBERLIN, S. & Headey, D.D. 2014, 'Land pressures, the evolution of farming systems and development strategies in Africa: a synthesis', *Food Policy*, 48, 1–17.

JICK, T. D. 1983, Mixing Qualitative and Quantitative Methods: Triangulation in Action. In MAANEN, J. V. (ed.) *Qualitative Methodology*, SAGE, Beverly Hills, CA.

JORRE, St. J., G.A.CORNIA, VAN DER HOEVEN, R. 1992, *Africa's recovery in the 1990s: from stagnation and adjustment to human development. Summary*, Innocenti Publications, UNICEF.

KRUGMAN, P. 1998, 'Two Cheers for Formalism', *The Economic Journal*, 108, 1829–1836.

LEEDY, P. D. 2001, *Practical Research: Planning and Design*, Prentice Hall, Upper Saddle River, NJ.

MCGOVERN, M. 2011, 'Review: Popular Development Economics—An Anthropologist among the Mandarins' *Perspectives on Politics*, 9, 345–355.

MERRIAM, S. B. 2001, *Qualitative Research and Case Study Applications in Education*, Jossey-Bass, San Francisco.

MILLS, C. W. 1959, *The Sociological Imagination*, Oxford University Press, New York.

NUCAFE 2009, 'Farmers' Lists Eastern Uganda, National Union of Coffee Agribusinesses and Farm Enterprises', Unpublished document.

PETERS, P. 2013, 'Land appropriation, surplus people, and a battle over visions of agrarian futures in Africa', *Journal of Peasant Studies*, 40, 537–562.

POLLET, I. 2009, 'Cooperatives in Africa: The age of reconstruction - synthesis of a survey in nine African countries', Series on the status of cooperative development in Africa. Cooperative Facility for Africa, ILO, Geneva.

RAPSOMANIKIS, G. 2015, 'The economic lives of smallholder farmers', Food and Agriculture Organization of the United Nations (FAO), Rome.

RODRIK, D. 2016, 'An African Growth Miracle', *Journal of African Economics*, 1–18.

SIEGMAN, K. A. & BLIN, M. 2006, *The Best of Two Worlds: Between-Method Triangulation in Feminist Economics*, School of Oriental and African Studies, University of London, London.

UBOS 2010a, *Uganda National Household Survey 2009/10 Socio-economic module*, Uganda National Bureau of Statistics, Kampala, Republic of Uganda.

UCA 2008, *Household Survey Eastern Uganda*, Unpublished Document, UCA, Uganda Cooperative Alliance Eastern Regional Office.

UCDA 2017, 'Annual and Monthly Reports, 1995–2017', Uganda Coffee Development Authority, Kampala, Uganda, Available from: <www.ugandacoffee.go.ug>. [20 July 2018].

UN 2018, *2018 Revision of World Urbanization Prospects*, 16 May 2018. Available from: <https://www.un.org/development/desa/publications/2018-revision-of-world-urbanization-prospects.html>. [20 July 2018].

WEBB, E. J., CAMPBELL, D. T., SCHWARTZ, R. D. & SECHREST, L. 1981, *Nonreactive Measures in the Social Sciences*, Houghton Mifflin, Boston.

WEDIG, K. & WIEGRATZ, J. 2017, 'Agricultural Cooperatives under Neoliberalism: The Case of Uganda's Coffee Sector in Uganda', *Journal of Agrarian Change*, 18, 348–369.

# 2 Footloose labor in Uganda's coffee sector

The rising importance of wage-labor as a source of income in rural Africa has been pointed to for some time, indicating that the development of rural labor markets as 'a major source of class differentiation, inequality and impoverishment' (Oya 2010b, p. 1) need to be addressed by policy makers (Barrett et al. 2005; Bryceson et al. 2000; Davis et al. 2017; Hurst et al. 2005; IFAD 2011; Otsuka & Yamano 2008; Oya 2010a; Sender & Cramer 2005; White & Leavy 2003). Eastern Uganda's coffee sector is an example of how rapid population growth, small-on-average landholdings,[1] and growing numbers of the landless have made wage work a defining feature of economic life in rural areas. As a result, efforts to address the challenges entailed in the development of rural labor markets, including working conditions, access to training, and labor market segmentation based on social inequalities, are essential to the design and implementation of effective strategies for inclusive rural development. However, the persistence of smallholder farming as a major income source in rural Africa has long kept alive notions of low socio-economic differentiation among the rural population. The literature on everyday forms of resistance among peasants as a more or less homogeneous group has to some extent contributed to this view (*see*, for example, Scott 1985; Adnan 2007), but studies of everyday forms of *compliance and support* have pointed out that the image of classless peasant societies is erroneous (Kerkvliet 1990, 2009; Walker 2008). The data presented in this chapter illuminate how existing social and economic inequalities are reproduced in highly informal rural and urban labor markets.

The chapter starts with a discussion of the development of rural labor markets in Uganda, before exploring agricultural and non-agricultural working conditions and the nature of labor market regulation in Uganda's highly informal labor markets. Despite the increasing importance of wage work for large numbers of households in rural Africa, policy discussions on growth, employment, and rural development have been slow to address the role of rural labor markets, and as a result, their development remains inadequately understood. The focus of rural development policies in many low-income countries continues to lie in the growth and commercialization of well performing small farms, thereby largely ignoring the importance of multi-occupational rural income strategies while fostering an uncritical approach to weakly regulated agribusiness investments.

*Figure 2.1* Coffee workers in Kampala, Uganda

In Uganda certainly, and most likely elsewhere, the policy focus on farming to promote rural development obscures the extent of exploitative labor relations and the existence of a large and increasing pool of rural surplus labor that faces dismal working conditions, including wages below subsistence level.[2] Slow growth in labor demand creates a 'reserve army of labor' with poor economic prospects. The nature of jobless growth in Uganda is briefly discussed below, as part of an outline of the country's labor market. Subsequently, the chapter presents evidence from Uganda's coffee sector and two fast-growing non-agricultural economic sectors – construction and hospitality (hotel and gastronomy). The data indicate that informal employment, poor working conditions, and low labor productivity are widespread for low- and higher-skilled jobs in agricultural and non-agricultural labor markets. The evidence allows for conclusions on how the absence of effective state regulation of labor markets contributes to perpetuating a cycle of low productivity and poverty wages.

The discussion on working conditions explores the linkages between the persistence of low skill levels in the labor force and the prevalence of informal labor relations. The coffee sector data point to very limited access to training for the large low-skilled section of the labor force. Casual agricultural workers show great interest in acquiring more and better skills and are willing to pay for it, but due to the generally low-skilled nature of agricultural processing, employers mostly fail to invest in labor. The survey in the hotel and construction sectors complements the evidence from agricultural workers and additionally covers workers with higher technical and vocational skills levels. The data offer highly differentiated results on the barriers against employers' and workers' investment in training in the context of high informality. Overall, the weak institutional framework fails to provide favorable conditions for investment, especially from employers, in improving labor supply quality. National labor market and training policies seemingly fail to address the close linkages between better labor productivity and working conditions: while the government addresses the extremely low value added per worker in Uganda[3] with policies to improve labor market-oriented skills levels, there seem to be hardly any effort to improve the enforcement of employment protection legislation.

The data presented in the third and last part of this chapter illustrate the discriminatory nature of the social regulation of labor market transactions: based on social binaries such as gender or ethnicity, inequalities in the households and the broader social sphere are reproduced within the context of labor relations. In the coffee sector, women are consigned to particularly low-paid jobs, and access to employment opportunities for both men and women is largely regulated by structures of kinship and ethnicity. In particular among male workers in coffee processing factories, labor gang leaders play an important role as informal brokers who negotiate jobs and payment rates with employers. They effectively control access to jobs and they might enforce wage increases that would not have been achieved by individual workers, but because there are no universal or skills-based rights to membership in labor gangs, inequalities among this section of the labor force are likely to be significant.

The evidence from the hotel and construction sectors present a similar situation with regard to skilled non-agricultural jobs. Given the large and growing pool of surplus labor also in urban and semi-urban areas, employers act as patrons, rather than as buyers of services, allowing for severe exploitation of workers, which is only minimally offset by notions of social obligations. As opposed to the 'Africa works' approach developed by Chabal and Daloz (1999) and Chabal (2009), the data from rural and urban Uganda indicate that the everyday politics of patrimonialism that shape the terms and conditions of labor relations are embedded in the dominant mode of production. Therefore, they contribute directly to reproducing the social relations of power and inequality underlying existing patterns of distribution and access to resources.

The chapter concludes by showing that the development of effective formal labor market regulation as well as organizational structures to represent workers' interests could have significant positive effects on labor productivity. First, better regulation of labor relations, including contract enforcement but also employment protection legislation, would reduce the transaction costs and risks associated with employers' and workers' investments in training, and help to create favorable conditions for their amortization. Second, labor organizations that represent the majority, rather than a fraction of the labor force, are able to pressurize employers and the state to improve working conditions, including the provision of more and better training for all sections of the labor force. Without public sector support, workers with low levels of education and training are likely to experience significant disadvantages in access to on-the-job training, because employers' investments in training tend to be skewed towards the more educated (Adams 2010). Given that the majority of wage workers in Uganda's coffee sector are also small producers, cooperatives could play an important role in organizing large numbers of farmers-cum-wageworkers.

## 2.1 Rural labor diversification

Rural labor diversification has intensified for quite some time in Africa. Rural households in low- and middle-income countries have long depended on combinations of farming, employment (agricultural and non-agricultural), self-employment, and transfers (mainly remittances), and given the need to diversify risks and supplement meager incomes from small landholdings, small farmers in Africa are particularly likely to pursue multiple income strategies (IFAD 2011). Despite the relatively low levels of income diversification in Africa, compared with other world regions, few farming households in Africa today depend solely on farm production (*ibid.*). The region's youth bulge and the associated growth of the landless population, combined with insufficient non-agricultural employment opportunities, mean that the number of young people who depend on agricultural wage work will continue to grow for some time. Although employment in agriculture is hardly attractive, an estimated 65 percent of young people across the region are currently employed in agriculture for at least part of the year (IFAD 2016).

The evidence from Uganda's coffee sector portrays a similar picture: many small producers are in fact *farmers-cum-wageworkers*, who participate in some way in labor markets, mostly as post-harvest workers in processing factories and as harvest helpers on other farms. The coffee sector survey data presented indicate that more than half of the small coffee producers in Eastern Uganda depend on a combination of farming, wage work, and non-agricultural entrepreneurial activities (*see* Table 2.2). Among wage workers, the proportion that depends on multiple income sources and diverse economic activities rises to 74 percent (*ibid.*). Furthermore, as communal forms of labor exchange have increasingly been substituted with market-based transactions, even producers with the smallest landholdings are likely to employ some wage labor themselves, mainly for digging, harvesting, and transport.[4]

In the absence of a functioning social security system, asset-poor households depend on multiple income-generation strategies to spread economic risks, bridge financial bottlenecks, and open up new sources of income. In Uganda, fast population growth, intensifying soil depletion and an inheritance law that divides family land into ever smaller and more disjointed plots is increasing the dependence of small farmers on wage work, and a significant part of employment demand is likely to occur in rural areas. According to the national household survey in 2016/17, 75.5 percent of Uganda's population still lives in rural areas (UBOS 2017, p. 21) and given that the country has one of the world's highest annual population growth rate (above 3 percent), Uganda's rural population continues to grow despite a rapid urbanization process. Recognizing the role of labor markets for inclusive rural development is thus important for two interrelated reasons. First, it takes full account of the diverse types of work that rural people depend on, thereby offering a sound empirical basis for the analysis of economic development and social change. Second, it brings back issues of power and inequality into the discourse on rural development, which has come to be neglected due to persistent images of homogeneously 'poor' rural Africans.

The notion of low inequality among 'the poor' has been accompanied by a focus on fostering entrepreneurship among asset-poor, low-skilled sections of the population. The promotion of micro businesses reflects an attempt to achieve poverty reduction on the basis of individual empowerment, but without a significant redistribution of resources. This approach to inclusive economic development fails to address the role of state institutions to mitigate the effects of existing inequalities, including social protection against exploitative employment relations, and the need for increased public investment (for example, into large-scale infrastructure development) to create more equal conditions for entrepreneurial activities.[5] It therefore neglects the fact that many micro-businesses are unlikely to develop beyond precarious and exploitative self-employment arrangements, as long as structural inequalities limit their growth potential. By recognizing the role of employment for disadvantaged and largely rural sections of the population, the narrow focus on individual empowerment and participation is substituted by a more comprehensive discussion of poverty reduction, which takes into account social relations of power, inequality, and dependency.

During the 1990s, the role of urban labor markets for poverty reduction in sub-Saharan Africa started to be more widely discussed, but the existence and socio-economic impact of rural labor markets was still largely ignored (*see*, for example, van der Geest & van der Hoeven 1999; Lachaud 1994). Some anthropological and economic studies already, at the time, pointed to the prevalence and diversity of wage-labor relations and activities in rural Africa, including the standard labor economist's definition of wage-labor as well as more subtle or indirect wage forms (Reardon 1997 on Zimbabwe; Kevane 1994 on Sudan; Duncan & Howell 1992 on sub-Saharan Africa; Vaughan 1998 on Malawi and Zambia; Perry 2000 on Senegal). Also, Byerlee and Spencer (1977, p. 16) noted even earlier that large parts of the adult rural population in tropical Africa participated in the labor force in some way. However, until today, data on Africa's rural labor markets remain highly insufficient, despite the recognition, some years ago, that the understanding of labor markets in developing countries is arguably about where the understanding of poverty was some thirty years earlier (Fields 2007).

So far, there are only a small number of country-based studies of rural labor markets in Africa, which point not only to the significant role of rural labor markets for current processes of rural economic development, but also to the insufficiency of current theoretical and methodological approaches to their analysis (*see*, for example, Cramer et al. 2008 and Oya & Sender 2009 on Mozambique; Cramer & Sender 1999, Sender 2000, and Sender & Johnston 1995 on Eastern and Southern Africa; Pontara 2010 on Mauritania; Rizzo 2011a on Rwanda and Ethiopia). Such country studies have started to expand the current understanding of how relations of power and inequalities that structure transactions in poorly regulated, highly informal labor markets affect the socio-economic outcomes of poor rural households in low-income countries. The data from Uganda presented in this book confirm the importance of this endeavor for better understanding the factors that shape rural economic development. By showing that the majority of coffee-growing households also depend on wage-employment, and how these labor relations affect socio-economic wellbeing, this book contributes to deconstructing an enduring image of Africa's rural poor as largely self-sufficient farmers and contributes to a much-needed debate on the role of labor markets for inclusive rural development.[6]

### *The labor market in Uganda*

The distribution of Uganda's labor force[7] across economic sectors illustrates the country's continued dependence on agriculture: in 2017, agriculture still provided 69 percent of total employment, while industry and services provided 6.9 and 24.1 percent respectively, and these figures have hardly changed over the past nearly two decades (ILOSTATS, accessed 5 January 2018; *see* Figure 2.2). Indeed, while the share of the labor force in services increased slightly, from 22.1 percent in 2000 to 24.1 percent in 2017, the share in industry has in fact *fallen* from 7.7 to 6.9 during the same time (*ibid.*). Compared with the development of the sectors' value added of GDP, these figures indicate serious

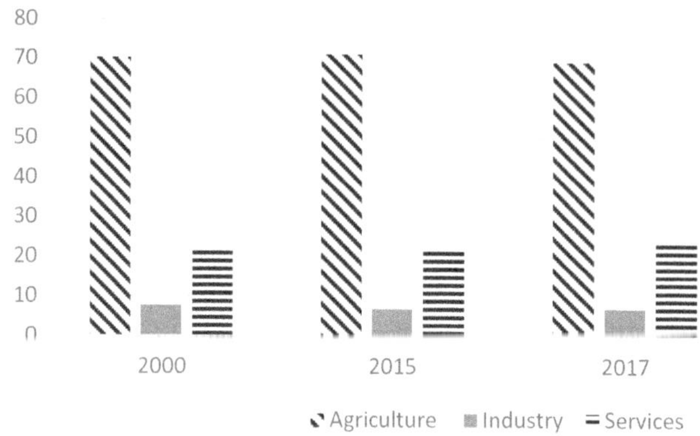


*Figure 2.2* Share of employment by sector

barriers to inclusive growth. Starting in the late 1970s and continuing into the mid-2000s, shares of GDP for industry and services increased significantly, but the growth rate has since flattened for services and become negative for industry (World Bank Data, accessed 5 January 2018). Thus, the past increases in the shares of GDP for industry and services have still not been matched by corresponding changes in the distribution of the labor force across sectors, while the reduction in value added by agriculture has stalled at a high level (between 23 and 26 percent) in the early 2000s (*ibid.*). Together, these developments cast serious doubts about the pace of progress towards a structural transformation of Uganda's economy.

The mismatch between the GDP shares of the modern emerging sectors and the distribution of labor across sectors is visible throughout the research area. Thus, the technology used in BCU's coffee-processing factory in Mbale town, which is leased out to the multinational buyer Kyagalanyi, is no longer serviced by Ugandan technicians, as was the case until the early 2000s. Today, according to the machine attendant and the manager, Swiss engineers are flown in from Kenya, because there is no suitably skilled labor available for the job. Other processing factories, in Kapchorwa town as well as in rural locations, were not operating at all at the time of the fieldwork, due to a lack of functional machinery and sufficient electricity.

The survey data from Uganda's coffee sector (*see* Survey I, Table 1, Chapter 1) further illustrate that the dependence on agriculture frequently involves wage work in addition to farming. Thus, even those small producers who give farming as their main occupation are likely to depend on non-farming activities, which often includes agricultural wage work, for parts of their income. From the sample of surveyed coffee growers, 51 percent depended on a combination of wage work and non-agricultural self-employment in addition to farming (*see* Table 2.1). For 23 percent of coffee growers, wage work is their main additional source of income: they depend either on agricultural or on non-agricultural wage work or on a combination of both. Furthermore, even those small producers who stated non-agricultural self-employment ('own business') or other types of farming outside of coffee as their main additional source of cash income were likely to conduct some casual wage work at different times of the year, usually in the agricultural sector.

The coffee sector data also point to the importance of wage work in rural Uganda as a *qualitative* factor of income-generation strategies, because wage work was often perceived as a particularly regular or reliable source of income. At 27 percent, more than a quarter of the surveyed coffee growers with small or average landholdings (up to five acres) emphasized that wage work was their most regular source of income, compared with non agricultural self-employment (20 percent) and farming (53 percent).[8] Even some of those coffee growers who also run a non-agricultural business confirmed that wage work, including seasonal agricultural jobs, was their most regular source of income. For example, Joseph Wobweni, a farmer and wage worker from Sironko district, explained:

> Growing coffee has become a gamble. Prices change frequently and if the harvest is spoiled one year, because of diseases, too little rain, or landslides, there may be no money from your coffee. If you have a *boda-boda* service [taxi], your bicycle can break in an accident, and if you lack the money to repair it, you have to wait. Wage work is tiresome, but you know the money will come, even though it is little.

The surveyed wage workers in the coffee sector invariably stressed that wage work was their most regular source of income, even though more than a third also had other sources of income. Thus, 29.9 percent also cultivated crops, and 7.8 percent engaged in non-agricultural entrepreneurial activities in addition to wage work. For 36.4 percent, other types of wage work outside the coffee sector were vital, while 26 percent of the surveyed wage workers had no additional sources of income.

*Table 2.1* Proportion of small coffee producers with regular additional sources of income, by type of income (in percentage)

| *Type of regular additional source of income* | *Prevalence* |
|---|---|
| Agricultural wage work | 6.3 |
| Non-agricultural wage work | 7.9 |
| Combination of agricultural and non-agricultural wage work | 8.7 |
| ***Cumulative percentage for both types of wage work*** | ***22.9*** |
| Non-agricultural self-employment (own business) | 28.1 |
| ***Cumulative percentage for all types of additional work other than farming*** | **51** |
| Other types of export crop farming | 2.4 |
| N.A. (no additional regular sources of income stated) | 46.6 |

The increasing dependence on wage work among rural people in low-income countries is associated with increasing wealth differentiation and disruptive effects on the social coherence of rural households (Bryceson 1999). Against this background, the development of effective state regulation of labor market transactions to enforce labor rights is essential for the generation of inclusive rural development processes and to insure against a rise in extreme levels of poverty. However, current methods of data generation on work and employment in Uganda and elsewhere in Africa are still slow in recognizing the importance of wage work as a source of income for rural populations. Thus, Uganda's national statistical data indicate which proportion of the labor force performs its work mainly within the agriculture and fishery sector, but the proportion of employment compared with farming within the sector remains unclear (UBOS 2010a, p. 39; UBOS 2017).

A major reason for the lack of relevant data is the way that information is acquired. Most labor market and household surveys, including those conducted by Uganda's National Bureau of Statistics, ask for respondents' main economic activity during the previous seven days. In rural areas, the answer is likely to be farming, which is conducted throughout the year, given the prevalence of intercropping and multiple harvests for many crops. Wage work, on the other hand, is often seasonal and tied to post-harvest periods. Furthermore, agricultural wage work, the most common form of rural employment,[9] has a low social status and respondents are likely to mention other income sources first. Among the Bagisu and Sabin people of Eastern Uganda, anyone who farms, no matter how small the landholding, or engages in non-farm self-employment, prefers to portray him or herself as a farmer or entrepreneur, even if agricultural wage work makes up an important part of his/her total yearly income and work. For the large numbers who depend on seasonal agricultural wage work, farming and non-farm self-employment, mentioning either farming or entrepreneurial activities may be the more dignified response.[10]

As indicated above, employment opportunities outside agriculture remain highly insufficient in Uganda. In addition, their quality tends to be poor. As the *African Economic Outlook* has noted repeatedly, new jobs in manufacturing are created largely in informal and micro-enterprises. Many of these jobs are precarious and low-paid, limiting the positive effects on welfare levels that can be expected from a growth of employment in manufacturing. With large investments foreseen in the country's transport and energy infrastructure, fueled by the discovery of oil in Western and Northern Uganda, non-agricultural wage work on large, labor-intensive construction projects has increased significantly in recent years (GoU 2010; EIU, 2017). However, given the lack of enforcement of employment protection legislation in Uganda, the quality of low-skilled employment thus created is unlikely to contribute significantly to improved welfare levels. Furthermore, the low level of skills among Uganda's labor force means that highly-skilled jobs are often filled by migrant workers from neighboring countries or from the home countries of foreign investors. The data from the hotel and construction sectors confirm this. Thus, employers' representatives explained that management posts are frequently filled with skilled staff from Kenya, in particular in the hotel sector, and also South Africa.

### *The socioeconomic effects of income diversification*

Given that poverty in Uganda, and indeed throughout Africa, will remain predominantly rural for some time to come, the process of rural income diversification, which accelerated throughout the region from the late 1980s onwards, should provoke wide interest among scholars and policy makers in the development of rural labor markets. Increasing dependence on wage-labor and non-farm self-employment, in a context of weak or non-existent employment protection legislation and severely deficient rural markets (most notably a lack of financial services), is likely to impede poverty reduction efforts due to high inequality and low levels of labor productivity. However, policy debates on rural poverty have been dominated by a body of literature on livelihood approaches, which is largely restricted 'to situational analysis underpinned by assumptions of economic optimization on the part of decision-making households, while ignoring the broader process of depeasantization' (Bryceson 1999, p. 171).

The 'sustainable rural livelihoods' approach essentially views rural income diversification as a household-based coping strategy that reduces vulnerability to the uncertainties of agricultural production and imperfect rural markets (*see*, for example, Ellis 1998; Carswell 1997; Carney 1999). Processes of differentiation and the formation of class interests caused by changes in wage-labor activity therefore receive little attention, because the focus on multi-occupational households as economic actors and basic analytical units obscures relations of power and inequalities that are embedded within the dominant mode of production and thus may cut across individual households. The analytical focus on the household's consumption security emphasizes its members' well-being, but it is less likely to capture the effects of income diversification on distributional patterns in the wider social environment.

A focus on household-based livelihood strategies further creates the problem of implying harmonious efforts by household members to spread risks under adverse economic conditions. The effects of unequal bargaining power within individual households on the well-being of their members, including socio-economic outcomes in the labor market and in education, have been critically analyzed by Kabeer (1997, 2003). Processes of inter-household bargaining are continuous, they are characterized by significant inequalities, and they are likely to produce shifting agreements that entail at least partially conflicting income-generation strategies among individual household members. As a result, changes in wage-labor and non-agricultural self-employment activity are likely to affect distributional patterns within the household and the wider social and economic environment.

In Uganda's coffee sector, the effects of changes in wage-labor activity on intra-household distributional patterns are clearly visible. Women who work as coffee graders generally spend up to ten hours daily, six days a week, in the factory. They may go home over lunch-time to feed smaller children and elderly relatives with food prepared in the early morning hours, and they are likely to do more domestic chores when they arrive home from the factory, but they have little or no time left to take care of their vegetable and crop gardens. Although coffee graders only work for part of the year, seasonal wage-employment and essential agricultural tasks may overlap, thereby reducing a woman's income from local and export cash crops. Men generally exert more control over unpaid family labor than women, which allows them to do seasonal wage work while ensuring sufficient work on their crops. Sauda Mugide, a coffee grader at Kyagalanyi factory in Mbale town, emphasized the conflicts created by multiple demands on her labor:

> I need the work here [in the factory], but it is difficult to look after my crops at the same time. I cultivate a very small plot of land with maize, tomatoes and onions. The income I make from them is important, but the land is owned by my husband. If I do not succeed in cultivating it in one season, he might take it.

While recognizing the threat of intra-household conflict over resources due to her wage job, Sauda Mugide stressed that she and her colleagues struggle to retain their jobs at the factory, because that provides an important and regular part of their income over the year.

This example illustrates the extent to which rural income diversification may directly affect social and economic differentiation, because it contributes to changes in distributional patterns within households. In the absence of institutional mechanisms that support disadvantaged groups, such as female casual workers, to better manage the processes of diversification, potential gains may be lost. As a result, 'income diversification may serve to exacerbate rather than alleviate inter-household economic differentiation' (Bryceson 1999, p. 174). Also, the cost of spreading risks over different activities can be high if households (or individuals) sacrifice the gains of specialization and concentrated investments (Collier and Gunning 1999). However, diversification, even among the extremely poor, is more than a distressed reaction to acute deprivation, because it can present a way to unlock new income sources. It is therefore essential to better understand the potential conflicts caused by diversification, both within the household and the labor market, to support the formation of representational structures and inform institutional development processes aimed at reducing transaction costs for disadvantaged groups. In this way, the likely exacerbation of inequalities due to diversification could be contained to merely reflecting some rising out of indignity. As Milanovic (2010) notes, the likely exacerbation of inequalities due to diversification may have wealth-creating effects for disadvantaged groups, *if* institutional mechanisms exist that minimize the preservation of positions of power by the 'haves' versus the 'have-nots'.

## 2.2 Working conditions in agriculture and beyond

Based on new evidence about working conditions in the coffee as well as the hotel/gastronomy and construction sectors, this section explores the quality of employment in Uganda's agricultural and non-agricultural labor markets. Qualitative data from the coffee sector as well as survey data from the hotel and construction sectors illustrate poor and precarious working conditions, including for higher-skilled non-agricultural workers. The poor quality of working conditions in African agriculture has been noted before (Mwamadzingo 2003; IUFAHTA 2009; World Bank 2007), but the lack of substantial data at the country level, especially for rural labor markets, remains profound. A closer look at the major sources of data on working conditions in Uganda illuminates some of the main data gaps and the associated challenges for the development of effective policy responses.

As the National Organization of Trade Unions pointed out, workers continue to face an erratic wage system with little transparency, and without a minimum wage. Regulations on working hours are non-existent, and non-compliance with health and safety standards remains widespread (Ssenkabirwa 2010). Labor inspections, the government's key instrument for scrutinizing the quality of working conditions, are supposed to be carried out in work places by the district labor officers 'to ensure that national labor standards are being followed' (UBOS 2007, p. 61). So far, however, a large number of district labor offices have never reported any inspections, thereby creating areas for which no government documentation of working conditions is available. The failure to conduct inspections is largely caused by a lack of funds at the district level to realize company visits, while the government's failure to publish any results of realized inspections indicates by obfuscation that the shortcomings in working conditions are likely to be serious.

An additional source of data on working conditions is the national statistics on complaints about breaches of work contracts, which can be filed at district labor offices. This is usually done by workers, but in rare cases also by employers. For most districts, data are available on the total number of complaints and on the settlement of each case, indicating whether a complaint was settled 'in favor of employees', 'in favor of employers' or 'not settled' (*see*, for example, UBOS 2007, p. 61 for the Kampala district office). However, no information is available on the nature and gravity of the documented contract breaches. Thus, the available statistics do not allow for any conclusion to be made on the actual quality of working conditions. Equally, the measures taken to settle a dispute are not disclosed, and no information is available on the follow-up of settlements, that is, to indicate whether a settlement agreement has been enforced. This not only limits the use of the available figures, but also calls for a cautious interpretation of settlements "in favor of employees".

Furthermore, the available statistics only represent a fraction of the labor force, namely the small number of formal employees. The data provide no information about the working conditions faced by the majority of labor market participants. To reiterate, less than 20 percent of the labor force is categorized as employed. Of these, the majority is in temporary employment, which is almost invariably informal and without a work contract. The small number of skilled workers in permanent employment may or may not have a work contract. Thus, the labor market survey and coffee sector case study, as discussed in more detail below, show that even permanent employment may be informal, based on oral agreements or a letter of appointment that fails to meet basic contractual standards. More than 80 percent of the labor force is categorized as self-employed and thus not covered by the national statistics on working conditions. As was discussed above, this category hides large numbers of unpaid family workers who have little power to negotiate their terms of work, but as 'self-employed' they remain invisible in the relevant statistics.

Lastly, the large numbers of micro and small entrepreneurs do not surface in the statistics on working conditions due to their status as self-employed. However, many of them are survival-oriented, rather than growth-oriented, entrepreneurs and their economic activities often depend on highly exploitative relations with more powerful economic actors. These relations generally form part of the wider social environment of the survival entrepreneur and cannot easily be severed, no matter how abusive they are. Thus, the situation of many survival entrepreneurs may be more like informal employment, and working conditions may be dismal, but neither labor inspections nor national statistics on work-contract breaches will provide information on the predicament they face.

In short, Uganda's national statistics provide no information on working conditions for the majority of the labor force. The database on the minority of formal, permanent employees is inadequate because of a lack of detail regarding information on work-contract breaches and the small coverage of the labor inspections. However, the country-wide labor market survey conducted for this research in the hotel and construction sectors, as well as the coffee sector data provide relevant insights into the working conditions of disadvantaged labor market participants. While they represent no substitute for reliable national statistical data, they illuminate major aspects of working conditions faced by low- and higher-skilled[11] workers in Uganda's urban and rural labor markets. The picture that emerges is one of highly informal employment for low-skilled casual labor and more permanent, higher-skilled workers alike. The quality of working conditions is generally low, but important differences are identified depending on the type of employer.

### *Income Poverty*

The World Bank, in its Uganda Poverty Assessment 2016, noted significant reductions in monetary poverty, stating that the share of the population living on $1.90 PPP per day or less had reduced from 53.2 percent in 2006 to 34.6 percent in 2013 (World Bank 2016). However, national statistics, measuring 'the percentage of individuals estimated to be living in households with real private consumption per adult equivalent below the poverty line for their region' noted an increase of poverty from 19.5 percent in 2012/13 to 27 percent in 2016/17 (UBOS 2017, p.84–85). Certainly, the lack of employment protection in Uganda creates socio-economic conditions that continue to force large parts of the labor force to accept wages below the subsistence minimum. The latest national statistical figures that are available on wage levels show that in 2009/10, the median monthly nominal wage for rural workers in the private sector stood at UGX 60,000 (approximately €17 in 2010). This translates into an income below or close to the international poverty (UBOS 2010b, p. 13). Wages below subsistence level have been noted for the agricultural sector throughout sub-Saharan Africa (World Bank 2007, p. 202; Sender & Cramer 2005). With nearly 70 percent of Uganda's employment provided by the agricultural sector, widespread poverty among the labor force is therefore likely to persist for some time (ILOSTATS accessed 5 January 2018). While the potential for the creation of skilled jobs in the agricultural sector is limited, improvements in welfare levels could be achieved through better regulation (Sender & Cramer 2005).

In Uganda, relevant policies have so far not been implemented. The average income from low-skilled, casual jobs, which make up the bulk of employment in the sector, are lower than in smallholder farming, although neither the income from smallholder farming nor that from casual wage work generally suffice to cover basic living costs (Fox 2009; unstructured interviews with coffee workers). In Uganda's coffee sector, coffee sorters earned daily wage that were close to or at the international poverty line. Most men work as transport workers and tend to earn about two or three times as much, but their work is physically too strenuous to be done by older men or those suffering from malaria or other illnesses. Thus, most men have shorter earning spans than women, both throughout the year and throughout their lifetimes.

However, income poverty is by no means confined to the agricultural sector, even though extreme income poverty is concentrated in rural areas. The data from the non-agricultural labor market collected for the present study illustrate a combination of low wages, short-term and insecure employment, and poor working conditions, including a widespread irregularity in the payment of wages. The skilled workers surveyed in the construction and hotel sectors named low wages as the most important reason for "low work ethics", a complaint frequently heard by employers. Irregular payment ranked twice, before the insecurity of employment and a more general perception of poor working conditions.[12] In the unstructured interviews, skilled workers said that their wages were too low to cover minimum living costs for an individual with dependents, emphasizing that this was a general problem within their sector. For the assessment of wage levels, the insecurity of employment also needs to be taken into account, because short contracts lead to frequent suspensions of earnings, making figures on daily, weekly, or monthly wages unsuitable as a determinant of income over the year.

Data on the regularity of payment was collected to provide additional information on the extent of income poverty. In the hotel and construction sectors, employers were asked if they had encountered difficulties paying their skilled workers during the previous two years. A majority had. In both sectors, 43 percent of employers admitted to irregularities in paying their semi- and higher-skilled workers during the previous two years, against 57 percent who declared regular payments (*see* Table 2.2). According to workers, the non-payment of wages also frequently occurred as a foot-dragging method of avoiding severance payments, because affected workers will eventually leave without being formally dismissed.

In Uganda's coffee sector, wages seem to be paid regularly, but in the absence of relevant state regulation, payment delays or cuts might be used informally by employers in the context of labor conflicts. Skilled workers of cooperatives or multinational companies that buy coffee (MNCs hereafter), generally indicated regular payments. These workers include machine attendants and supervisors at the coffee processing stations and factories, as well as extension workers.[13] However, fluctuation among skilled workers in the coffee sector was high, and extension workers often mentioned conflicts with past employers. This indicates a lack of functional mechanisms to achieve settlements of labor conflicts, including payment regularities, which contributes to the high fluctuation of workers. Casual workers of cooperatives and MNCs indicated that payments, on a daily or weekly basis, were *generally* regular, but might be delayed or interrupted in case of labor conflicts.[14] Overall, workers as well as producers pointed out that the "new" cooperatives founded after the liberalization of the coffee sector, but also the MNCs that have entered the market since, are more reliable and "trustworthy" than the formerly monopolistic Bugisu Cooperative Union (BCU).

## *Working conditions*

The qualitative and quantitative research carried out among coffee workers indicates that working conditions in the sector fall visibly short of international standards. Information was collected through a questionnaire-based survey (*see* Survey I, Table 1.1, Chapter 1), semi-structured interviews and through participant observation, which included unstructured interviews with coffee sorters, transport and storage workers and machine attendants (*see* Table 1.2, Chapter 1).[15] As with questions on the regularity of payment, questions regarding the employers' adherence to health and safety standards at the workplace were not

*Table 2.2* Employers (%) who made irregular payments to skilled workers in previous two years

| *Payment irregularities occurred* | *Hotel sector* | *Construction sector* |
|---|---|---|
| Yes | 42.6 | 42.6 |
| No | 57.4 | 57.4 |

included in the questionnaire-based survey, but information was collected through unstructured interviews and informal work place visits.[16]

Overall, few workers seem to have written work contracts or binding oral agreements with their employers. Furthermore, basic health and safety measures are generally not implemented in the factories and warehouses of the three largest employers in Eastern Uganda's coffee sector, which included Kyagalanyi, Kawacom, and the BCU, which had recently begun to buy coffee and employ workers again.[17] Thus, coffee sorters typically work on the factory floor, in a climate with high levels of dust. On the coffee processing stations, they work long hours in the sun, even though the aisles between the coffee drying stands could be provided with shade easily and at low cost. Overall, simple protective appliances are largely missing, whether in transport and storage, picking and drying or machine operation. Gumutindo, a relatively young and fair-trade-certified cooperative, is a noteworthy exception, keeping up high health and safety standards with simple protective equipment as well as regular instructions on safe work behavior for all its workers. The same divergence was apparent with regard to the existence of work contracts. All the surveyed agricultural wage workers employed by the three biggest employers worked without a work contract.

In the construction and hotel sectors, the quality of working conditions was explored through a questionnaire-based survey that covered work contracts, access to training and employers' appreciation (financial or otherwise) of good-quality work (*see* Table 1.1, Chapter 1). A limited amount of participant observation, including unstructured interviews, was conducted to acquire additional information, for example on health and safety at the workplace. The construction and hotel sectors were selected because they provide growing numbers of jobs throughout the country, including the poorer northern and Eastern regions, thereby providing data on the structure of labor relations in particularly poor as well as the wealthiest regions of Uganda. The sample included a total of 131 questionnaire-based interviews with employers and workers in 101 companies. In each company, one top manager or the company head (generally the owner) was interviewed, and in about a third of the companies, one questionnaire-based interview was conducted with an employee to cross-check employers' statements with workers' perspectives. Furthermore, ten unstructured interviews with workers were conducted outside the work places to complement the difficult generation of data on working conditions within companies. The visits to 54 hotels and 47 construction companies, which took part when conducting the interviews, also provided insights into current working conditions in both sectors.

The informality of employment in Uganda extends beyond the agricultural sector to urban labor markets. Thus, in the hotel and construction sectors, a significant proportion of skilled workers, in addition to all *leja-leja* [18] workers, depend on informal employment arrangements. Only 55 percent of all surveyed employers claimed to generally sign contracts with all of their skilled workers, while 27 percent said that they signed contracts with 'some' and 17 percent admitted to not signing work contracts at all (*see* Table 2.3).[19] Furthermore, the unstructured interviews with skilled workers showed that many contracts are in fact so-called letters of appointment that fail to specify basic contractual elements, such as the duration of employment, the level of payment, working hours, and the job description. Spot tests of contracts were conducted where possible and they confirmed workers' accounts.

No employer provided work contracts for low-skilled, *leja-leja* workers, who are employed on a daily or weekly basis and make up the majority of the labor force in the surveyed companies. Also, workers indicated in both sectors that the number of written contracts for skilled labor might be lower than suggested by employers, because work contracts may be promised at recruitment, but not delivered.

Employment insecurity is high in both sectors. For skilled construction workers, the duration of work engagements is generally bound to the length of a particular project, which may be limited to a few weeks or extend over a year or more. However, according to workers' accounts, employment is frequently interrupted in the context of longer projects due to a lack of liquidity of the constructor or delays in bureaucratic procedures. A representative of workers in the construction sector confirmed that workers frequently experience such interruptions, effectively making the vast majority of jobs short-term. In the hotel sector, contracts tend to be permanent, although they usually fail to specify a notice period for either side. The particularly high level of fluctuation in the hotel sector, which was frequently bemoaned by employers, indicates that the existing contracts fail to significantly improve employment security.

Given the sensitivity of the subject, no questionnaire-based data were collected on adherence to health and safety standards at the work place. Neither employers nor workers could be expected to talk freely about the shortcomings in a documented interview. Some workers complained about "dirty" and "hazardous" conditions during unstructured interviews held outside the work place, and observations during informal work place visits served as a further source of information. Overall, visits to companies throughout the country provided valuable insights, especially because the first visit was often made unannounced to arrange a date and time for interviews.[20] On the basis of these visits, no clear relationship between company size or location and the quality of health and safety conditions was apparent. Poor conditions were found in big

*Table 2.3* Skilled workers that have written contracts (%), employers' account

| *Contract provision* | *Both sectors* | *Hotel sector* | *Construction sector* |
|---|---|---|---|
| All skilled workers have contracts | 55.4 | 63.0 | 46.8 |
| Some skilled workers have contracts | 27.4 | 24.0 | 31.9 |
| No skilled worker has contract | 17.2 | 13.0 | 21.3 |

*Table 2.4* Skilled workers that have written contracts (%), workers' account

| *Sector* | *Hotel sector* | *Construction sector* |
|---|---|---|
| Contract provided by employer | 58.8 | 46.2 |
| Contract not provided by employer | 41.2 | 53.8 |

and small hotels and construction companies, in the capital city as well as in more remote towns, such as Gulu or Lira. In many cases, employers failed to implement low-cost measures, such as the provision of rubber boots and plastic helmets for construction workers or gloves for kitchen staff.

Particularly poor working conditions for women point to significant gender-based inequalities in all surveyed sectors. Within agricultural processing, typically "male jobs", such as transport, loading, and storage of coffee bags, involve equally poor health and safety conditions as those jobs typically done by women, such as coffee picking. However, the coffee sector survey shows that "male jobs" are significantly better paid. Therefore, men can afford to work somewhat shorter hours, which gives them more time for recreation and participation in social and political life. In both the hotel and the construction sectors, higher-skilled and better-paid jobs are more likely to be given to men than to women. As a result, men tend to be in a stronger position than women to negotiate the terms and conditions of work with their employers.

Given that the national average of hours spent daily on child care responsibilities and household chores is 8.6 for women and only 1.4 for men (UBOS 2007, p. ix), the low pay for typically "female jobs" is particularly distressing. In the agricultural sector, many casual jobs are paid on a piece-rate basis, as is the case for the almost exclusively female task of coffee picking. Thus, these jobs are typically associated with particularly long working hours, because workers try to increase their meager earnings. As a result, women tend to perform extremely long working days to fulfill what are often excessive demands on their labor. Fox (2009) estimates that Ugandan women spent on average 170 hours per month (a full-time job) on household chores. However, this is not reflected in the national statistics, which only provide an average of hours of paid work per day, based on all economic sectors, including public sector employment. Accordingly, it is estimated that women have on average six hours of paid work per day against 7.3 for men (UBOS 2007). This figure hides significant differences between economic sectors and is hardly a meaningful estimation of men's and women's actual workload.

### *Access to training in informal labor markets*

The data discussed in this section shows that despite an unmet demand for skilled labor in non-agricultural economic sectors, employers and workers in Uganda's highly informal labor markets face significant disincentives to invest in training. The demand for skilled labor in the hotel and construction sectors is high, but an examination of training provision in both sectors shows that in the context of a highly informal labor system and a lack of contract enforcement, risks for employers are high that investments in skills training will not pay off.

The countrywide labor market survey in the hotel and construction sectors confirmed that employers see low labor productivity as a serious barrier to companies' growth. However, many fail to recognize that the poor quality of working conditions and a lack of access to training are major reasons for low labor productivity. Uganda's National Development Plan has directly associated 'negative attitudes towards work, reflected in low human productivity and low entrepreneurial spirit' with 'backward cultural practices, beliefs, attitudes and a lack of national ethical values in political, social and economic spheres' (GoU 2010, p. 31–32). In contrast, the present study suggests that the combination of low wages, inadequate health and safety conditions, and low levels of education and skills are the main reasons for low labor productivity. Both employers and workers in the hotel and construction sectors unanimously stressed the need for more and better skills to improve economic prospects, echoing previous insights that limited education and skills are a major cause of poverty (UNDP 2005, p. 13).

Since the start of its national campaign for Universal Primary Education (UPE) in 1997 and the successive introduction of free secondary education in 2007, access to general education has been improved considerably in Uganda. However, the labor force (UBOS 2010b, p. xvi; GoU 2010) and persons aged 15 and above (UBOS 2017) still have low educational attainment levels. In 2009/10, the proportion of workers without a formal school certificate was at 17.1 percent (UBOS 2010a) and in 2016/17, 11.9 percent of the population aged 15 and above had no formal schooling. The proportion of people aged 15 and above who have some secondary education stood at 18.7 percent in 2016/17, while 8.6 percent had completed secondary education (UBOS 2017, p. 44). Improvements in the quantity and quality of vocational skills training have lagged behind the development of general education, mainly because of the higher costs and the limited ability of Uganda's vocational education and training system to reach rural areas (Wedig 2010).

Given the limited coverage of formal vocational education and training services and the still low educational attainment of Uganda's labor force, non-formal education and training remains a major source of skills development. The survey data from the coffee sector further indicate that most farmers-cum-wageworkers in the sector lack the general education qualifications to enter Uganda's formal Business, Technical and Vocational Education and Training (BTVET) system. In the construction and hotel sectors, the situation is similar. Against this background, workers in both sectors tend to rely heavily on training provided by employers, but the quantity and quality of on-the-job training is limited. Low-skilled, *leja-leja* workers, who are employed on a daily or weekly basis, generally have no access to training. Skilled workers often receive some kind of on-the-job training, but training sessions are often short and of low quality. Across both sectors and regardless of company size, 58 percent of employers had provided at least one training opportunity to skilled workers during the past two years (*see* Table 2.5). Skilled workers in the hotel sector are much more likely to receive training, but unstructured interviews with workers indicated that many training sessions consist of not more than a briefing for workers. Workers in larger companies are more likely to receive training than those in smaller companies. Thus, 77 percent of companies with more than fifteen skilled workers had provided training in the previous two years, compared with 42 percent of companies with fewer than fifteen skilled workers.

The quality of training varies, but employers frequently stressed that they lack the didactical and methodical knowledge to provide adequate training. Furthermore, the quality of training is likely to be reduced by employers' reluctance to make investments in improving the quality of their work force. Thus, the duration of training sessions is frequently limited to a few hours per worker. Participant observation in some companies, as well as comments made by respondents during the unstructured interviews with workers, suggest that simple briefing sessions for workers to inform them of work place regulations may be declared as 'training' by employers. Overall, few companies cooperate with professional training institutes to ensure minimum quality standards, although employers generally emphasize that they need additional in-house competencies to improve the quality of trainings.

### *Barriers to improving labor supply quality*

The high informality of employment in Uganda's labor market perpetuates disincentives for workers and employers to invest in training. Employers face a relatively high risk that their investment in improving the skills of their work force will not be amortized, because it is difficult to retain workers. Investing in training for an informal work force is generally risky, because given poor working conditions and the widespread lack of labor contracts, workers are likely to leave at the next opportunity of earning a slightly better income. Without effective labor market regulation, there are few incentives for individual companies to invest in the provision of better working conditions and to build up a permanent work force. Furthermore, the formal skills development system largely fails to provide competent partners for the provision of training, in particular in companies within the informal economy. Thus, formal BTVET institutions have only recently started to cooperate with the largest, most formalized companies, but for the large number of small, more or less informal enterprises, it is virtually impossible to provide training in cooperation with a

*Table 2.5* Companies that provided trainings (%) during previous two years

| *Training provision* | *Both sectors* | *Hotel sector* | *Construction sector* |
|---|---|---|---|
| Yes | 58.4 | 70.4 | 44.7 |
| No | 41.6 | 29.6 | 55.3 |

formal institute. In the absence of a regulatory framework for non-formal training, assessing the quality of non-formal training institutes and not-for-profit providers is difficult and costly for employers.

For workers, the lack of job security, low labor market mobility, and poor working conditions are major barriers to investing in job-specific skills. Prospects for transferring new skills into positive labor market outcomes are low, which reduces the readiness of workers to invest in training. The high flexibility of Uganda's labor market is heavily skewed in favor of employers, because mobility is limited for large sections of the labor force (for example, women) by the social regulation of labor market transactions. As a result, many labor market participants have restricted opportunities to enter higher-skilled and better-paid jobs regardless of their training and are thus less likely to invest. Furthermore, the hire-and-fire politics that characterize employment in Uganda's extremely flexible labor market support contribute to factitious labor relations, low work ethics, and low productivity.

The weak development of labor organizations directly reduces the quantity and quality of skill training for workers in two interrelated ways. First, workers lack bargaining power *vis-à-vis* the state to enforce increased public and private sector investments in training. There are a number of institutional mechanisms to promote the provision of labor-market-relevant, good-quality skills training on the basis of targeted public investments and the engagement of enterprises (Adams 2008). These include voucher systems, training levies and the development of qualification frameworks for both formal and non-formal training, but also dual training approaches to establish long-term social contracts between enterprises and for the state to create lasting public-private partnership systems for the provision of vocational and technical training. The extent to which particular instruments are relevant and practical in a particular socio-economic, political, and cultural context varies, but the probability of success of any reform that requires long-term cooperation increases significantly if all actor groups command bargaining power within the relevant negotiation processes. There is a widespread failure in policy discussions on social and economic development to recognize the "beneficiaries" or buyers of training services as an economic interest group. While rights-based approaches to education and training rightly emphasize greater equality in access to resources, they have so far insufficiently addressed the role of skills as an essential economic asset itself.

Second, workers are largely unable to exert pressure on employers to invest in the provision of training. Trade unions and workers' associations have played an important role in the development of non-formal, on-the-job education and training opportunities for workers throughout the industrialized world (Ashton 1996). Because the formal BTVET system in Uganda is unlikely to provide services outside urban or semi-urban areas for some time to come, expanding the quantity and improving the quality of non-formal training is essential to reach large sections of the labor force. However, without organizational structures to represent their interests *vis-à-vis* employers, workers lack bargaining power to negotiate improved conditions for the acquisition, utilization and further development of skills.

Overall, the data on the provision of in-service training in Uganda indicate that in a highly informal labor market environment, significant barriers to investments in the development of skills persist for both employers and workers. The social regulation of labor market transactions is highly discriminatory, reducing the role of skills as a basis for access to jobs. Furthermore, even skilled workers face high job insecurity and poor working conditions, reducing the likelihood that investments in training can be amortized. In the absence of institutional rules, enforced by the state, that create incentives and obligations for employers to invest in lower-skilled workers, the provision of in-service training in the private sector is likely to be skewed towards better educated and higher-skilled workers. Given the lack of a functional and effective social dialogue between employers, workers, and the state, the ability of workers to press for an expansion of the training services offered by companies and the state is severely limited. As a result, a large and growing proportion of the labor force is excluded from training opportunities, perpetuating a cycle of inadequate labor supply quality, low productivity and poor prospects for workers.

## 2.3 The discriminatory nature of informal labor market regulation

Given the weak development of formal labor market institutions in Uganda – in particular, the almost complete lack of implementation of existing employment protection legislation – informal institutional mechanisms are crucial for regulating labor market transactions. This section explores the dominant patterns of social and economic differentiation that structure the organization of labor relations in Uganda. Based on data from the coffee, hotel, and construction sectors, I argue that the logic of neoliberal market reforms, according to which employers' demand for higher-skilled labor should improve the economic opportunities of workers in a deregulated labor market, was not realized in Uganda. The empirical evidence presented below illuminates how poor working conditions are reproduced in a context in which informal institutions based on dominant social norms and practices emerge as key mechanisms to define access to jobs and regulate claims within labor relations. This takes on highly discriminatory forms, as social and political denominators of identity, most notably gender and ethnicity, are associated with expectations of skills, competencies, and entitlements, thereby shaping access to jobs and higher wages.

The lack of workers' rights in informal labor markets has been documented (ILO 2002a and b), and the discriminatory nature of the "social regulation" of labor markets has been illuminated by in-depth case studies, most notably on India (Breman 1996, 2001, 2003; Harriss-White 2003). In Uganda, the absence of effective state regulation and the widespread lack of formal labor organization have similarly created labor markets that are highly informal and characterized by inequalities based on social categories of gender, ethnicity, and clan membership.[21] Contributors to the debate on rural class formation in Africa have pointed out that the 'intersection of lineage structures, gender relations, and generational cycles with processes of capitalist development are critically important for assessing the extent to which [...] social differentiation is developing into an identifiable structure of classes with distinct and conflicting interests' (Cousins et al. 1992, p. 12, cited in Oya 2004, p. 292). These intersections between historically specific social, cultural, and political factors on the one hand, and the dominant mode of production on the other hand, are examined below by exploring the extent to which social binaries, most notably those based on gender and ethnicity, shape access to employment in Uganda's labor market.

The close association of notions of identity with access to resources in the labor market links unequal power relations within the household and the wider social and political environment to economic discrimination, thereby naturalizing the latter and making it more persistent (Tilly 1998)[22]. As has been shown for India and Nigeria, the social regulation of the informal economy relies on the construction of identity through social binaries of gender and ethnicity, but also on the basis of kinship and other networks, such as new evangelical churches, for determining access to resources (Basile & Harriss-White 2003; Harriss-White 2003; Meagher 2010). Similarly, the social regulation of labor market transactions in Uganda is based to a large extent on social categories that bestow identity and thereby shape distributional patterns. An in-depth analysis of 'identity economics' as part of informal institutional arrangements, as presented by Meagher (2010) for Nigeria, goes beyond the scope and focus of this study. However, the idea that the social construction of identity plays a significant role in consolidating distributional patterns, rather than creating fluidity and space for negotiation, is useful for contextualizing the following analysis of informal labor relations in Uganda into a larger discussion of poverty, inequality, and economic development.

A dominant aspect of the social regulation of labor market transactions is the decisive role of personal relations, rather than impersonal rules, to regulate the distribution of power and access to resources. As noted by North et al. (2009), personal relations are likely to represent the principal form of regulation in the context of closed-access societies, in which institutions are largely dominated by powerful individuals. Transferred into a labor market context, recruitment processes and the terms and conditions of employment are likely to be determined by the interests of elites who have preferential access to institutions.[23] In the absence of impersonal rules that ensure, at least to a significant extent, the competition for jobs on the basis of skills while also guaranteeing minimum subsistence rights, workers depend on securing protection from elites in order to realize and defend their interests. The analysis of fresh labor market data indicates that a crucial way to secure protection from elites seems to be membership of social groups that are defined by concepts of kinship or ethnicity. While the numbers of workers with personal relations to powerful individuals are naturally restricted, social relations based on concepts of kinship or ethnicity allow greater numbers of workers to demand access to some form of preferential treatment or protection by powerful individuals.

The structure of labor relations in Uganda, therefore, provides an example of social organization in a 'limited' rather than an 'open-access society' (North et al. 2009). North, Wallis, and Weingast explain how in 'open-access societies' formal institutions allow for the cooperation of large groups on the basis of laws that regulate social interaction regardless of an individual's social, economic, and political power. This ideally allows individuals to access and benefit from institutional arrangements regardless of their membership of or protection by elite coalitions. In the context of an open-access order, the distribution of jobs and mobility within the labor market therefore depends on the assessment of workers' skills and competences on the basis of impersonal rules, such as technical standards or the approximation of knowledge acquired by years of work experience. Furthermore, the terms and conditions of employment are regulated at least to some extent by impersonal rules, rather than by personal negotiations between employers and job seekers.

However, even within an open-access order, inequalities based on wealth, gender, religion, and other social categories persist and affect access to resources. In the labor market, they are of particular relevance for two interrelated reasons. First, the 'pseudo-commodity' labor (Storper & Walker 1989) differs from other resources, because it is integral to its owner who, therefore, needs protection from exploitation and self-alienation within labor market transactions (*see*, for example, Breman 1995; Braverman 1974). Second, access to employment in any society depends to a large extent on education and training processes that are characterized by significant inequalities within both formal educational institutions and the wider socio-economic environment that determines the definition and distribution of human capital (*see*, for example, Bourdieu 1997, 1990; Bourdieu & Passeron 1977; Kabeer 2003, 2008; Bowles & Gintis 1975, 1976). Impersonal rules, such as skills standards to guide access to jobs, or labor rights to regulate employment conditions, are important means of mitigating such inequalities, but labor relations in any society are likely to remain to some extent rigged by discriminatory practices.

In Uganda, the persistence of discriminatory practices in labor market transactions is aggravated by a profound lack of enforcement of impersonal rules aimed at improving access to resources for disadvantaged groups. As a result, there is a close interrelation between the terms and conditions of employment on the one hand, and workers' social status and identity on the other. The latter is to a large extent defined by bounded social categories (in Tilly's sense of the term) such as kinship, ethnicity, or gender and the associated access to material wealth. The meanings of particular social categories that regulate labor market transactions are subject to change, and may be shaped and extended to accommodate changes in the composition of the labor force. In Uganda, as elsewhere, workers from other parts of the country or from abroad are generally conceptualized in terms of the ethnic "other'", as opposed to "locals".

The data from the hotel, construction, and coffee sectors illustrate the importance of social categories of kinship, ethnicity, and gender for the regulation of labor market transitions in rural and urban Uganda. Based on dominant social norms and practices, employers' expectations and assessments of job seekers' skills and competencies are inextricably linked to existing inequalities from the wider social sphere, which are subsequently reproduced and reinforced within the labor market.[24] The discriminatory nature of the social regulation of labor relations is illustrated with regard to recruitment processes, access to jobs and mobility within the labor market. It is shown that categorical inequalities based on gender lead to a particularly profound labor market segmentation that is likely to relegate women to low-paid jobs.

## *The social regulation of labor relations*

The effects of changes in modes of production and trade on the reproduction of inequalities in the wider social and political sphere have been carefully analyzed elsewhere (*see*, for example, Parry et al. 1999; Rukmini 1998). The inequalities examined in the present analysis of Uganda's rural and urban labor market are rooted in repeated patterns of behavior and organizational forms which are closely related with and possibly functional to the dominant mode of production.[25] In labor markets with effective democratic structures of organization, formal institutional mechanisms generally mitigate existing inequalities to a certain extent through targeted subsidies and social protection schemes, which allow for a partial redistribution of resources. The informal institutional mechanisms that dominate the regulation of labor market transactions in Uganda have an effect to the contrary: they deepen existing inequalities through an association of naturalized social denominators of inequality with access to economic resources.

In the construction sector, according to employers and workers, personal recommendations are essential for access to skilled jobs. Furthermore, the value of recommendations seems to be closely associated with concepts of kinship, clans, and ethnicity. Just over half, 54 percent, of the surveyed employers relied mainly on friends' and family members' recommendations when hiring skilled workers, while an additional 21 percent predominantly took in so-called 'walk-ins', who inquire about jobs informally (*see* Table 2.6). The unstructured interviews with workers further indicated that job applications by 'walk-ins' are rarely successful if the job seeker fails to subsequently secure a recommendation through patronage networks, which are often established on the basis of clan membership. Such networks imply a number of social obligations. Thus, the worker may be forced to take up inadequately paid work to "pay off" her/his own or another clan member's debts, or the employer may need to provide work to an undesirable candidate.

In the hotel sector, similar tendencies regarding patronage networks were found, despite significant differences in the structure of the skills demand. Overall, a larger number of skilled or semi-skilled workers are needed, such as waiters, customer care staff, chefs, and receptionists, while the number of low-skilled *leja-leja* workers tends to be smaller than in the construction sector. Overall, the importance of advertising vacancies in local media is somewhat higher, with 28 percent of employers indicating it as their main recruitment method. Nevertheless, personal contacts remain decisive, with 31 percent of employers relying predominantly on recommendations made by friends and family members. While 27 percent largely recruit 'walk-ins', workers again indicated that personal recommendations are likely to be decisive for these applications, too. Furthermore, the questionnaire-based interviews with workers in the hotel sector did not entirely confirm employers' statements regarding the use of advertisements as a method of recruitment, indicating that recommendations from friends and family might play a more significant role instead.[26]

In both the hotel and the construction sectors, the decisive role of personal contacts for access to jobs was not limited to skilled workers, but applied to low-skilled *leja-leja* workers as well. These workers are usually hired either on a daily or weekly basis. In particular, male workers in the construction sector often operate through local labor gangs, the leaders of which act as brokers between job seekers and employers. Women depending on low-skilled, *leja-leja* jobs, most of them in the hotel sector, seem to rely more heavily on personal recommendations, either by clan or family members with a higher status or by friends or relatives who already work for the respective employer.

A similar situation prevails in the coffee sector, where the large majority of workers do low-skilled casual work.[27] As in the construction sector, male applicants for casual work in coffee processing factories largely depend on membership of local labor gangs for access to jobs. On a daily or weekly basis, the labor gang leaders negotiate with the factory managers, who are responsible for the recruitment of casual workers, how many men will be employed. These negotiations take place at the factory gate, and their success depends to a significant extent on the quality of the personal working relations between the gang leader and the factory manager. The distribution of transport and storage jobs, the main type of casual work available to low-skilled men, is organized in this way. Therefore, a casual worker who is trying to hire out in the coffee sector needs to "belong" to a labor gang leader who is able to successfully place his members. For this study, only limited data was collected on the internal organization of labor gangs, but the interviews with casual workers illustrated that there are no formal, skills-based application procedures. Instead, the factors that determine access to membership of gangs seemed to include ethnically defined ties, including clan membership, but also personal contacts to individuals with a high social status.

The vast majority of women work as coffee sorters in the processing factories or in the processing field stations that are scattered on the slopes of Mt Elgon, partly in remote rural areas.[28] Coffee sorters are employed as *leja-leja* workers on a weekly basis during the bi-annual harvest seasons. Access to jobs for these women seems to be less organized, but casual female workers tend to belong to loose, informal support groups that are used to communicate recommendations of new applicants to the employer. These groups are generally founded outside

*Table 2.6* Most common recruitment methods (%) during previous two years

| *Recruitment method mostly used by employer* | *Hotel sector* | *Construction sector* |
|---|---|---|
| Advertisement | 28.4 | 13.9 |
| Agency | 13.6 | 11.1 |
| Friends and family | 30.7 | 54.2 |
| Walk-ins | 27.3 | 20.8 |

the work place, either in the village or in the neighborhood, as is the case for factory workers in Mbale municipality. Thus, they are multiple-purpose networks for the provision of mutual support within and outside the labor market. Female workers perceived membership of these groups as helpful, but not as essential for access to jobs.

### *The role of gender in recruitment*

The segmentation of the labor market along the lines of gender illuminates the role of bounded social categories, rather than universally applicable rights and standards, for access to jobs. Expectations regarding personal characteristics relevant to recruitment, such as honesty or the propensity to be hard-working, are created on the basis of concepts of gender and determine recruitment decisions in important ways. Given the lack of state regulation, there are no effective institutional mechanisms to contest this effect. Thus, Kagundu and Pavlova (2007, p. 1) estimate that in Uganda, 'a substantial portion of the gender wage differential results from employer-driven differences in treatment' – in particular, but not exclusively, in rural areas.

In both the construction and the hotel sectors, gender stereotypes shape employers' expectations and assessment of workers' skills, leading to the concentration of women in low-skilled and low-paid jobs. Furthermore, the actual workload performed by women tends to be undervalued, both financially and socially. In both sectors, employers frequently described apparently widespread notions of women being physically and mentally unfit or too 'weak' for specific jobs. A widely voiced view in the hotel sector was, for example, that women 'cannot stand the heat' of electric ovens and cookers and are therefore ill-suited to work as chefs. Men were generally perceived as more prone to being dishonest, but also as physically and mentally strong and more hard-working. The notion of men's superior work performance stands in stark contrast to the current gendered division of labor in Uganda. As household data from Eastern Uganda as well as more recent interviews with female workers and farmers indicate, women tend to work longer hours than men and are generally responsible for some of the physically most strenuous tasks in the household and farms, such as digging and fetching water (UCA 2008; interviews).

The gendered division of labor in the coffee sector is equally pronounced. Among low-skilled casual workers, women work exclusively as coffee sorters, while men work in transport and storage. Both types of jobs are characterized by poor working conditions, as described in the previous section of this chapter, although men tend to earn higher wages. Thus, the concentration of women in particularly low-paid jobs is to some extent repeated within the coffee sector. The gendered segregation of coffee labor markets is also pronounced in the higher-skilled job sections: throughout the fieldwork area, the vast majority of managers as well as all extension workers, supervisors, and machine attendants were male. Underlying this segregation were similar gender stereotypes as those found in the hotel and construction sectors. In semi-structured and unstructured interviews, casual workers, supervisors, and some managers emphasized the supposed suitability of men and women respectively for certain jobs. Further barriers of access to skilled jobs for women are the fairly remote locations of field processing stations and the lack of technical knowledge, as the only female processing station manager in the Mt. Elgon area explained.

The persistence of gender stereotypes that legitimate serious discrimination against women in the labor market points to the continued importance of critically assessing *how* women are integrated into economic development processes. A number of country studies from the 1980s onwards, in particularly from East Asia, have illuminated how socially constructed and culturally accepted notions of femininity have provided legitimization for the creation of new economic inequalities within processes of economic development (Elson 1981, 1999; Judd 1990; Lee 1995; Razavi 1999). Economic liberalization has since expanded employment opportunities for women throughout the developing world, but the ways in which women are integrated into new markets continue to be closely linked to their subordination (Seguino & Grown 2006).

Among employers, gender stereotypes seem to be a fundamental part of socially acceptable perceptions of workers' dispositions and skills. Gender-based occupational segmentation was generally perceived as a "natural" condition by employers and to some extent by workers. Given the pervasiveness of gender stereotypes as a foundation of people's frame of reference in everyday life, women tend to comply with them. Because dominant social norms and practices are an integral part of how people construct and understand the world, they influence the perceptions and choices of advantaged and disadvantaged groups (Bourgeois 2001). Thus, inequalities based on gender tend to be naturalized, thereby shaping behavioral patterns of both women and men in ways that contribute to the reproduction of such inequalities (Tilly 1998; Strathern 1980; Ortner 1974). Overall, the lack of formal regulation creates insecure conditions for men and women, but the creation and reproduction of gender stereotypes that discriminate against women is particularly widespread. Due to the absence of legislation to reduce women's double work burden and to mitigate the disadvantages that women experience in the labor market due to their reproductive work, the vulnerability of women workers is particularly severe.

### *The role of ethnicity and regional origin in recruitment*

Employers' preference for employing "locals" for the majority of jobs available (with the exception of very few high-skilled positions that may be filled by foreigners), can be understood as yet another aspect of the role of bounded social categories for the regulation of labor market transactions. The term 'local' is utilized by Ugandan employers to refer to members from the dominant ethnic group in a particular area, and it generally excludes residents with a different ethnic background, even if they are long-term residents in the local area. Within the research area, the Bugisu people are the dominant ethnic group in four out of five districts and anyone else, regardless of years of residence, is generally considered a non-local. The fifth district has a largely homogeneous population of Sabin people among whom disapproval of ethnically mixed families remains particularly strong. During data collection, numerous incidents of domestic conflict illustrated the reasons for the ethnic definition of being local. Thus, a woman who is beaten by her husband is likely to seek protection at her parents' household, which may be located in another district if she has a different ethnic background. The geographical and cultural distance limits the husband's ability to force his wife to return. As a result, non-local women who flee their conjugal home are literally hunted down by their husbands and other family members to prevent them from leaving the area. Local wives, on the other hand, are often allowed to leave, because negotiations with their families can be arranged easily.

Employers' explanations of the apparent advantages of employing "one's own people" generally center on the positive effects of shared social and cultural values, which are seen to create greater loyalty towards the employer and improved communication. However, employers' anecdotes and the unstructured interviews with workers indicate that employers can also expect increased levels of control over workers who have a common clan membership or at least the same ethnic origin.[29] This control rests on complex structures of social obligations that interlink wealth and social status with notions of ethnicity and kinship and are generally skewed in favor of employers. Thus, workers from the same clan have preferential access to jobs, but they are likely to be treated as an extension of unpaid family labor and are often subjected to irregular payment.[30] Overall, employment relations are often portrayed in similar ways to patriarchal kinship relations, characterized by a patron who looks after his dependents. Correspondingly, inequalities that exist within the household, the community or the wider social sphere are transferred into the labor market context and often amplified as they are expressed in terms of unpaid wages, dismal working conditions, or a lack of personal development opportunities for the worker.

Against the background of widespread poverty, family or clan members of a worker frequently place demands for support on his or her employer, such as covering a medical bill. This will push the worker into a relation of indebtedness with the employer. In a similar vein, hiring "one's own people" allows employers to utilize a worker's financial debts to wealthier clan members as an instrument of negotiation. By offering paid work, the employer provides an opportunity for the worker to repay his or her debts, making a refusal or even quitting a job on the grounds of inadequate working conditions socially unacceptable. This seems to be a widespread condition for women working as room maids or in the kitchen of hotels. In the unstructured interviews, some workers explained that payment irregularities frequently occur, but because of outstanding debts to the employer, either by themselves or by clan members, they are obliged to hold out, even over months, waiting for their wages to be paid. One woman aptly explained:

> How can I offset my debts against my unpaid wages? He is a big man and when I request him to pay me, he says I have eaten here every day [lunch in the hotel kitchen] and he will eventually pay me when there are more customers. It is hard to get another job around here, and as long as I have outstanding debts with him [the employer], it is even harder, because it will be known. If I ask for a job somewhere else, I will appear to have run away from my debts.
>
> Female hotel worker, Mbale municipality

Overall, the role of ethnicity, clan membership and kinship in recruitment processes is likely to create information asymmetries to the disadvantage of job seekers and workers. In the absence of employment protection legislation, employers' privileged access to information about applicants from the same clan may be used to enforce acceptance of poor working conditions. Thus, relatedness to a locally powerful employer generally opens up job opportunities, but it also increases the likelihood of exploitation. In smaller companies, workers from the same clan as the employer may work under conditions similar to those faced by unpaid employees, because workers' requests for payments can be offset more easily by outstanding social obligations based on kin or clan relations. Comments made by respondents in the unstructured interviews with workers indicated that in the case of large companies, the relation between recruitment decisions and ethnicity or clan membership is less obvious.

Due to the high informality of employment, the generation of reliable quantitative data on the geographic and cultural (or ethnic) origin of workers was not possible. However, the survey data indicate that the importance of social relations based on kinship, clan membership, and ethnicity for recruitment decisions is reflected in employment numbers. In the construction sector, the majority of workers in any company were locals, namely men and women with the same ethnic background. Thus, 68 percent of the surveyed employers did not recruit significant[31] numbers of workers from different regions, while 32 percent said they did. When asked about the reasons for employing non-local workers, employers invariably pointed to a lack of adequately skilled labor, which forces them to employ people from other regions. The proportion of foreign migrant workers from neighboring countries was not perceived as significant by any surveyed employer. However, this estimation may be skewed as employers may have tried to portray themselves as patrons of local, and certainly of Ugandan, people, an image that would be threatened by large numbers of foreign workers.

In the hotel sector, the recruitment of workers from other regions was more significant, in particular inside the largest towns (Mbale and Jinja) and in Kampala, where refugees from the North and migrant workers from throughout the country are concentrated. Thus, only half (48 percent) of the surveyed hotels overwhelmingly recruited locals, while the other half (52 percent) recruited significant numbers of non-locals. The employment of foreigners for managerial jobs was widespread, but according to employers, no hotel had a significant number of foreign workers below the managerial level. However, it should be noted that the number of foreign and Ugandan non-local workers was possibly understated by employers who were keen to portray themselves as patrons of local people.

To summarize, the terms and conditions for selling and buying the 'pseudo-commodity' labor (Storper & Walker 1989) are negotiated in social and political processes that reach well beyond the sphere of other commodity markets. The data presented above indicate that the social regulation of labor market transactions contributes to maintaining existing inequalities, because the prevalent social norms and practices that legitimize the terms and conditions of employment are based on durable inequalities (in Tilly's sense of the term). These discriminate against large sections of the labor force, most notably on the basis of gender as well as complex structures of social obligation and notions of indebtedness.

## *Labor organization in the coffee sector*

An analysis of the processes of "depeasantization" is not the aim of this book; however, some conclusions about the potential effects of rural income diversification on structures of socio-economic organization in rural labor markets – which may act as a driver of change in labor market regulations – can be drawn from the above presented data. Increasing wage-labor activity not only provides new opportunities for the generation of incomes, it also creates new forms of exploitation and dependency that are likely to shape informal structures of socio-economic organization. Given the lack of employment protection legislation in Uganda and the weak development of trade unions in particular in the agricultural sector, there are multiple barriers to the development of effective representational structures among casual wage workers in the coffee sector. However, the data from Uganda's coffee sector point to the prevalence of informal labor organization among male factory workers as well as sporadic labor action among women workers, in particular at the processing stations in rural areas. More research is necessary to explore the conditions for and the effects of the formation of informal labor organization among male and female workers in rural areas.[32] The limited data on rural labor organization collected for this study shed some light on the development of collective action among casual agricultural workers and point out existing knowledge gaps.

In contrast to the organization of small producers in cooperatives, formal economic organization among agricultural wage workers in Uganda is largely non-existent. Throughout the country, the formal structures for the representation of rural wage workers' interests are weak or are missing altogether. The coverage of the National Trade Union of Agricultural and Plantation workers is minimal and membership numbers in other unions that include significant numbers of rural workers, such as Fisheries and Allied Workers; Hotels, Food, Tourism and Allied Workers; and Farm and Agro-based Workers, are equally small (UBOS 2007, p. 35–36; interviews, *see* Table 1.2, Chapter 1). Furthermore, unions across the economy lack political influence, and accusations of a widespread management bias have been made (Barya 2010; Devereux 2005).

The weak development of an identity as wage workers among the agricultural labor force seems to be perpetuated on the one hand by the lack of trade union activity within the agricultural sector and on the other hand by a low social status of casual agricultural wage work in comparison with farming. The national union for agricultural wage workers implemented no activities in Uganda's coffee sector at the time of data generation, and none of the surveyed casual workers or respondents in the semi-structured interviews was a member. Although some casual workers are organized in growers' cooperatives, and are thus familiar with formal economic organization, none of the casual agricultural workers who were interviewed for the present study had any connection with a trade union or had ever benefited from one. In the semi-structured interviews with small producers, the low social status of agricultural wage work was repeatedly pointed out, while casual workers with land holdings, however small, emphasized their activity as farmers in addition to wage work.

The prevailing ideology of self-employment as farmers is likely to impede the formation of widespread collective action among casual workers. Thus, farmers-cum-wage workers throughout the research area were likely to emphasize their identity as farmers, rather than wage workers. When interviewed in their homes, villages, or on their coffee farms, coffee producers rarely talked about their wage work without being specifically asked about it. During focus group discussions, relations of inequality and exploitation within coffee production and marketing, both at the household level and within the wider socio-economic environment were vividly discussed, while the dependence on wage work was frequently down-played. Direct questions about the importance of wage work for a particular group or person were often responded to with explanations about the secondary role of seasonal jobs. This representation of wage work as a marginal activity contrasts with its role as the most important additional source of income for a quarter of organized farmers (*see* Table 2.7).

While the vast majority of surveyed cooperative members emphasized the benefits of and the barriers to being thus organized, no one highlighted the need for similar support structures during their activities as wage workers. This

*Table 2.7* Prevalence (%) of regular additional income sources for cooperative members

| *Type of main regular additional source of income* | *Prevalence* |
|---|---|
| Wage work (agricultural and non-agricultural) | 25.1 |
| Non-agricultural self-employment (own business) | 29.8 |
| Not applicable (no major additional sources of income) | 45.1 |

apparent disregard of labor organization is not, however, a sign of its insignificance. Throughout the research area, workers organize informally, mostly to secure access to jobs and partly to improve working conditions. Furthermore, when probed on the issue of wage work, workers, many of whom are farmers as well, explain that they value their jobs as an essential and fairly regular source of income. Although casual workers equally emphasized their identity as farmers, all the interview respondents in coffee processing factories and field stations also confirmed that they held a 'good job' because it presented an opportunity to earn a regular income for part of the year. Although agricultural wage work undoubtedly is of low social status due to its association with low skills and possible landlessness, workers appreciate it as an income source that is perceived as more secure than smallholder farming in a liberalized economic environment. Thus, Nathan Wakadala, a transport and storage worker, explained that although he estimated his yearly income from crops to be higher than his wage, he largely relied on the wage money to pay his regular expenses.

Informal organizational structures and sporadic labor action were found both in Kyagalanyi's large processing factory in Mbale town and in the processing stations, also managed by Kyagalanyi, that are scattered on the slopes of Mt. Elgon.[33] Male workers, who are mostly responsible for loading and off-loading trucks and storing coffee bags in the factory warehouses, tend to be members of labor gangs. Women, who largely work as coffee graders, both at the processing factory in Mbale town and at the processing stations in rural areas, tend to belong to loose, informal support groups. The labor gangs regulate access to jobs in transport and storage, where workers are generally selected on a daily basis at the factory gate. The gang leaders directly negotiate the number of jobs with the factory manager, as well as sporadic increases in overall wage levels.[34] Men's labor gangs are somewhat more formal than the support groups of female workers. Coffee graders are employed on a weekly basis and mainly rely on 'personal recommendations' by other workers to secure access to jobs. Such recommendations are frequently given within existing support groups of women who cooperate outside the workplace, either in their village or their neighborhood.[35]

Men's labor gangs seem to have tight control of access to jobs. Nathan Wakadala explained that without the labor gang, getting a job in transport and storage would have been impossible for him. At the same time, factory managers also maintain close relations with gang leaders as a way to maintain control over the labor force. There is a large pool of surplus labor, but the manager nevertheless depends to some extent on the gang leaders, because the latter manage the provision of the right number of workers on a daily basis and ensure that the hired labor is working hard under the given conditions. Labor gang leaders therefore have a strategic position between workers and employers, which they utilize to negotiate access to jobs and wage levels on behalf of workers, but also to extract shares of members' wages for their services.

Thus, men's labor gangs have ambiguous effects, and they potentially hinder rather than enable the formation of broader alliances of workers across work places and employers. On the one hand, they ensure a relatively reliable access to jobs for members and they are presumably more effective in negotiating higher wages than individual workers.[36] On the other hand, labor gangs contribute to a fragmentation of the work force into a large number of competing groups that are not connected with each other by an overarching organizational framework. In addition, labor gangs seem to lack internal democratic structures of representation, while their leaders may maintain close relations with factory managers and with each other.[37] Against this background, labor gangs might provide footholds for exploitation by barring individual workers from membership on the grounds of existing social divisions and inequalities, thereby effectively inhibiting the formation of class interests. Also, in the absence of relevant organizational mechanisms to protect members' interests, labor-gang leaders may start to extract increasing shares of members' wages.

An exploration of these issues goes beyond the scope of this study and more research is needed to evaluate the internal organizational structures of labor gangs and their effects on socio-economic outcomes. The present data indicate that they *potentially* strengthen workers' ability to defend their interests, but in their current form, this potential remains limited. The nature of informal labor organizations such as labor gangs seems to create barriers to the formation of an identity of workers that cuts across individual labor gangs. Further research into the ethnic, cultural, and social composition of labor gangs could shed more light on the possible linkages between the prevalence of labor gangs and the lack of broader alliances of workers in labor unions or less formalized workers' associations. The organizational weakness of Uganda's national union and its various sector-specific organizations, which remain largely inactive in rural Uganda, certainly contributes to the lack of formal labor organization across the coffee sector or even the agricultural sector at large. However, it is unlikely to represent a sufficient explanation.

Women's informal support groups are very loose organizational structures, generally without an appointed leader, and they have a much weaker influence on access to jobs than labor gangs. Most women apply for their jobs individually, not as a group or through a group leader, but the factory manager frequently follows the recommendations given by members of such groups, generally for fellow group members. Newcomers thereby gain access to jobs in the factory or processing station on the basis of informal support networks built outside the work place. Typically, these support networks have no influence on wage levels or working conditions, because group-based activities are limited to bringing members into the factory, but are not utilized to represent workers' interests in negotiations with the management. This is effectively not possible, because workers neither necessarily belong to support groups, nor are the latter connected with each other. Thus, support groups are generally not able to effectively control access to jobs.

However, female workers at coffee processing stations in rural areas engage in sporadic labor action to press for specific improvements in working conditions. Thus, during the fieldwork for this research, coffee graders at Kyagalanyi's processing station in Sironko district went on strike to enforce the payment of lunch money and a lunch-time break that was long enough for women to feed their babies, have food themselves and sit in the shade to rest.[38] In the case of this strike, a relatively large informal support group that was made up of women from neighboring villages played an essential role. During the formation of the strike, one woman emerged as a temporary leader who took over negotiations with the station manager. The result of the strike was the introduction of a small cash payment for lunch, as well as a slightly longer lunch break. However, the station manager was fired shortly afterwards on the grounds of differences of opinion with the operational manger. Thus, women workers' temporary, informal groups may provide an effective basis for *ad hoc* labor protests and they might contribute to the development of greater organizational capacities among workers. At the same time, they do not provide permanent organizational structures, and thus might not be able to sustain and up-scale achieved improvements in working conditions.

The discussion above has shown that the social relations underlying widespread poverty among the working population in Uganda need to be understood within the context of historically specific labor market structures that are shaped by neoliberal economic reforms, ineffective state institutions, and dominant social norms and practices that regulate labor market transactions. In contrast to cooperative members, wage workers in Uganda are likely to interact on an informal and often individual basis with employers and the state. The weak development of trade unions and social dialogue significantly limits their negotiating power, while the social regulation of labor market transactions on the basis of social binaries impedes the formation of class interests. Formal labor organizations are not a panacea for the creation of equity in labor market transactions; in fact, they may be driven by elite interests, but they tend to *mitigate* inequalities while also providing a platform for generating institutional change, such as the development and enforcement of employment protection legislation.

Given the increasing importance of multi-occupational income strategies for rural households, cooperatives could provide impulses for the development of formal labor organization at the primary level. One form of organization, which is centered on production and trade, might therefore spill over into greater organizational capabilities around labor to improve working conditions. The widespread recognition of the importance of smallholder agriculture for inclusive rural development has led to a renewed interest in cooperatives, and since their revival in rural Africa in the early 2000s, they are again supported by governments and donors as effective institutions for enhancing market access for small producers, increasing rural incomes and local food security, and promoting rural employment (Kariuki & Place 2005; Poulton et al. 1998; Dorward et al. 2004). However, this renewed interest in cooperatives and the associated discourse of the Social and Solidarity Economy (SSE), largely conceptualizes cooperatives as an instrument of rural poverty reduction that is essentially non-threatening to current patterns of distribution in global agricultural value chains. Overall, the debate about the SSE – and about cooperatives as its flagship organizational form – promotes a narrow view of the role of collective action among small producers. Furthermore, as farmers-cum-wage-workers, small producers are part of the laboring classes (Bernstein 2008, p. 18), and cooperatives are the single most important form of collective action among this large and disadvantaged population section. It is hoped that the data that have been presented above will contribute towards a more politicized discussion of economic organization among poor working people – in particular, but not exclusively, in rural areas.

## Notes

1 At less than one hectare per farm, average land holdings in Uganda's coffee sector are small (Ribbink et al. 2005; data collected for this study). Under the prevalent land heritage systems in Uganda, family plots are divided into ever smaller plots, usually among sons or other male relatives.

2 There is no aggregate data on wage levels per economic sector in Uganda. However, interviews with government officers and workers in agricultural and non-agricultural labor markets indicated that most workers are unable to secure a modest living standard from their wage.

3 Value added per worker in Uganda has in the past been estimated to be 68 percent lower than in India, 96 percent lower than in China and 28 percent lower than in Tanzania (GoU 2010, p. 205).

4 Willie Onyang Odwongo, a rural development specialist at the World Bank in Kampala, described how formerly widespread communal forms of balanced labor exchange have been monetized in rural Uganda. Growers throughout the research area confirmed his account.

5 Policies for entrepreneurship development in low-income countries are generally based on the assumption that many poor workers are self-employed and can benefit significantly from micro interventions aimed at creating economic opportunities at the local level (Rizzo 2011b). This assumption neglects the large and increasing numbers of people in urban and rural areas who face exploitative employment conditions that are unlikely to change without addressing structural inequalities (*ibid.*).

6 Information gathered from the unstructured interviews and participant observation in coffee-growing villages indicated that farmers who grow crops for local rather than export markets are even more likely to depend on additional wage work, because their income from farming tends to be lower.

7 The terms 'labor force' and 'working population' are used interchangeably and follow the definition used in Uganda's national household survey: youth, women and men between 14 and 64 years of age.

8 Coffee growers with relatively large holdings (above five acres) were excluded because they are generally able to secure themselves better against natural risks and could therefore rely on income from farming to a much greater extent. Most of them could invest in pesticides against diseases and they generally had several plots and were thus less likely to lose their entire harvest in landslides.

9 There is little data on how many rural dwellers commute to urban areas for non-agricultural wage work and how much informal labor is hired within rural areas. While the data on wage employment in the informal sector has improved significantly with recent household surveys, no breakdown for rural areas exists.

10 Aspects of social status are important in the context of data generation through surveys. In countries with a poor communications infrastructure, such as Uganda, labor market and household surveys are still largely conducted through personal interviews. Interviewers tend to be well-educated urban residents, who generally have a higher social status than their rural respondents. Furthermore, other community members are likely to listen to interviews, making the response to personal questions a representational exercise that can affect personal assessments of life circumstances.

11 The terms 'low-' and 'higher-skilled' are used to denote workers who are categorized according to the Uganda Vocational Qualifications Framework (UVQF) somewhere between the skills levels 1 and 3. The levels are defined as follows: Level 1 'works with a lot of supervision', level 2 'works longer intervals without supervision' and level 3 'can be left to supervise others' (MoES 2008). No category of workers in this study is considered to be 'unskilled', based on the assumption that no person has *no* skills and any job demands *some* skills. This assumption was confirmed when working – for not more than a few hours at a time - alongside female coffee sorters in factories in Mbale. This work is often considered 'unskilled', but it took considerable concentration and dexterity for the *other*-skilled, European researcher to perform for any stretch of time.

12 The non-agricultural labor market survey concentrated on interviewing employers, including only a small sample of 30 workers, because questionnaire-based interviews that focus, amongst other things, on working conditions are generally not permitted by employers. However, visits to 101 companies as well as unstructured interviews with skilled workers outside the workplace complemented the data collected from employers and helped to qualify the employers' views.

13 Cooperatives and large commodity buyers employ their own extension workers, also called business managers or field officers, to advise small producers. They also take on a control function to enforce agreements with producers on output volumes to be sold to a particular cooperative or company.

14 The regularity of payments to agricultural wage workers was not covered by the survey, due to resistance by factory managers against formally recorded information on this question. However, the questionnaire-based interviews with workers provided opportunities to discuss payment regularity informally with the respondent.

15 Participant observation was carried out during numerous visits to villages over the course of five months, as well as two months in the largest coffee processing factories, storage places and coffee processing stations in the research area. These were run by two MNCs, Kyagalanyi and Kawacom, and by the cooperatives BCU and Gumutindo.

16 Factory managers had to report to their superiors about the research conducted on the company's premises and a copy of the questionnaire was sent to headquarters in Kampala. On the advice of the local managers, questions on payment regularity and adherence to health and safety standards were taken out. Subsequently, all qualitative data collection was treated with a generous 'don't ask – don't tell' policy and the researcher and her assistants were able to move around freely inside the factory to speak to workers.

17 BCU was only employing a few workers at the time, but the lack of health and safety appliances for the workers in its factory were clearly visible.
18 *Leja-leja* is Lugandan, and roughly translates into 'helper'. It is the term used for low-skilled, casual workers in most regions of Uganda and is understood throughout the country.
19 The survey results show that employment is more formalized in the hotel than in the construction sector. Thus, 63 percent of hotel managers and owners had written contracts with all semi- and higher-skilled workers, against 47 percent in the construction sector. Only 13 percent declared having no work contracts at all, against 22 percent in the construction sector.
20 The lack of up-to-date business registries in Uganda meant that many companies could not easily be contacted by telephone. Frequently, a personal visit, although time-consuming, was the most promising strategy.
21 Religion is a further social category that may serve to regulate labor market transactions. However, because the majority of the population within the fieldwork area belongs to the same group of Protestant Christian churches, religion was not included in this current survey.
22 Tilly's (1998) analysis of inequality illuminates the crucial organizational work of social binaries based on categories of gender, ethnicity, kinship, or religion. As such binary pairs are associated with access to resources, they contribute to creating, maintaining, and naturalizing economic inequalities.
23 However, it should be noted that even in open-access societies in which the enforcement of impersonal rules is highly advanced, members of social, political, and economic elites are still likely to have better access to some institutions, such as universities or professional clubs.
24 The role of widely accepted norms and practices for the reproduction of inequalities within the labor market explains why such inequalities tend to persist to some extent – or disappear very slowly – even in a context of effective state regulation aimed at creating more equal access to jobs and wages.
25 *See*, for example, Seguino & Grown (2006) for a discussion of how the liberalization of the economy in low-income countries impedes the transformation of gender inequalities in the labor market. The authors show that the reproduction of gender inequalities is closely linked to the structures of globalized capitalism.
26 Due to the small number of interviews with employees, no figures are given.
27 The largest coffee processing factory in Eastern Uganda, run by Kyagalanyi, employed approximately one thousand *leja-leja* workers during the time of the fieldwork, but only around a dozen skilled workers, including field officers, supervisors, and machine operators. This estimation, given by the factory management, applies to the busy, bi-annual harvest/post-harvest season, which lasts about two months. The skilled workers tend to be employed throughout the year.
28 At the time of the fieldwork in 2009, there were few female skilled workers. Gumutindo employed female operational managers in its main office in Mbale municipality, while Kyagalanyi, the Ugandan branch of a large MNC, employed one female field station manager. All extension workers, supervisors, and machine attendants in the factories and field stations were male.
29 In the case of joint ethnic origin, it is often possible – and, indeed, a widespread practice – to establish some degree of relatedness within employment relations, usually based on membership in related clans.
30 The hotel sector provided numerous examples of this situation, in particular in small hotels with around a dozen permanent employees in total.
31 Generating exact numbers was not possible, because employers either keep no records or prefer to give estimations only, because most workers are informally employed. The term 'significant' is used to describe the employers' phrase of "a visible proportion of workers", such as ten percent or more.

32 Due to gender-based labor market segregation within the agricultural sector, informal labor organization differs significantly between male and female workers.

33 At the time of the research, only a few processing factories, all located in Mbale municipality, were functional. The qualitative data were collected in the largest coffee processing factory of Eastern Uganda, run by Kyagalanyi, and in Kyagalanyi's processing station in Busulani, Sironko district.

34 No such increases were negotiated at the research locations during the times of data collection.

35 As noted in Chapter 5, women in rural areas often belong to informal groups aimed at providing mutual support in different spheres of life. Without specific objectives, the economic effects of such groups are difficult to measure and may frequently be negligible. However, in this case, they seem to have some positive effects on access to casual agricultural jobs.

36 No substantial data were collected on the effects of labor gangs on wage levels. Also, no negotiations for higher wages took place at the factory in Mbale during the times of data collection. However, supervisors at the factory confirmed that gang leaders represent workers in negotiations over wages, and it can be assumed that a small number of representatives are better able to negotiate than individual workers, who can be easily undercut by other workers competing for the same jobs.

37 An analysis of the internal organizational structures of labor gangs and other informal organizational structures among wage workers, such as women's support groups, goes beyond the scope of this study. More research is necessary to explore how access to such gangs and groups is regulated and the extent to which their organization follows democratic principles.

38 None of the processing stations offer shaded workplaces for coffee sorters. This represents a significant strain on workers, who work up to ten hours a day, because the main post-harvest period, when coffee sorters are employed, is during the dry season.

## References

ADAMS, A. V. 2010, 'The Role of Skills Development in Overcoming Social Disadvantage', Technical Note to Inform UNESCO's 2012 Global Monitoring Report on Education, UNESCO, Paris.

ADAMS, A. V. 2008, 'Skills development in the informal sector of sub-Saharan Africa', World Bank, Washington, DC.

ADNAN, S. 2007, 'Departures from Everyday Resistance and Flexible Strategies of Domination: The Making and Unmaking of a Poor Peasant Mobilization in Bangladesh', *Journal of Agrarian Change*, 7, 183–224.

ASHTON, D. N. & GREEN, F. 1996, *Education, training, and the global economy*, Edward Elgar Publishers, Cheltenham, UK, Brookfield, VT.

BARRETT, C. B., CLARK, M. B., CLAY, D. C. & REARDON, T. 2005, 'Heterogeneous constraints, incentives and income diversification strategies in rural Africa', *Quarterly Journal of International Agriculture*, 44, 37–60.

BARYA, J.J. 2010, 'Trade unions, liberalisation and politics in Uganda', in *Trade unions & party politics: labour movements in Africa*, Edited by Björn Beckman, Sakhela Buhlungu and Lloyd Sachikonye, HSRC Press, Cape Town, 219 p.

BASILE, E. & HARRISS-WHITE, B. 2003, 'Corporatist capitalism: The politics of accumulation in South India', In: R.J. BENEWICK, M. B. & COOK, S. (eds.) Asian politics in development: Essays in honour of Gordon White. Frank Cass, London.

BERNSTEIN, H.2008, Agrarian Change in a Globalising World: (Final) Farewells to the Peasantry?, Paper presented at the Journal of Agrarian Change Workshop on Agrarian Change: Lineages and Prospects, SOAS, University of London, London, 1-2 May 2008.

BOURDIEU, P. 1997, *The Forms of Capital*, Oxford University Press.

BOURDIEU, P. 1990, *The logic of practice*, Stanford University Press.

BOURDIEU, P. & PASSERON, J.C. 1977, 'Reproduction in education, culture and society', *Trans.Nice,* Sage, London.

BOURGOIS, P. 2001, 'The Power of Violence in War and Peace: Post-Cold War Lessons from El Salvador', *Ethnography*, 2(1), 5–34.

BOWLES, S. & GINTIS, H. 1976, *Schooling in capitalist America: Educational reform and the contradictions of economic life*, Basic Books, New York.

BOWLES, S. & GINTIS, H. 1975, 'The Problem with Human Capital Theory - A Marxian Critique', *American Economic Review*, 65, 74–82.

BRAVERMAN, H. 1974, *Labor and monopoly capital: the degradation of work in the twentieth century*, Monthly Review Press, New York.

BREMAN, J. 2003, *The labouring poor in India: patterns of exploitation, subordination, and exclusion*, Oxford University Press, New Delhi, New York.

BREMAN, J. 2001, 'An Informalised Labour System: End of Labour Market Dualism', *Economic and Political Weekly*, 36, 4804–4821.

BREMAN, J. 1996, *Footloose Labour: Work and Life in the Informal Sector Economy of West India*, Cambridge University Press, Cambridge, UK.

BREMAN, J. 1995, 'Labour, Get Lost: A Late-Capitalist Manifesto', *Economic and Political Weekly*, 30, 2294–2300.

BRYCESON, D. F., KAY, C. & MOOIJ, J. 2000, *Disappearing peasantries? Rural labour in Africa, Asia and Latin America*, Intermediate Technology, London.

BRYCESON, D. F. 1999, 'African rural labour, income diversification & livelihood approaches: a long-term development perspective', *Review of African Political Economy*, 26, 171–189.

BYERLEE, D. & SPENCER, D. S. C. 1977, 'Small farms in West Africa: a descriptive analysis of employment, incomes, and productivity in Sierra Leone', Njala University College.

CARNEY, D. 1999, *Approaches to sustainable livelihoods for the rural poor*, Overseas Development Institute ODI Poverty Briefing, London, UK.

CARSWELL, G. 1997, 'Agricultural intensification and rural sustainable livelihoods: a 'think piece'', *IDS Working Paper 64*, IDS, Brighton.

CHABAL, P. 2009, *Africa: the Politics of Suffering and Smiling*, Zed books, London and New York.

CHABAL, P. & DALOZ, J. P. 1999, *Africa Works: the Political Instrumentalization of Disorder*, Indiana University Press, Bloomington.

COLLIER, P. & GUNNING, J. W. 1999, 'Explaining African Economic Performance', *Journal of Economic Literature*, 37, 64–111.

CRAMER, C., OYA, C. & SENDER, J. 2008, 'Lifting the Blinkers: A New View of Power and Poverty in Mozambican Rural Labour Markets', *Journal of Modern African Studies*, 46, 361–392.

CRAMER, C. & SENDER, J. 1999, 'Poverty, Wage Labor and Agricultural Change in Rural Eastern and Southern Africa', International Fund for Agricultural Development (IFAD), Rome.

COUSINS, B., WEINER, D. & AMIN, N. 1992, 'Social Differentiation in the Communal Lands of Zimbabwe', *Review of African Political Economy,* 19, 3–24.
DAVIS, B., DI GIUSEPPE, S., & ZEZZAC, A. 2017, 'Are African households (not) leaving agriculture? Patterns of households' income sources in rural Sub-Saharan Africa', *Food Policy*, 67, 153–174.
DEVEREUX, S. 2005, 'Can minimum wages contribute to poverty reduction in poor countries?', *Journal of International Development*, 17, 899–912.
DORWARD, A., KYDD, J., MORRISON, J., UREY, I. 2004. "A Policy Agenda for Pro-Poor Agricultural Growth", *World Development* 32(1): 73-89.
DUNCAN, A. & HOWELL, J. 1992, *Structural Adjustment and the African Farmer*, ODI, London.
EIU 2017, *Country Report Uganda*, Economist Intelligence Unit, London.
ELLIS, F. 1998, 'Household Strategies and Rural Livelihood Diversification', *Journal of Development Studies*, 35, 1–38.
ELSON, D. 1999, 'Labor Markets as Gendered Institutions: Equality, Efficiency and Empowerment Issues', *World Development*, 27, 611–627.
ELSON, D. 1981, "Nimble Fingers Make Cheap Workers': An Analysis of Women's Employment in Third World Export Manufacturing', *Feminist Review*, 7, 87–107.
FIELDS, G. S. 2007, 'Labor Market Policy in Developing Countries: A Selective Review of the Literature and Needs for the Future', *Working Papers ILR Collections*, Cornell University.
FOX, L. 2009, 'Sharing the Growth in Uganda: Recent Labor Market Outcomes and Poverty Reduction', *Draft Note*, USAID.
GOU 2010, 'National Development Plan 2010/11–2014/15', Government of Uganda, National Planning Authority, Kampala, Republic of Uganda.
HARRISS-WHITE, B. 2003, 'Inequality at Work in the Informal Economy: Key Issues and Illustrations', *International Labour Review*, 142, 459–470.
HURST, P., TERMINE, P. & KARL, M. 2005, 'Agricultural Workers and their Contribution to Sustainable Agriculture and Rural Development', Food and Agricultural Organisation (FAO); International Labour Office (ILO); and International Union of Food, Agricultural, Hotel, Restaurant, Catering, Tobacco and Allied Workers' Associations (IUF), Rome.
IFAD 2016, 'Rural Development Report 2016: Fostering inclusive rural transformation', International Fund for Agricultural Development (IFAD), Rome.
IFAD 2011, 'Rural Poverty Report 2011: New realities, new challenges: new opportunities for tomorrow's generation', International Fund for Agricultural Development, Rome.
ILO 2002a, 'Decent work and the informal economy', International Labour Conference 90th Session Report VI Sixth item on the agenda, International Labour Organisation, Geneva.
ILO 2002b, 'Decent Work and the Informal Economy', Abstracts of Working Papers, International Labour Organisation, Geneva.
ILOSTATS, Available from: <www.ilo.org>. [5 January 2018].
IUFAHTA 2009, 'Working conditions in the African cut flower sector', International Union of Food Agricultural Hotel Restaurant Catering Tobacco and Allied Workers Association (IUFAHTA).
JUDD, E. R. 1990, 'Men Are More Able: Rural Chinese Women's Conceptions of Gender and Agency', *Pacific Affairs*, 63, 40–61.

KABEER, N. 2008, 'Gender, Labour Markets and Poverty. An Overview', *Poverty in Focus: Special Issue on Gender Equality*, 13, 3–5.

KABEER, N. 2003, 'Gender inequality in educational outcomes: a household perspective', *Background paper prepared for the Education for All Global Monitoring Report 2003/4 Gender and Education for All: The Leap to Equality*, UNESCO, Paris.

KABEER, N. 1997, 'Women, Wages and Intrahousehold Power Relations in Urban Bangladesh', *Development and Change*, 28, 261–302.

KAGUNDU, P. & PAVLOVA, O. 2007, 'Gender wage differentials in Uganda: Evidence from the Uganda National Household Survey', Andrew Young School of Policy, Atlanta.

KARIUKI, G. & PLACE, F. 2005, 'Initiatives for rural development through collective action: the case of household participation in group activities in the highlands of central Kenya', CAPRi Working Paper 43, IFPRI, Washington D.C.

KERKVLIET, B.J.T. 2009, 'Everyday politics in peasant societies (and ours)', *The Journal of Peasant Studies*, 36:1, 227–243.

KERKVLIET, B.J.T. 1990, *Everyday politics in the Philippines: class and status relations in a central Luzon village*, University of California Press, Berkeley, CA.

KEVANE, M. 1994, 'Village Labor Markets in Sheikan District, Sudan', *World Development*, 22, 839.

LACHAUD, J. P. 1994, *The Labour Market in Africa*, International Labour Organization, Geneva.

LEE, C. K. 1995, 'Engendering the Worlds of Labor: Women Workers, Labor Markets, and Production Politics in the South China Economic Miracle', *American Sociological Review*, 60, 378–397.

MEAGHER, K. 2010, *Identity Economics: Social Networks and the Informal Economy in Nigeria*, James Currey, Woodbridge, UK.

MILANOVIC, B. 2010, *The Haves and the Have-nots: A Short and Idiosyncratic History of Inequality*, Basic Books, New York.

MoES 2008, 'BTVET Act', Ministry of Education and Sports, Kampala, Republic of Uganda.

MWAMADZINGO, M. 2003, 'Addressing the Decent Work Deficit in African Agriculture: Priority Issues', ILO, SRO, Geneva.

NORTH, D. C., WALLIS, J. J. & WEINGAST, B. R. 2009, *Violence and Social Orders: A conceptual Framework for Interpreting Recorded Human History*, University Press, New York, Cambridge.

ORTNER, S. 1974, Is Female to Male as Nature is to Culture? In: ROSALDO, M. & LAMPHERE, L. (eds.) *Woman, Culture, and Society*. Stanford University Press, Stanford, CA.

OTSUKA, K. & YAMANO, T. 2008, 'The Role of Rural Labor Markets in Poverty Reduction: Evidence from Asia and East Africa', World Bank, Washington D.C.

OYA, C. 2010a, 'Rural Inequality, Wage Employment and Labour Market Formation in Africa: Historical and Micro-Level Evidence', *Working Paper No. 97.*, International Labour Organisation, Geneva.

OYA, C. 2010b, 'Rural Labour Markets in Africa: The Unreported Source of Inequality and Poverty', *Development Viewpoint Number 57.*, School of Oriental and African Studies, London.

OYA, C. 2004, 'The Empirical Investigation of Rural Class Formation: Methodological Issues in a Study of Large- and Mid-Scale Farmers in Senegal', *Historical Materialism*, 12, 289–326.

OYA, C. & SENDER, J. 2009, 'Divorced, separated and widowed female workers in rural Mozambique', *Feminist Economics*, 15, 1–31.

PARRY, J. P., BREMAN, J. & KAPADIA, K. 1999, *The Worlds of Indian Industrial Labour*, SAGE, New Delhi; London; Thousand Oaks.

PERRY, D. 2000, 'Rural Weekly Markets and the Dynamics of Time, Space and Community in Senegal', *Journal of Modern African Studies*, 38, 481–486.

PONTARA, N. 2010, *A Critical Examination of Theoretical and Methodological Approaches to Low-income Country Labour Markets: A Case Study of Mauritania*. Doctoral dissertation, School of Oriental and African Studies (SOAS), University of London.

POULTON, C., DORWARD, A., KYDD, J. 1998, 'A new institutional economics perspective on current policy debates', *Smallholder Cash Crop Production Under Market Liberalization: A New Institutional Economics Perspective*, CAB International, Wallingford, UK.

RAZAVI, S. 1999, 'Export-Oriented Employment, Poverty and Gender: Contested Accounts', *Development and Change*, 30, 653–683.

REARDON, T. 1997, 'Using Evidence of Household Income Diversification to Inform Study of the Rural Nonfarm Labor Market in Africa', *World Development*, 25, 735–741.

RIBBINK, G., NYABUNTU, P. & KUMAR, S. 2005, 'Successful Supply Chains in Uganda: A study of three successful chains in the coffee, dried fruit and fresh vegetables sectors', DFID; ILO, Geneva and London.

RIZZO, M. 2011a, 'Rural wage employment in Rwanda and Ethiopia: A review of the current policy neglect and a framework to begin addressing it', International Labour Organization, Geneva.

RIZZO, M. 2011b, *The Struggles of Informal Transport Workers in Tanzania: Debunking the Myth of Micro Solutions*, Centre for Development Policy and Research, School of Oriental and African Studies, London.

RUKMINI, D. V. 1998, Women's Employment Status by Marital Status in Harayana. *In*: CHEN, M. A. (ed.) *Widows in India*. SAGE, New Delhi.

SCOTT, J. C. 1985, *Weapons of the weak: everyday forms of peasant resistance*, Yale University Press, New Haven, CT.

SEGUINO, S. & GROWN, C. 2006, 'Gender Equity and Globalization: Macroeconomic Policy for Developing Countries', *Journal of International Development*, 18, 1081–1104.

SENDER, J. 2000, 'Struggles to escape poverty in South Africa: results from a purposive rural survey', Department of Economics, School of Oriental and African Studies, London.

SENDER, J. & CRAMER, C. 2005, 'Unequal prospects: disparities in the quantity and quality of labour supply in sub-Saharan Africa', *Social Protection Discussion Paper Series*. Social Protection Unit, World Bank, Washington, D.C.

SENDER, J. & JOHNSTON, D. 1995, 'A fuzzy snapshot of some poor and invisible women: farm labourers in South Africa', Dept. of Economics, School of Oriental and African Studies, University of London, London.

SSENKABIRWA, A. M. 2010, 'Workers want Employment Policy', *The Monitor*, Kampala.

STORPER, M. & WALKER, R. 1989, *The capitalist imperative: territory, technology and industrial growth*, Basil Blackwell, Oxford.

STRATHERN, M. 1980, *No Nature, No Culture: The Hagen Case. Nature, Culture and Gender*, Cambridge University Press, Cambridge.

TILLY, C. 1998, *Durable inequality*, University of California Press, Ltd., Berkeley and Los Angeles, California.

UBOS 2017, 'Uganda National Household Survey 2016/17', Uganda National Bureau of Statistics, Kampala, Republic of Uganda.

UBOS 2010a, 'Uganda National Household Survey 2009/10 Socio-economic module', Uganda National Bureau of Statistics, Kampala, Republic of Uganda.

UBOS 2010b, '2010 Statistical abstract', Uganda National Bureau of Statistics, Kampala, Republic of Uganda.

UBOS 2007, 'Report on the Labour Market Conditions in Uganda', Uganda National Bureau of Statistics, Kampala, Republic of Uganda.

UCA 2008, 'Household Survey Eastern Uganda', UCA, Uganda Cooperative Alliance Eastern Regional Office, Unpublished Document.

UNDP 2005, 'Uganda Hum Dev Report', United Nations Development Programme (UNDP).

VAN DER GEEST, W. & VAN DER HOEVEN, R. 1999, *Adjustment, employment & missing institutions in Africa: the experience in Eastern & Southern Africa*, International Labour Office, Geneva.

VAUGHAN, M. 1998, Exploitation and neglect: rural producers and the state in Malawi and Zambia. In: BIRMINGHAM, D. & MARTIN, P. (eds.) *History of Central Africa: The Contemporary Years, since 1960*. Longman, London and New York.

WALKER, K.L.M. 2008, 'From Covert to Overt: Everyday Peasant Resistance Politics in China and the Implications for Transnational Agrarian Movements', *Journal of Agrarian Change* 8(2 and 3), 462–488.

WEDIG, K. 2010, 'Linking labour organisation and vocational training in Uganda: lessons for rural poverty reduction', Focales: AFD Research Department, Agence Francaise de Developpement, Paris.

WHITE, H. & LEAVY, J. 2003, 'Labour Markets in Rural Africa: What Do Models Need to Explain', IDS.

WORLD BANK DATA, Available from: <https://data.worldbank.org>. [5 January 2018].

WORLD BANK 2016, *Uganda Poverty Assessment 2016*, World Bank, Washington D.C.

WORLD BANK 2007, *World Development Report 2008: Agriculture for Development*, World Bank, Washington D.C.

# 3 Cooperatives as a driver of inclusive rural development

This chapter examines the political-economic conditions under which cooperatives may function as an instrument for achieving inclusive social and economic development. The first section examines the origins and development of the Social and Solidarity Economy (SSE), which provides a conceptual framework for the potential role of cooperatives to the achievement of greater equality in the distribution of access to resources and benefits of economic growth. The discussion contributes to a re-politicized debate on the SSE and cooperatives as one of its central forms of economic organization. The section calls for a stronger engagement within the international debate on development, with the activist ideas of the SSE movement, which aims to transform neoliberal economies into more just, equal, and sustainable systems of social and economic exchange. The second section of the chapter provides a brief history of cooperatives in Africa and the past political-economic conditions encountered by small producer organizations in the region. It outlines the historical development of cooperatives under colonialism and reviews the main reasons for the widespread failure of large, state-controlled agricultural cooperatives in the post-independence era to realize a significant redistribution of resources and profits in favor of small producers. The third section takes a closer look at current political-economic conditions for the operation of cooperatives by analyzing cooperative policies and agricultural development and investment strategies in Uganda and some of its East African neighbors.

## 3.1 The Social and Solidarity Economy (SSE)

The concept of the social economy emerged during the 19$^{th}$ century and refers to economic activities in any sector that are based on shared individual ownership, rather than stock or shareholder ownership. Thus, member-owned organizations, such as cooperatives and credit unions or other mutual associations, which are controlled by the democratic one-member one-vote principle, with open and voluntary membership, make up the social economy. Charles Dunoyer's 1830 publication *Nouveau traité d'économie sociale* first made the concept more widely known, and the earliest cooperatives appeared in the United Kingdom and throughout Europe in the following decades.[1] Other principles of the social economy, which partially follow from the democratic, member-based ownership and control principle,

*Figure 3.1* Gumutindo Cooperative, Training session in Mbale district

include the priority of social objectives over the interests of capital, the union of members' interests on the one hand and general social benefits or societal interests on the other, the realization of solidarity among members and among cooperatives and mutual associations, and the reinvestment of surpluses into services for members and into activities that are considered to further general societal interests.

The extension of the democratic ownership of businesses to all means of production has been promoted by some advocates of the social economy (*see*, for example, Jantet 2008). Under this condition, the social economy forms the basis for a comprehensive alternative development model to capitalism. But even if a fundamental transformation of the economic order on the basis of an all-encompassing new ownership structure is not achieved nor desired, the widespread presence of social economy enterprises can contribute to incremental structural changes by democratizing public policy through the principle of co-construction (Vaillancourt 2009). The basic condition for this to happen is a state that is open to the participation of civil society stakeholders and market forces in the design and implementation of services to the public (*ibid.*), however, the social economy also contributes to the existence of such a state by building and strengthening democratic institutions.

During the 1980s and 1990s, concepts of the social economy which emphasized the social *purpose* of enterprises, rather than their ownership structure emerged in the anglophone literature (Poirier 2013). According to this notion, social enterprises can be cooperatives, non-profits, or for-profits with a social purpose, and they often focus on social sectors, such as health, child-care, care of the elderly, or social work (*ibid.*).

Within the anglophone literature and in international debates on development, the term "third sector" has increasingly been used interchangeably with this purpose-based definition of the social economy (and with the concept of the SSE), even though this brushes over differences in the definitions of the two terms. The North American concept of the third sector, as adopted by the John Hopkins Project[2], defines it as the non-profit sector, which in the context of neoclassical economic theories of institutional choice is de facto a third-ranked option for when market- and state-based solutions to social and economic problems fail (Laville 2011).

The third sector notion severely limits the transformative power the social economy, because it applies the non-distribution constraint of non-profit organizations as a basic criterion for social economy enterprises, which by definition excludes cooperatives and mutual associations and neglects the possibility of widespread standards adoption by for-profit enterprises as a social economy instrument to extend the prioritization of the general interest to the logic of for-profit, market-based solutions (*ibid.*). A perhaps more potent criticism is the implicit hierarchization between 'market-based enterprises', 'state interventions' and 'non-profit solutions', which promotes, in Laville's words, a "shift towards a valorization of civil society as an alternative to the intervention of the state", because "the non-profit sector is summoned to justify the withdrawal of the state" (p. 5). Finally, it profoundly misrepresents the history of cooperatives and mutual associations, which regularly abstain from distributing any surplus to members and only have a limited legal ability for distribution, because the generation of returns on capital investments is not their primary objective (*ibid.*).

Widespread use of the term 'solidarity economy' started in the 1990s, and a first international meeting that focused on the concept took place in 1997. The concept of the solidarity economy is usually understood to promote a more radical, transformative notion of change than the social economy: while the latter is generally portrayed as a part or sector of the economy that is made up of collective enterprises or enterprises with a social purpose, the solidary economy entails a vision of an alternative economy altogether. Although some writers on the social economy have emphasized the transformative potential of democratic, member-based ownership structures, the concept itself offers little in terms of a roadmap for achieving the institutional changes that could lead to a far-reaching expansion of collective enterprises across the economy and society. The solidarity economy seeks to change this by proposing a pluralistic, context-sensitive approach to the creation of a post-capitalist economy.

Thus, the purpose of the solidarity economy is to "re-orient" (Kawano 2013) the institutions within the political and economic spheres toward social and environmental objectives. This vision, however, does not necessarily entail an opposition to capitalism, but promotes the transformation of the "life-damaging and growth-addicted features of low road capitalism" (p.5) into the "high road strategies" that reflect places "the values of justice, inclusion, balance, diversity, ecological sustainability, and financial viability" (Lewis & Swinney 2008). According to this view, the solidarity economy cuts across all three types of economies: the market-driven capitalist system, the planned economy, and the third system, which consists of social enterprises, voluntary organizations, and a family economy. Achieving the transformative goals of the solidarity economy depends not on the system that the dominant economic activities and strategies are part of, but on whether the latter are guided by the above-named *high road* values (*ibid.*). Yvon Poirier, member of the RIPESS Board of directors and RIPESS representative at the UN Inter-Agency Taskforce on SSE describes the transformative goals of the solidarity economy as follows:

> The solidarity economy seeks to change the whole social and economic system and puts forth a different paradigm of development that upholds solidarity economy principles. It pursues the transformation of the neoliberal capitalist economic system from one that gives primacy to maximizing private profit and blind growth, to one that puts people and planet at its core. As an alternative economic system, the solidarity economy thus includes all three sectors – private/for-profit, public and the third sector. The solidarity economy seeks to re-orient and harness the state, policies, trade, production, distribution, consumption, investment, money and finance, and ownership structures towards serving the welfare of people and the environment. What distinguishes the solidarity economy movement from many other social change and revolutionary movements in the past, is that it is pluralist in its approach - eschewing rigid blueprints and the belief in a single, correct path; the solidarity economy also values and builds on concrete practices, many of which are quite old, rather than seeking to create utopia out of thin air. Thus, the solidarity economy explicitly has a systemic, transformative, post-capitalist agenda. The social economy is a sector of the economy that may or may not be part of a transformative, post-capitalist agenda, depending on whom you are talking to. (Poirier 2013, pp. 75–76)

The concept of the Social and Solidarity Economy (SSE) emerged in the late 1990s from a critical debate about the ways in which the social economy had been accommodated to the interests of political and economic elites in maintaining the neoliberal status quo. Regional activist forums in Spanish and French speaking countries started to bring the two concepts together and in 2002, the Intercontinental Network for the Promotion of the Social and Solidarity Economy (RIPESS) was formed. The SSE includes the above-discussed concepts of the social economy into the broader and more comprehensive vision of a post-capitalist solidarity economy and society. It emphasizes the original ideas of the social economy as collective enterprises (mainly cooperatives and mutual associations), but also includes non-profit organizations. The SSE thus attempts to transcend de-politicized conceptualizations of the social economy as a remedy to state- and market failures and creates an inclusive, alternative development model.

In contrast to earlier concepts of the social economy, the SSE was created as a rival concept to the dominant system of neoliberal economics, with the clearly defined goal to overcome and replace the status quo. In order for the SSE to function as a driver of transformation, substantial social, economic, and political change processes need to be realized. A basic but potentially the most far-reaching of these change processes is a shift from the idea of the supposedly autonomous, self-maximizing individual as the underlying logic and legitimization of economic activities to a morally informed decision-making process that focuses on the needs of communities or social groups (McMurty 2013, p. 11). Neither the market nor the state should be at the center of economic decision-making. Thus, the community or civil society should have the power to guide economic decision-making (*ibid.*). However, many writers remain vague on how to achieve and maintain this balance between market and state, which is perhaps indicative of the continuation of a de-politicized debate about the SSE. Based on the ideas promoted by RIPESS activists, the role of civil society as a center of economic decision-making emerges clearly: to develop an economy that follows the principles of solidarity[3], a large-scale transfer of ownership to collective enterprises, such as cooperatives and mutual associations, is necessary, accompanied by a widespread recognition within and across societies that fundamental societal challenges cannot be solved on the basis of a supposedly autonomous self-maximizing individual.

Furthermore, the SSE will only function effectively as a driver of transformation if it operates within the context of institutional structures that promote justice, equality, emancipation, inclusion, diversity, social cohesion, ecological sustainability, and economic viability (Utting 2013; Lewis 2013). This would ensure, for example, the implementation of rules that are essential to realize the principles of solidarity, such as the internalization of all foreseeable social and environmental costs and risks in economic strategies. The realization of these far-reaching change processes and the development of the SSE as a transformative power occur in a dialectic relationship, with complex interlinked processes that initiate and strengthen each other. McMurty (2013) describes this clearly when stating:

> While there are many different philosophical, economic, social and political frameworks that have engaged with part or all of the SSE, the fundamental belief remains that individuals and communities must themselves articulate their capacities once the "rules of the game" are set. I wish to turn this premise on its head and argue that what is crucial for the SSE to realize its moral and economic, and thereby Promethean, potential is for the first premise to be a critical understanding of the "rules of the game" and a conscious movement to build alternatives which meet the needs of communities which have been excluded and oppressed by these structural conditions. (McMurty 2013, p. 12)

Thus, the key to unlocking the transformative potential of the SSE is its ability to ensure the rights and strengthen the capacities of economically, socially, and/or politically marginalized groups to effectively represent their interests in the development of institutions that regulate economic and social relations and shape patterns of distribution across society. For this to occur, social economy enterprises must be able to establish equitable partnerships with private and public actors (Lewis et al. p. 35).

### *Market-based, local development-focused, and transformative SSE*

There are numerous studies on the diverse outcomes of efforts to develop the SSE in different countries and world regions. Utting *et al.* (2014), in their review of over 70 of these studies recognize how social enterprises, based on different forms of collective action, have started to successfully address interconnected local and global barriers to inclusive and ecologically sustainable economic development. Two major issues that arise from their discussion are first, the ways in which finance affects SSE and the need for solidarity finance schemes that can be upscaled, and second, the role of the state in enabling the SSE through public policy, support programs, and supranational initiatives. Last but not least, they emphasize that the ability of SSE organizations to thrive depends on the nature of collective action among producers, consumers, and citizens, and the instruments they develop to facilitate participation, claims making, and bargaining.

Before exploring the role of the state further (and discussing public policies towards cooperatives in present-day East Africa in the next section of this chapter), it is worth looking more closely at the nature of collective action, or how the SSE is likely to develop. McMurty (2013, p.9) identifies two main and interrelated barriers to the ability of the SSE to fulfill its transformative goals. One is the lack of capacity among large numbers of people in neoliberal economies and societies, and the other is widespread social alienation. For example, cooperatives experience a lack of financial resources and human capacities despite rapid economic growth and significant wealth accumulation among elites. It is these rising inequalities in neoliberal economies that Uganda's small coffee producers frequently describe as the "times of division", which can hamper the formation of collective action (for a detailed discussion, *see* Chapter 5).

Marques (2014) and McMurtry (2013) identify three main forms of potential (or already happening) SSE development, of which only the third reflects the emancipatory ideal. They describe these forms respectively as first, the market-oriented SSE or the 'Trojan Horse', second, the local development model or the 'Frankenstein Monster' and third, the SSE as a project of social transformation, the 'Prometheus' model.

The market-oriented SSE echoes the third-sector concept of the social economy: It is made up of enterprises or projects for which a firm adopts selected aspects of social and solidarity economic strategies "with the objective of lowering costs, benefiting from tax exemption and other subsidies from the state, or acting as subcontractor for private companies or as providers of public services" (Marques 2014, p. 13). Such market-oriented forms of SSE may also include public initiatives that were developed to temporarily reduce societal problems, such as unemployment, without addressing its root causes (*ibid.*). Marques points out how such public policies, which fall short of pursuing a transformative agenda, reflect the tendency of the liberal welfare state to subordinate social objectives to economic ones.

Similarly, McMurtry (2013, p. 12) illuminates how social policies that measure impact exclusively by economic growth and job creation indicate that growth-based objectives are taking precedent over social objectives. As a consequence of successful (growth-based objectives) market-based initiatives, the state may withdraw from the provision of services to vulnerable social groups. An example are job and income creation programs in the microfinance sector that have been used to justify reductions in social welfare spending without contingency plans to ensure the protection of vulnerable groups in the future (Utting et al. 2014). In many African countries, donor-funded programs to strengthen job creation through social enterprises unintentionally help to reduce pressure on governments to increase investments in health and education and implement redistributive policies. In the context of extreme inequality, widespread poverty, and a lack of protection of political rights, the longer-term socioeconomic effects can be devastating.

In the market-based model, the SSE is hardly distinguishable from the conceptualization of the social economy as a third sector and it certainly stabilizes neoliberal structures more than challenging them. Lacking any agenda to change the institutional structures that reproduce inequalities by representing elite interests, this type of SSE has no transformative power. One answer to the obvious question why such forms of SSE are not only supported by political and economic elites with an interest in protecting the status quo, but are also welcomed by large numbers of people, including marginalized groups, is the absence of an alternative epistemology with strong ontological foundation, which allows us to think about social and economic relations in different terms than is prescribed by orthodox economics, with its ontological construct of *homo economicus* and a positivist logic to explain what is possible (Dash 2013).

In the local development model or Frankenstein Monster, the SSE is complementary to the state and the market and contributes to social cohesion by addressing state and market failures. In this model, the SSE is a *de facto* instrument for maintaining and strengthening the neoliberal status quo, because it provides remedies for the social, economic, and political crises created by far-reaching neoliberal reforms without questioning their basic legitimacy. Like the market-based SSE, this type of social economy often exploited as an instrument of the state (Utting et al. 2014, p. 11; Vaillancourt 2009, p. 292), serving as a band-aid to the socio-economic inequalities that necessitated their formation, while strengthening the institutions that protect the status. This is why Dash (2013) stated unequivocally that the issue is "not just economic; it is systemic—ideological, institutional and epistemological" (p. 1).

Finally, the SSE may develop as a project of social transformation or Prometheus: a grass-roots initiative that provides the basis for transforming the capitalist institutions that drive processes of neoliberal globalization.

## *The role of the state in the development of a transformative SSE*

If the SSE is to emerge as a new development paradigm it must provide a pathway to creating "a protective state that is much more active in economic life and in the task of redistribution while permitting 'greater control by the citizen of both the market and the state'" (Garreton 2007, quoted in

Vaillancourt 2009, p. 283). In short, in a transformative, Prometheus-type SSE, the state must be willing to protect social justice and to share its control over the social and economic spheres with different non-state actors. To achieve this, fundamental institutional changes are necessary, which can only be realized if social economy actors participate in policy design and implementation processes as equal partners alongside the state and traditional private sector actors, a process that Vallaincourt (2009) calls *co-construction* (policy design) and *co-production* (policy implementation).

Of these two concepts, co-construction is considered indispensable for triggering economic democratization processes, because it engages civil society actors at an institutional rather than an organizational level (p. 289). Vallaincourt describes an ideal of "democratic, solidarity-based co-construction" (p. 293) characterized by four features. The first is that of participation: The state, while retaining ultimate decision-making power, engages multiple stakeholders before taking policy decisions (p. 293). The second is the rejection, by the state, of partiality to any given category of stakeholders ('sector'). The third feature is described as a "deliberation between the best of representative democracy and the best of participatory democracy" (p. 294), by engaging state, market, civil society leaders, and other socio-economic and socio-political stakeholders. This includes the active promotion of a better understanding between the various stakeholders and the state. The final feature is that the immediate inclusion of the social economy, as public policy and programs are defined. Crucial to realizing this criterion is the successful establishment of a partnership between state and social economy, rather than an instrumentalization of the latter by the former (*ibid.*).

The final feature addresses what McMurtry (2013) called the necessary democratization and localization of "key levers of the economy" (p. 12), which he clarifies as meaning "that a clearly articulated 'third' player (the SSE) be given a meaningful seat at the political and economic table" (p. 13); meaningful, both in the sense that they are considered and that they have the capacity to participate effectively. This is an important distinction between participation that is best described as inconsequential involvement and participation that allows the exertion of influence over outcomes. However, against the background of the often-meaningless invitations to participate in local development activities, offered to marginalized groups in low- and middle-income countries in countless poverty-reduction programs in the past (thereby turning the term into an empty buzzword), participation needs to be "meaningful" in order not be harmful.

In addition to co-construction, Vaillancourt (2009) offers a description of the co-production ideal type, in which the social economy is called upon to implement a policy, for example by delivering a particular public service (p. 285). Whether this results in McMurtry's Promethean scenario or in a Trojan Horse, depends on the policy, which, despite a democratic, solidarity-based co-construction policy, may or may not center around social and sustainable goals.

The utilization of the social economy as a service provider by the state brings up Marques's (2014) and McMurtry's (2013) critiques of the market-based local-development forms of the SSE, as the state may be supporting "neo-liberal policies by cushioning the adverse social effects" (Haarmann & Haarmann 2011, p.18) they helped to create. Successful protection against this subordination of social to economic objectives also depends on context-specific institutional structures and historical circumstances, which shape social and economic expectations and the ability to unmask adverse social effects (Amin 2009). Thus, Vaillancourt's framework needs to be contextualized within the specific institutional realities that shape relations of power between the state and social economy actors. Saguier & Brent (2013) usefully assert that the extent to which a social economy is taken seriously by the state as an economic alternative is evident through the types of policies to which SSE actors are permitted to contribute. Where the utilization of SSE principles remains limited to (those) social policies that are treated as secondary, SSE is reduced to a poverty reduction tool rather than a means of economic transformation.

### *The realization of the SSE*

Worldwide, the relationship between the capitalist state and the social economy has been overwhelmingly paternalistic, and the state has co-opted the sector to address state and market failures. Realizing the SSE's potential as an alternative development model depends on whether the SSE 1) is legitimized and mainstreamed by the state through various institutions along with its solidarity principles, 2) is invited to contribute in the design and implementation of core policies that shape national economic and social development 3) has the capacity to participate effectively in these processes, and 4) is able to maintain its autonomy.

There are no historical or current examples where a transformative SSE has been established on a national scale, but even on a local scale, development strategies that rely on market-based and local-development forms of the SSE are widespread. Certainly, in rural Africa, the utilization of social economy actors as a temporary remedy to extreme inequality and increasingly deadly effects of environmental degradation prevail. This is despite an official rhetoric that uses a terminology of transformative change: Government programs that explicitly strengthen agricultural cooperatives, often with international donor support, frequently fail to address conflicts of interests between transnational buyers with considerable market power and organized small producers who strive towards value addition and the ability to export processed commodities. By creating the image of a win-win in this context – promising the realization of inclusive rural development without redistribution – such programs effectively utilize cooperatives as a tool for creating Trojan Horse-style solutions to the adverse social and economic effects of neoliberal policies.

The empirical evidence presented in Chapter 5 about the organizational structures of Uganda's coffee sector cooperatives, and their direct socioeconomic effects on small producers' economic prospects, sheds light on the nature and role of existing forms of the SSE in African export agriculture today. Chapter 6 then takes up questions surrounding the role of corporate power in Africa's buyer-driven agricultural value chains and the strategies by transnational corporations vis-à-vis cooperatives. The chapter illuminates how recent developments point to the increasing prevalence of third-sector model of a social economy: social enterprises in the form of CSR projects, financed by TNCs, are common and try to substitute for cooperatives with political advocacy power and a redistribution agenda.

Before turning to the discussion of these micro-level data, the broader political and economic framework conditions that shape the development of the SSE and the likely influence of cooperatives on institutional changes at the national level need to be better understood. Section 3 of this chapter examines existing state institutions and policies in Uganda and other East Africa states, which directly support and regulate cooperative activities in export agricultural production and marketing processes. Prior to this regional policy analysis, a brief history of cooperatives in Africa illuminates organizational objectives and performance under European colonial regimes and during the phase of state control from the 1960s to the 1980s, up to the collapse of cooperatives at the onset of neoliberal reforms. The short account not only confirms that cooperatives in Africa, as elsewhere, have largely followed reformist, rather than radical transformative agendas, but it also points to the importance of the political-economic framework conditions in shaping the large-scale failure of cooperatives to change distributional patters to the benefits of small producers.

## 3.2 Cooperative performance and capacity for advocacy

The potential virtues of cooperatives have continued to animate their proponents despite the weak performance of many agrarian cooperatives in the 1960s and 1970s (Develtere et al. 2008, p. 367). At the onset of neo-liberal reforms, when cooperative development had reached a long-term low, Braverman (1991, p. 27) concluded that the "cooperatives' failure may be due to unfavorable conditions rather than to inadequacy of the approach itself". Since the early 2000s, there has been a renewed interest in cooperatives as an instrument to promote inclusive economic development (Pollet 2009; Wanyama et al. 2009; Develtere et al. 2008; Agarwal 2010; Deininger & Liu 2009). The combination of business with socio-economic objectives within cooperative enterprises has contributed to their representation as a superior way of reducing poverty and inequality (Birchall 2004). In particular with regard to Africa, the combination of business and social concerns characteristic of cooperatives is often seen as a suitable approach to poverty reduction that apparently responds to existing "communal" cultures in many African countries (for a discussion of this view, *see* Develtere et al. 2008).

However, this combination of objectives is not exclusive to cooperatives, and the capacity of this organizational form to represent the interests of resource-poor small producers may depend more on historically specific institutional structures, both formal and informal, within local communities, within the wider socio-economic environment and at the national policy level.[4] Next, the general ideas and objectives of cooperatives are briefly outlined, indicating the major external and internal factors that limit their capacity to realize these goals. These include shortcomings in the wider institutional framework within which cooperatives operate, but also the existence of social and economic inequalities that have characterized cooperatives throughout the developing world in the past, despite their claims to promote the contrary.

## *The cooperative idea(l)*

Generally, cooperatives are meant to be voluntary, group-based and democratically controlled enterprises through which members improve their living standards by gaining control over the productive activities from which they derive their livelihoods (Develtere et al. 2008; Ofeil 2005 in Wanyama et al. 2009). With a clear political mandate to strengthen the bargaining power of disadvantaged groups *vis-à-vis* stronger economic actors and the state, cooperatives directly address inequality by pooling resources and providing capacity-building measures, such as training, advisory services, and technical equipment. Like trade unions, cooperatives provide permanent organizational structures that are capable of representing the interests of disadvantaged sections of the population at the national level. Ideally, they represent an effective means of accumulation among the laboring classes, because they enable the formation of strong economic actors that represent the interests of disadvantaged groups within institutional development processes that shape the terms and conditions of economic exchange (Hare 2088; Deininger 1993).

In a context of widespread poverty and a liberalized agricultural sector, cooperatives represent an organizational response to the socio-economic challenges faced by small producers. In order to leverage the opportunities provided by dynamic price developments, small producers need to respond strategically to market incentives, but financing the storage of crops and bearing delayed payments caused by bulk selling puts strains on poor rural households that require cooperative solutions. Organized responses enable the accumulation of capital and improve the bargaining power of small producers *vis-à-vis* stronger economic actors (Rauch & Alff 1997, p. 157). When operating individually, small producers are forced to sell when prices are low, because the costs of professional storage facilities to withhold crops are likely to outstrip the capacities of individual producers. Equally, the ability to pay for transport when prices surge—as buyers are likely to come to the villages only when prices are low – necessitates joint efforts by poor rural producers. However, without public sector support, either in the form of direct subsidies or on the basis of privileged terms of trade and financial services, cooperatives tend to be unable to offer pre-payments and to make initial investments into storage facilities. Thus, without supportive state institutions, the initial set-up and successful development of agrarian cooperatives is unlikely.

In addition, rural producers in a liberalized, but far from perfectly functional, market face high costs of information. Price fluctuations for crops, inputs, processing, and related services need to be monitored to enable informed decisions and planning in response to market incentives. Cooperatives can help poor smallholder farmers to build up the necessary information infrastructure at relatively low costs. First, the vertical organizational structure of cooperatives, which connects villagers to district and national level institutions, ideally provides access to information for all members, not simply for those households with above average education and wealth. Second, cooperatives reduce the cost of information through the provision of horizontal organizational structures that can bridge existing gaps in the available information infrastructure. Thus, the present fieldwork in Uganda indicates that one individual or household with a mobile phone in each primary group usually provides information to around thirty small producers. However, rural communities are far from homogeneous and existing inequalities and hierarchies are likely to impede the flow of information to cooperative members (*see* Chapter 5 for a discussion of empirical material from Uganda's coffee sector).

Overall, the socio-economic effects of cooperatives in the developing world have been mixed. Success stories from agrarian cooperatives in Asia, Latin America, and Africa can be juxtaposed with studies showing weak or even undesirable socio-economic effects (for positive examples, *see*, for example, Baviskar 1980, on India; Borda 1971, on Ecuador; Kodama 2007, on Ethiopia; Ibhawoh & Dibua 2003, on Tanzania; Tefft 2004, on Mali; for adverse cases, *see*, for example, Uphoff 1993; Tendler 1983; Neven et al. 2005; Chirwa et al. 2005). Early on, observers argued that agrarian cooperatives failed to generate the widespread structural change necessary for a robust improvement of rural living standards.[5] Thus, a worldwide study concluded that "rural cooperatives have seldom achieved the development goals set out for them by economic and social planners. This has been most clearly evident when the goals have included structural changes" (UNRISD 1975, p. 11). The persistence of social and economic inequalities within cooperatives has been documented across the world, indicating gender-based inequalities in particular (Peek 1983, on Nicaragua; Lin 1990, on China; Goyal 1966, on India; Pinstrup-Andersen 2001; Agarwal 2010).

Up to today, the conclusions regarding the complex social, economic, and political conditions under which cooperatives may contribute to the reduction of poverty and which determine their effects on existing structures of social and economic inequality remain diverse. However, the negative effects of close interlinkages between political elites and cooperatives have been identified as a barrier to the generation of social change processes and a factor relevant to the reproduction of inequalities within rural communities (for examples, *see* Brass 2007a, on Peru; Attwood & Baviskar 1988, on India; Bernard & Spielman 2009, on Ethiopia). Thus, cooperative performance has been reduced by the misuse of resources, both by the state and by local elites. At the local level, dominant social norms and practices within disaggregated rural communities have frequently been implicit in the diversion of resources for the protection of elite interests.

## *A brief history of agrarian cooperatives in Africa*

As has been indicated in the previous section, cooperatives have not necessarily been voluntary, democratic, or self-controlled organizations, as they are theoretically expected to be. In sub-Saharan Africa, the historical development of cooperatives illuminates how they have been used in ways contrary to their members' interests. The introduction of cooperative approaches on the African continent goes back to colonial rule, when agricultural cooperatives were established by the British, French, Belgian, and Portuguese colonial administrations, mainly to protect the interests of the colonial administrations, rather than the rural African population (Develtere 1994, Develtere et al. 2008). Cooperatives were set up to organize farmers involved in the production of export crops, to improve agricultural productivity, and to handle quality control, transport, and export on behalf of the colonial administration (Develtere et al. 2008, p. 28). Thus, cooperatives were established and utilized to intensify extraction from the agricultural sector in the colony to support the colonial administration and, most importantly, the metropolitan area. Furthermore, cooperatives provided organizational structures that allowed increased control over the large rural populations by relatively small colonial administrations.

Due to the differences between the British indirect rule and the French policy of 'assimilation', there were variations in the organizational structures of cooperatives and the scope of application or the services covered. For the most part, agricultural cooperatives under colonial rule were meant to improve agricultural production and processing methods, organize the supply of farming inputs and provide structures for the provision of insurance as well as financial services. The British emphasized productivity enhancement in the agricultural sector – the sole base of African economies at the time – to maximize commodity exports to Britain and thereby support industrialization efforts at home (Wanyama et al. 2009, p. 3). Thus, British policies were more focused on protecting the interests of white settler farmers than on promoting functional institutional structures beyond the minimum necessary to keep production going.

French policies put a stronger focus on establishing rather extensive structures of insurance, loan schemes, and extension services. This more elaborate development and employment of cooperatives as modernizing institutions can be ascribed to the aim of French policies to modernize and 'civilize' African societies by assimilating them to the French one (*ibid.*). However, these differences were never absolute as both colonial administrations were aimed at maximizing the profits extracted from African agricultural producers while simultaneously maintaining control over the rural population that was being squeezed so vigorously. Furthermore, the gradual development of the French policy of assimilation into a more and more 'indirect' form of rule towards the end of the colonial period, as argued by Mamdani (1996a),[6] meant that these differences became increasingly blurred.

In the Belgian as well as the Portuguese colonies, cooperative development was characterized by a stronger paternalistic element and was used deliberately to keep control over an underprivileged African population (Wanyama et al. 2009, pp. 3–4). Under the Belgian administration, the predominantly rural population was allowed to form agricultural cooperatives to improve their meager incomes from farming, but their success in serving their members' interests was closely watched and curtailed by the colonial power. Thus, when African cooperatives started to compete with private Belgian enterprises, they were quickly restricted to a range of activities that did not pose a threat to colonial interests (*ibid.*). A look at the Portuguese administrations in Angola and Mozambique produces a similar picture. Agricultural cooperatives were constrained by colonial policies to function as appendages of agencies created to serve the economic interests of the colonial government (Develtere et al. 2008). Thus, attached to the Coffee Institute of Angola as well as the Cotton Institute of Mozambique were agricultural cooperatives that were effectively run by a management responsive to the interests of the colonial government, rather than to those of members (*ibid.*).

The distinct cooperative models that developed and spread under colonial role have been described as the unified model, the social economy model, the social movement model, and the producers' model (Develtere et al. 2008, p. 5).[7] None of the cooperative sectors in African countries followed an exclusive or 'pure' version of one of these models, but each can be associated with one of the major European colonial powers. The latter promoted organizational objectives and structures that best reflected their own social and economic policies and/or were embedded in their own cooperative culture at home, but Develtere's distinction takes account of the major characteristics of different African cooperative movements, without suggesting that the latter represented replicas of European cooperative traditions (*ibid.*, p. 4).

The unified model, most prominent in British colonies, closely reflects British colonial policies aimed at creating a single cooperative movement with a unique legal form (Develtere et al. 2008, p. 5). Primary cooperatives were formed at the village level, secondary cooperatives in the intermediate level, and an apex body at the top. The effective organization of cash crop producers to improve productivity, large-scale quality control, and post-harvest treatment was central to the unified model. In contrast, the social economy model, prevalent in the francophone countries, entailed the establishment of various organizational forms, such as mutual societies, associations, foundations, and trusts. The distinctive characteristic of each individual organization was its shared social and economic objectives, rather than a cooperative approach to achieve them (*ibid.*). Thus, organizations that belong to the social economy model could be described as following group approaches, but not necessarily a cooperative production and/or marketing strategy.

The social movement model reflects the Belgian cooperative tradition in which cooperatives were first and foremost used as an instrument of collective action (*ibid.*). As Develtere suggests, this focus on the collective action dimension of cooperative approaches certainly influenced cooperatives in Central Africa (*ibid.*). However, it should be noted that throughout the Belgian colonies, attempts by African cooperatives to develop into effective instruments of collective action were suppressed and responded to with paternalistic policies to protect colonial interests. The interventionist policies of the Belgian colonial administration, which used an exceptional level of brutality to keep Africans in underprivileged and subservient positions, effectively prevented the development of strong social organizations such as trade unions, women's, or farmers' organizations.

The producers' model, rooted in the Portuguese cooperative system, refers to organizations of agricultural producers that were established as instruments to improve agricultural production and marketing (*ibid.*). This model shows overlap with the unified model, as it equally concentrates on improving agricultural productivity and making the marketing of cash crops more effective. Similar to the unified model, organizations in the producers' model tradition are first and foremost concerned with economic objectives, as opposed to the organizations that form part of the social economy and the social movement traditions. However, the unified model in particular was characterized by a high level of government control to realize objectives beyond members' interests, while the producers' model was focused more strongly on improving members' living standards. The *sui generis* model was not introduced by any of the colonial powers, but developed through the agency of local actors out of a mix of foreign and local ideas and mainly in countries where colonial powers had little influence, namely Ethiopia, Sierra Leone, Liberia, and Egypt (*ibid.*), rather than colonial administrations (*ibid.*).

Despite the differences between the cooperative traditions that were introduced to and developed on the continent, all but the *sui generis* model were strongly influenced by the colonial administrations' needs to maintain control over large geographical areas and diverse societies. The unified model was almost exclusively focused on realizing the export crop strategy of the British colonial administration, while the social economy model included organizations aimed at the development of local social and economic structures to 'assimilate' African societies to French prototypes. Members' interests were not promoted to stand at the core of these organizations, except when they overlapped with colonial interests.

Post-independence, government control over the large agrarian cooperatives remained tight, with many organizations following an essentially path-dependent development (Develtere et al. 2008, p. 3). The development of cooperatives in Anglophone African countries post-independence remained closely tied to governments' policies on cash crop export.[8] From the 1960s and up to the early 1990s, before structural adjustment reforms led to a widespread reduction of governmental control, there was a notable degree of continuation from colonial to post-independence strategies on cooperatives as a way to organize agricultural production and export.[9] Later on, under the national marketing boards, agricultural cooperatives were utilized to extract surplus from agricultural production to invest into urban development and strategies for industrialization, albeit with limited success. While the organization of cash-crop farmers, the management of post-harvest treatment and the storage and transport of cash crops were managed through cooperatives, it was the marketing boards which supervised all quality controls and exports, effectively making cooperatives an appendage of state-controlled marketing boards.

The strategy of government control of export revenues from agricultural production reflected the need of the newly established African governments to generate the funds for the development of their national economies and to assert control over fragmented societies in more or less artificial territories

(Ghose 1983; Sandbrook 1985). The promotion of industrialization through investments into infrastructure and manufacturing was at the time seen as the single most important strategy to promote rapid economic development. Improving the living standards of the urban population, in particular through food subsidies, was further perceived as necessary to ensure political support and foster the development of an urban middle class. These objectives were to be funded by revenues produced in agriculture, by large, but often desperately poor, populations of small producers.

In many cases, public provision failed to provide critical services to the agricultural sector, leading to the critique of state-led agricultural development that constituted a turning point towards market-led agricultural reforms throughout the developing world in the early 1980s (Bates 1981). An historical analysis of different institutional pathways for agricultural development has since shown that the dichotomy between public- and private-sector based provision promoted during the past three decades is misleading, because it fails to recognize and learn from the range of successful state interventions for the development of agricultural markets, in particular in East Asian and European Countries (Chang 2009). However, the way in which governments throughout the developing world were taking control of agrarian cooperatives from the 1960s onwards undoubtedly meant that cooperatives became gateways to political power, accelerating trends towards corruption and estrangement from cooperative objectives at the management levels.

Most of the formerly monopolistic cooperatives collapsed under the pressures of agricultural liberalization, but new organizations have been founded since the 1990s and cooperatives remain a widespread form of economic organization in the region's still predominantly rural and agriculture-based economies (Pollet 2009; Develtere et al. 2008). Thus, across Eastern and Southern Africa, "cooperative presence was significant" by the end of the 2000s, although there was still insufficient evidence about their activities, progress and difficulties (Pollet 2009, p. xii). Overall, it can be said that although wage work is increasingly important throughout the continent, cooperatives continue to shape the relations of economic exchange for large numbers of people, while trade unions still play a limited role for shaping the prospects of rural wage-labor, in particular but not exclusively in the agricultural sector.

## 3.3. Cooperatives and the state in Uganda

The section examines the ways in which African governments engage with producer cooperatives as part of their agricultural development strategies. Uganda serves as an example of the large group of African countries in which governments, as part of implementing neoliberal reforms in the 1980s and '90s, have ended state ownership and management of cooperatives and have eventually embraced producer organizations, more or less prominently, as a civil society driven solution to poverty and inequality. This relatively new approach to cooperatives is reflected in and communicated through an official rhetoric that seems to follow the progressive ideas and concepts of the SSE by promoting agricultural cooperatives as an effective instrument to achieve inclusive economic development in the agricultural sector. However, the same rhetoric seems to suggest that the cooperative movement can grow and function successfully, despite the simultaneous consolidation and even further expansion of market power by a small number of international corporations in Africa's export-oriented agricultural value chains.

A review of Uganda's cooperative policies and institutions illuminates how the state's engagement with cooperatives is essentially top-down, thereby undermining the autonomy/democracy principles of the cooperative movement. State support to cooperatives often remains ill-defined with regard to the transformative goals of the cooperative movement, and many of the existing laws are either deficient in their enforceability or directly fail to tackle the main barriers for a cooperative-friendly economic and political environment. The discussion below does point to the slow but noteworthy expansion of cooperatives' capacities to engage in political advocacy at the national level. At the same time, Uganda's National Cooperative Policy seems to offer only a tightly confined space in which cooperatives may advise the government on policies that relate directly to cooperative issues, while they remain barred from influencing other policy processes that affect rural production and marketing conditions (Wanyama 2012). The analysis clearly shows that current state-cooperative relations reproduce institutional structures that create adverse political and economic conditions for the cooperative movement. The section reinforces the claim, formulated above, that a re-politicized debate on the SSE in rural Africa is needed to address the power asymmetries that limit the growth of cooperatives by structuring export-oriented agricultural markets in favor of large corporate actors.

### *Uganda's cooperative policy*

In the post-colonial period, cooperative policy in most African countries was integrated into national development plans and policies, rather than taking the form of a dedicated document (Schwettmann 2014). For many newly-independent African governments, creating vibrant cooperatives with large memberships was part of a political strategy of nation-building. Government control over export revenues from agricultural production was meant to finance industrialization efforts, increase food security, and strengthen government control in the newly-built states (Ghose 1983; Sandbrook 1985). In some countries, governments used the potential of cooperatives to contribute to achieving general welfare and widespread political participation as a key instrument of political control, for example in Tanzania, Ethiopia, and Tunisia, while in others, for example in Kenya, public sector support to cooperatives was more strongly focused on achieving the objectives of social enterprises (Schwettmann 2014). In Uganda, state-cooperative relations were fairly antagonistic (Bunker 1987), but throughout Africa, cooperative policy advanced and legitimized increasing state control over cooperatives, often accompanied by a de facto exclusion of cooperative members from the development of policies that directly affected them.

When the implementation of far-reaching neoliberal reforms in the early 1990s, which included the dismantling of co-operative banks, led to the collapse of state-subsidized cooperative activities, most countries revised their laws and regulations pertaining to cooperatives. Amidst growing pressures for democratization, these revisions mostly included consultative processes with cooperatives and civil society more generally (Schwettmann 2014). From the mid-1990s onwards, governments across Africa started to design dedicated cooperative policies (*ibid.*). The fast recovery of the cooperative movement in form of new and revived organizations that started to operate in Africa's liberalized markets certainly advanced this development. Using the examples of Uganda, Kenya, and Tanzania, this section discusses the extent to which current cooperative policy in the region provides an effective political framework for supporting the realization of cooperative goals.

Uganda's National Cooperative Policy was launched in 2011 (MTIC 2011) and is implemented by the relatively recently restructured Ministry of Trade, Industry, and Cooperatives (MTIC)[10]. It refers to cooperatives as a sector, rather than a form of organizing economic exchange, and thereby arguably promotes a type of social economy that is more reminiscent of the above-discussed 'third-sector' than an SSE that functions as a driver for the transformation of neoliberal structures across all sectors of the economy. The 2016 amendment Bill aims to contribute to the diversification of the cooperative movement into non-agricultural economic sectors, which could be interpreted as a move towards a more transformative understanding of cooperatives (MTIC 2016). However, other government activities, such as the nature of its support to SACCOs (as discussed below), indicates a trend towards increased government control over cooperatives.

Since the Policy was launched, the government of Uganda (GoU) has realized notable improvements to the political-economic conditions for cooperatives, most of which were initiated and/or advanced significantly by lobbying activities of Uganda's cooperative umbrella organization, the Uganda Cooperative Alliance (UCA)[11]. These improvements include the 2015 establishment of a Warehouse Receipt System (WRS) authority to realize the development of an e-WRS, which could greatly extend the ability of the existing WRS to improve farmers' access to loans from financial institutions (Katunze et al. 2016), the exemption of Saving and Credit Cooperatives (SACCOs) from income tax since July 2017 (Rwothungeyo 2017), and the planned re-opening of a national Cooperative Bank.

However, there are also serious shortcomings that the policy either has not yet addressed with any concrete initiatives, or fails to recognize at all. In its National Development Plan II, the GoU states the creation a cooperative-friendly economic and political environment as a goal, but there are few concrete suggestions as to how to achieve this (GoU 2015). As for the Cooperative Policy, Okello & Ahikire (2013, p. 11) pointedly note: "the objectives are about everything; the entire development aspirations of the country are here indicated as if they can wholly be achieved under cooperatives. This overloading of the cooperative policy risks resulting into a paralysis of implementation".

A detailed discussion of all areas for improvement in the Cooperative Policy is not the objective of this book, but the most important shortcomings are named below. First, the existing laws and regulations governing cooperatives need to be updated, a cause that the UCA prominently lobbies for (The Independent, 2017a). Cooperatives still fall under the 1991 Cooperative Law, which has become partly incompatible with newer financial laws. The UCA General Secretary Ivan Asiime specifically criticizes section 73 of the law, which refers to settling loan disputes, stating that it has "led many cooperatives to lose money in bad loans because the process of recovering the money is long" (Kyatusiimire 2017a). Thus, the existing laws allow very limited options in the case of delayed loan repayment, or for recovering cooperative assets that were stolen during the war in the 1970s and early 1980s (Okello & Ahikire 2013). Another legal shortcoming refers to dispute settlement: when the need for litigation arises, existing laws fail to adequately protect cooperative interests, especially in the case of financial crimes (*ibid.*).

Second, the Department of Cooperatives within the MTIC is said to be underfunded, which hampers the conduction of regular audits and supervision and negatively affects measures designed to improve leadership capacities (Okello & Ahikire 2013; Nannonjo 2013). Extension services that are offered by district commercial officers through the Area Cooperative Enterprises (ACEs) – the secondary-level organizational layer of the UCA – also apparently suffer from a lack of funding (Nannonjo 2013). As the evidence discussed in Chapter 5 indicates, neither the quality nor the outreach of agricultural service provision suffices to improve production processes rapidly.

Third, the GoU's support to Savings and Credit Cooperatives (SACCOs) is at best poorly coordinated with the needs of an autonomous cooperative movement, or it is actively designed to undermine the latter. For example, MPs actively stimulate the formation of individual SACCOs and guarantee support, thereby making it hard for independent initiatives to compete (Okello & Ahikire 2013, p. 18). Such activities seem to challenge the UCA's method of SACCO development that seeks to achieve self-sufficiency for all supported SACCOs.

Forth, the consideration of fundamental cross-cutting issues seems to be subordinated to the short-term achievement of productivity and output growth, even though their neglect may already prevent the upscaling of short-term solution, or reverse positive outcomes sooner rather than later. Thus, the inclusion of women and youth, despite Uganda's enormous youth bulge and the significant role of women in agriculture as providers of labor and bearers of knowledge, is so far hardly emphasized. The minimum age requirement of 18 years to form or join a cooperative excludes large numbers of youth from the cooperative movement, and the participation of women is neither enforced through quotas, nor are there any larger programs that focus on strengthening women's capacities to participate and take on leadership roles. Furthermore, a meaningful inclusion of social-ecological aspects of cooperative development is so far missing. For example, the strong and important emphasis on modernizing the agricultural sector is not accompanied by measures to improve the implementation of social and environmental standards, and there is little emphasis on incentivizing context-specific innovations in sustainability. Last but not least, the minimum membership requirement of 30 members to form a cooperative is considered too high by many small producers (interviews). UNDP (2016, p. 36) states that "the recommended solution is to reduce the minimum to 3 persons, similar to that of the International Cooperative Alliance (ICA) guidelines".

All of the above-described shortcomings, despite being significant, could be addressed by the GoU. However, the overall top-down nature of the state's engagement with cooperatives, which undermines the autonomy and potentially the democracy principles of cooperatives, indicates that the current government may put the maintenance of political power over transformative goals in the cooperative sense. Thus, there is again a high concentration of power in the post of the registrar (UNDP, 2016), which is reminiscent of the pre-liberalization era. For example, it is the sole responsibility of the registrar to interpret the results of an inquiry into a cooperative society and decide whether it should be closed down. Neither the apex organization or a committee made up of cooperative representatives has a say in this decision. The registrar also appoints the liquidator and fixes his/her remuneration, which is paid out of the funds of the society (UNDP 2016, p. 35).

Secondly, the Cooperative Policy overemphasizes SACCOs at the expense of producer cooperatives. Okello & Ahikire (2013) as well as Wedig & Wiegratz (2017) report the view, voiced by organized small producers and representatives of production and marketing cooperatives, that SACCOs are meant to replace cooperatives rather than complement them. This would effectively substitute a political cooperative movement that has transformative social and economic goals with a de-politicized, third-sector type social economy model, because SACCOs essentially provide finance for small producers to function in a neoliberal economy; they do not seek a transformation the latter. The lack of harmonization of Uganda's Cooperative Societies Act with the EAC Cooperative Societies Act could also be interpreted in this way. Thus, the Ugandan Act fails to state some of the key objectives of cooperatives, including the protection of cooperative members from exploitation by traders and the principles of cooperation among cooperatives (UNDP, 2016, p. 32–33).

The potential trend towards heightened government control over cooperatives has been pointed to by analyses about state-cooperative relations in Uganda's coffee sector, which indicated an at time antagonistic attitude by the ruling NRM towards cooperatives with close relations to the political opposition (Wedig & Wiegratz, 2017). Furthermore, political initiatives to modernize the agricultural sector, such as the 2008 'six-farmers-model', which is still active in 2018, have reduced state support to producer organizations by focusing the distribution of agricultural subsidies on technical inputs for selected model farms. The 'six-farmers-model' was an intervention by the President's Office, which instructed the National Agricultural

Advisory Services (NAADS) to re-direct agricultural subsidies to individual producers who are selected by local government committees to serve as demonstration farmers (Joughin & Kjaer 2010, p. 70).

Speaking about the six-farmers-model, one manager at MAAIF's secretariat for the Plan for the Modernisation of Agriculture (PMA) suggested that the rural development agenda was being reshaped to increase government control over development processes at the local level (semi-structured interviews). In this view, the introduction of the initiative represents a move away from demand-oriented, horizontal structures of organization among producers (*ibid.*). Similarly, fieldworkers of the National Agricultural Advisory and Development Services (NAADS) in Eastern Uganda described an increasing emphasis on free agricultural inputs for model farms and a simultaneous reduction in public spending on training that would benefit larger numbers of producers.[12] Participant observation and interviews with organized producers in Eastern Uganda also indicated that the GoU, at the local government level, is fostering a political discourse that associated cooperatives with rebellious behavior and portrays them as detrimental for economic development and national unity. While this rhetoric is not part of official government communication, certainly not at the national and international level, producers and cooperative fieldworkers throughout the field work area reported difficult relationships with local politicians, who openly discouraged membership of cooperatives.[13]

Strategies of agricultural reform such as the six-farmers-model can certainly obstruct the development of cooperatives by promoting vertical organizational structures based on the model-farm status. Joughin, adviser to the Ministry of Agriculture, Animal Husbandry and Fisheries (MAAIF) at the time that the initiative was launched, emphasized that this effectively reduces the voice of producers in the distribution of public sector support while tightening political control over a large rural electorate. The development of an increasingly competitive political environment with the introduction of (some form of) multi-party elections in 2005 certainly contributed to the policy choice (*ibid.*). While the six-farmers-model has recently been criticized for slow implementation (Daily Monitor 2018), it remains part of the governments' agricultural development strategy.

On a more positive note, the relatively strong and increasing advocacy capacities of the UCA are noteworthy indicator that the cooperative movement is not necessarily in the process of ceasing its autonomy, or giving it up lightly. The significant role of the UCA in achieving the above-described improvements, especially with regard to the planned re-opening of the Cooperative bank, have already been noted. In addition, the UCA is petitioning government to award cooperatives at least 30% of all government contracts for agricultural inputs supply (Kyatusiimire 2017a) and it wants the GoU to increase public investment in cooperative education at secondary and tertiary formal education levels (Kyatusiimire 2017b).

Since 2016, the UCA has also petitioned parliament to create a well-funded independent Ministry of Cooperatives, in addition to having a Parliamentary Committee where all the concerns of cooperatives will be channeled (UCA

2017). This reflects the call of a long-term observer of Cooperative Policy in Africa: Wanyama (2012) argues that in order to change institutional structures in favor of its members, the cooperative movement needs an agency that can represent its interests at the national level authoritatively. Thus, an umbrella organization or apex body needs to be able to lobby for enabling policies that go beyond the cooperative policy itself and extend to all other policy areas that directly affect their business (*ibid.*). The recent request by the GoU to create an extensive database of cooperative members is a welcome move to improve existing data on the needs of cooperatives (The Independent, 2017b). As with all data extension, this could be used to further state control over cooperative unions, but the commissioning of UCA with the task is, at least, a reassuring sign.

## Notes

1 The British *Rochdale Equitable Pioneers Society*, established in 1844 by male weavers and skilled workers in related trades, is considered to have been the first cooperative.

2 The Comparative Nonprofit Sector Project (CNP), started in 1991 by the Centre of Civil Society Studies of the John Hopkins University, analyzes the scope, structure, financing, and role of the private nonprofit sector in countries around the world. (ccss.jhu.edu, accessed 24 June, 2018).

3 Based on conversations with SSE activists and the writings and presentation of RIPESS, the principles that guide economic enterprises in a SSE can be described as follows: i) conjunction of members/users' interests and the general interest ii) activities are based on principles of participation, empowerment, and individual and collective responsibility, iii) autonomy of the State, iv) democratic decision-making processes that imply the necessary participation of users and workers and v) primacy of the individual and of social objectives over capital.

4 State-owned companies have similarly combined business and socio-economic goals, but in their case, the combination represented a major source of critique during the 1980s and 1990s, mainly driven by the World Bank. These evaluations have correlated state ownership with politicization, inefficiency and the waste of resources (Galal 1991; Kikeri et al. 1992; Short 1984). However, the hypothesis that private enterprises are inherently more efficient in allocating resources has been widely criticized before and afterwards (for an interesting early critique, *see* Papandreou 1952).

5 The term 'robust' refers to improvements in living standards that can be expected to endure external factors such as food price fluctuations.

6 Mamdani (1996a) argued that colonial rule throughout Africa was *de facto* indirect rule, because local structures of political and economic organization were increasingly used to control large geographical areas and culturally diverse societies.

7 Develtere (2008 et al. p. 5) also distinguishes the indigenous or *sui generis* model, which includes pre-colonial forms of organization among small producers.

8 This brief review of post-colonial cooperative policies concentrates on Anglophone Africa, given that the empirical data presented in this book covers organizations that developed out of the British-influenced tradition of a unified model.

9 Although it should be noted that many African governments displayed a marked export pessimism and made limited efforts to maximize their revenues. *See* Sender and Smith (1986) on the development of capitalism in Africa.

10 Which was previously the Ministry of Trade, Tourism, and Industry (MTTI), of which the department of cooperatives already was a sub-section.

11 For more information on the UCA, see Chapter 5.

12 As one NAADS coordinator put it: "We used to teach farmers how to fish. Now we give out free fish to some few of them".

13 Primary cooperative meetings must finish before nightfall to avoid denunciations by local politicians of being 'rebels', which may have serious consequences of persecution. Geoffrey Wesuga, NUCAFE fieldworker in Sironko district, noted: "Local politicians are distrustful of our work. First, they didn't know our objectives, but we organized meetings with the local government to explain our activities. Today, they still discourage the formation of groups [primary cooperatives] in their rallies." (*see* Appendix 3.2, number 6).

## References

AGARWAL, B. 2010, 'Rethinking Agricultural Production Collectivities', *Economic and Political Weekly*, 45, 64–78.

AMIN, A. 2009, *The social economy: International perspectives on economic solidarity*, Zed Books, London.

ATTWOOD, D. W. & BAVISKAR, B. S. (eds.) 1988. *Who Shares? Cooperatives and Rural Development*, Oxford University Press, Delhi.

BATES, R. H. 1981, *Markets and states in tropical Africa: the political basis of agricultural policies*, University of California Press, Berkeley.

BAVISKAR, B. S. 1980, *The politics of development; sugar co-operatives in rural Maharashtra*, Oxford University Press, Delhi.

BERNARD, T. & SPIELMAN, D. J. 2009, 'Reaching the rural poor through rural producer organizations? A study of agricultural marketing cooperatives in Ethiopia', *Food Policy*, 34, 60–69.

BIRCHALL, J. 2004, *Cooperatives and the millennium development goals*, International Labour Office, Geneva.

BORDA, F. 1971, *Cooperative and rural development in Latin America: an analytical report*, UN Research Institute for Social Development, Geneva.

BRASS, T. 2007a, 'How agrarian cooperatives fail: Lessons from 1970s Peru', *The Journal of Peasant Studies*, 34, 240–287.

BRAVERMAN, A. 1991, 'Promoting rural cooperatives in developing countries: the case of Sub-Saharan Africa', World Bank, Washington, D.C.

BUNKER, S. G. 1987, *Peasants against the state: the politics of market control in Bugisu, Uganda, 1900–1983*, University of Illinois Press, Urbana.

CHANG, H. J. 2009, 'Rethinking public policy in agriculture: lessons from history, distant and recent', *Journal of Peasant Studies*, 36, 477–515.

CHIRWA, E., DORWARD, A., KACHULE, R., KUMWENDA, I., KYDD, J., POOLE, N., POULTON, C. & STOCKBRIDGE, M. 2005, *Walking tightropes: supporting farmer organizations for market access*, Overseas Development Institute, London.

DAILY MONITOR 2018, 'Farmers wait for government to fund model farms in vain', April 4, 2018, Daily Monitor, Kampala.

DASH, A. 2014, 'Toward an epistemological foundation for social and solidarity economy (No. 3)', UNRISD Occasional Paper: Potential and Limits of Social and Solidarity Economy.

DEININGER, K. 1993, *Cooperatives and the Breakup of Large Mechanised Farms: Theoretical Perspectives and Empirical Evidence*, World Bank, Washington D.C.

DEININGER, K. & LIU, Y. 2009, 'Longer-Term Economic Impacts of Self-Help Groups in India', World Bank, Washington D.C.

DEVELTERE, P. 1994, *Co-operation and development: With special reference to the experience of the Commonwealth Caribbean*, Acco, Leuven.

DEVELTERE, P., POLLET, I. & WANYAMA, F. O. 2008, *Cooperating out of Poverty: the renaissance of the African cooperative movement*, ILO and the World Bank, Geneva.

DUNOYER, C. 1830, 'Nouveau traité d'économie sociale', A. Sautelet, Paris.

GALAL, A. 1991, *Public enterprise reform: Lessons from the past and issues for the future*, World Bank, Washington D.C.

GHOSE, A. K. 1983, *Agrarian Reform in Contemporary Developing Countries*, St. Martin's Press, New York.

GOU 2015, *Second National Development Plan (NDPII): 2015/16–2019/20*, Republic of Uganda.

GOYAL, S. K. 1966, *Cooperative Farming in India*, Asia Publishing House, Bombay.

HAARMANN, C., & HAARMANN, D. 2011, *Solidarity economy—A chance for southern Africa: an introduction to the concept and practical experiences from Brazil*, ELM, VELKD, Misereor and the Karibu Foundation.

HARE, P. 2008, *Economic institutions matter, but they are not the full story. Improving Institutions for Pro-Poor Growth (IPPG)*, University of Manchester, Manchester.

IBHAWOH, B. & DIBUA, J. I. 2003, 'Deconstructing Ujamaa: The Legacy of Julius Nyerere in the Quest for Social and Economic Development in Africa', *African Journal of Political Science*, 6, 59–83.

JEANTET, T. 2008, '« L'économie sociale, une alternative au capitalisme »', *Economica*, 80 pages.

JOUGHIN, J. and KJAER, A. M. kjaer 2010, ''The Politics of Agricultural Policy Reform: The Case of Uganda', Forum for Development Studies, 37(1): 61–78.

KATUNZE, M., KUTEESA, A., MIJUMBI, T. & MAHEBE, D. 2016, 'Uganda Warehousing Receipt System: Improving Market Performance and Productivity', *African Development Review*, 29, 135–146.

KAWANO, E., 2013, February 26, *Social and solidarity economy: toward convergence across continental divides*, UNRISD.

KIKERI, S. & NELLIS, J. 1992, *Privatization: The lessons of experience*, World Bank, Washington D.C.

KODAMA, Y. 2007, 'New role of cooperatives in Ethiopia: the case of Ethiopian coffee farmers cooperatives', *African Study Monographs*, 35, 87–108.

KYATUSIIMIRE, S. 2017a, 'Cooperatives want new laws', *Chimp Reports*, 22 September 2017, Available from: <http://www.chimpreports.com/cooperatives-want-new-laws/>. [25 October 2017].

KYATUSIIMIRE, S. 2017b, 'Cooperatives boss wants govt to include cooperative studies in curriculum', *Chimp Reports*, 22 October 2017. Available from: <https://www.chimpreports.com/cooperatives-boss-wants-govt-to-include-cooperative-studies-in-curriculum/>. [25 October 2017].

LAVILLE, J.L. 2011, 'What is the third sector? From the non-profit sector to the social and solidarity economy: Theoretical debate and European reality', *European Research Network, WP 11/01.*

LEWIS, M. & SWINNEY, D. 2008, 'Social Economy? Solidarity Economy? Exploring the Implications of Conceptual Nuance for Acting in a Volatile World', BC-Alberta Social Economy Research Alliance Working Paper Series, September 2007, 17 pp.

LIN, J. Y. 1990, 'Collectivisation and China's Agricultural Crisis in 1959–1961', *Journal of Political Economy*, 98, 1228–1252.

MAMDANI, M. 1996a, *Citizen and subject: contemporary Africa and the legacy of late colonialism*, James Currey, London.

MARQUES, J. S. 2014, 'Social and solidarity economy: Between emancipation and reproduction (No. 2)', UNRISD Occasional Paper: Potential and Limits of Social and Solidarity Economy.

MCMURTRY, J. J. 2013, October, 'Prometheus, trojan horse or frankenstein? The social and solidarity economy as community creation, market wedge, or state monster (Draft)', In UNRISD Conference Potential and Limits of Social and Solidarity Economy.

MTIC 2016, 'Bill No. 14 Cooperatives Societies Amendment Bill 2016', Republic of Uganda, Available from: <http://parliamentwatch.ug/wp-content/uploads/2017/03/The-Cooperative-Societies-amendment-Bill-2016.pdf>. [07 May 2018].

MTIC 2011, *National cooperative policy. Ministry of Trade, Industry and Cooperatives*, The Republic of Uganda, Kampala.

NANNYONJO, J. 2013, 'Enabling agricultural cooperatives through public policy and the State: The case of Uganda', In a draft paper prepared for the UNRISD Conference. Available from: <http://www.unrisd.org/sse-nannyonjo>. [08 May 2017].

NEVEN, D., REARDON, T. & HOPKINS, R. 2005, *Case studies of farmer linking to dynamic markets in Southern Africa: The Fort Hare Farmers Group*. Michigan State University, Mimeo.

OKELLO, L., & AHIKIRE, J. 2013, 'The cooperative movement and the challenge of development: a search for alternative wealth creation and citizen vitality approaches in Uganda', ActionAid, Centre for Basic Research, and The Uhuru Institute, Available from: <http://www.actionaid.org/sites/files/actionaid/cooperatives_report.pdf>. [06 May 2017].

PAPANDREOU, A. G. 1952, 'Some basic problems in the theory of the firm', In: HALEY, B. F. (ed.) *Survey of Contemporary Economics*, Irwin, Homewood, IL.

PEEK, P. 1983, 'Agrarian Reform and Rural Development in Nicaragua, 1979–1981', In: GHOSE, A. K. (ed.) *Agrarian Reform in Contemporary Developing Countries*, St Martin's Press, New York.

PINSTRUP-ANDERSEN, P. & ROSEGRANT, M. W. 2001, *The Unfinished Agenda: Perspective on Overcoming Hunger, Poverty, and Environmental Degradation*, International Food Policy Research Institute, Washington D.C.

POIRIER, Y. 2013, In: *Developments in Solidarity Economy in Asia*, (eds.) Denison Jayasooria, Asia Solidarity Economy Council, Centre for Social Entrepreneurship Binary University, pp. 71–89.

POLLET, I. 2009, *Cooperatives in Africa: The age of reconstruction - synthesis of a survey in nine African countries*, Series on the status of cooperative development in Africa, Cooperative Facility for Africa, International Labour Organization, Geneva.

RAUCH, T. & ALFF, U. 1997, 'Jenseits von Ujamaa-Sozialismus und neoliberaler Strukturanpassungspolitik: Entwurf einer neuen Strategie der ländlichen Entwicklung in Tanzania', *Afrika Spectrum*, 32, 151–172.

RWOTHUNGEYO, B. 2017, 'Kasaija explains why SACCOs have been exempt from taxes', *New Vision*, June 14.

SAGUIER, M., & Brent, Z. 2014, 'Regional policy frameworks of social solidarity economy in South America', UNRISD Occasional Paper: Potential and Limits of Social and Solidarity Economy.

SANDER, S. & SMITH, S. 1986, 'Development of capitalism in Africa', Methuen, London.

SANDBROOK, R. 1985, *The politics of Africa's economic stagnation*, Cambridge University Press, Cambridge.

SCHWETTMANN, J. 2014, 'Cooperatives in Africa: Success and Challenges', A Contribution to the International Symposium on Cooperatives and Sustainable Development Goals: The Case of Africa, Berlin, 2 September 2014, ILO, Geneva.

SHORT, R. P. 1984, 'The role of public enterprises: An international statistical comparison', In: FLOYD, R., GRAY, C. S. & SHORT, R. P. (eds.) *Public enterprises in mixed economies: Some macroeconomic aspects*, World Bank, Washington D.C.

TEFFT, J. 2004, 'Mali's white revolution: smallholder cotton from 1960 to 2003', International Food Policy Research Institute.

TENDLER, J. 1983, 'What to think about cooperatives: a guide from Bolivia', The Inter-American Foundation, Washington D.C.

THE INDEPENDENT 2017a, 'This Week: Cooperative laws need to be reviewed – UCA', 1 October 2017, Available from: <https://www.independent.co.ug/week-cooperatives-laws-need-reviewed-uca/>. [13 October 2017].

THE INDEPENDENT 2017b, 'Government registers farmers to boost operation wealth creation', 11 June 2017, Available from: <http://allafrica.com/stories/201706120120.html>. [26 June 2017].

UCA 2017, Uganda Cooperative Alliance Petitions, Available from: <www.parliament.go.ug>. [May, 30, 2017].

UNDP 2016, 'Reengineering Cooperatives into Enablers of Agricultural Transformation in Uganda', UNDP Uganda, Kampala.

UNRISD 1975, 'Rural Cooperatives as Agents of Change: A Research Report and a Debate', *Rural Institutions and Planned Change* [Online], Vol VIII.

UPHOFF, N. 1993, 'Grassroots organizations and NGOs in rural development: opportunities with diminishing states and expanding markets', *World Development*, 21, 607–622.

UTTING, P., VAN DIJK, N., & MATHEÏ, M. A. 2014, 'Social and solidarity economy: Is there a new economy in the making? (No. 10)', *UNRISD Occasional Paper: Potential and Limits of Social and Solidarity Economy*.

VAILLANCOURT, Y. 2009, 'Social economy in the co-construction of public policy', *Annals of Public and Cooperative Economics*, 80(2), 275–313.

WANYAMA, F. 2012, 'Cooperatives and Policy Advocacy in Eastern Africa. Perspectives for Cooperatives in Eastern Africa', Friedrich Ebert Stiftung, Humura Resort Hotel, Kampala.

WANYAMA, F. O., DEVELTERE, P. & POLLET, I. 2009, *Encountering the Evidence: Co-operatives and Poverty Reduction in Africa*.

WEDIG, K. & WIEGRATZ, J. 2017, 'Agricultural Cooperatives under Neoliberalism: The Case of Uganda's Coffee Sector in Uganda', *Journal of Agrarian Change*, 18, 348–369.

# 4 Institutional change for cooperative growth

New institutional economics (NIE) is the most commonly used economic theory to explain institutional development processes in the context of broader social, economic, and political change processes. Furthermore, it is frequently used by international development practitioners to explain the role of institutions for enabling sustainable development processes. In fact, there is probably not a single other economic theory that has received more attention and has been widely drawn upon by international development and aid practitioners than NIE. This chapter examines its capacity as an analytical framework to understand the extent to which cooperatives are likely to improve the economic prospects of small producers and potentially casual wage workers in African export agriculture. Thus, the discussion assesses the explanations offered within the analytical framework of NIE, for how institutions, including the internal institutional structures of economic organizations, as well as informal institutional mechanisms that regulate labor market transactions, affect the ability of small producers and casual wage workers to defend their interests vis-à-vis stronger economic actors and the state[1]. The scope and limitations of different strands of NIE for understanding the development of historically specific institutions are outlined, and a political economy perspective is proposed to explain how relations of power and inequality shape the internal organizational structures of cooperatives as well as the wider institutional structures in which they operate.

The double focus on both small producers and wage workers is necessary in response to the increasing number of rural households in Uganda and throughout Africa that depend on a combination of small-scale farming and casual employment (see Chapter 1). The socio-economic challenges faced by rural people today overwhelmingly entail inequalities in the labor market, in addition to the poor quality of infrastructure and limited access to markets within small-scale agriculture. Against this background, a complementary analysis of the distinct institutional structures underlying the organization of smallholder agriculture and labor markets provides valuable insights into rural economic development and poverty reduction.

Institutions are understood as historically specific political settlements that regulate the distribution of power between contending social groups (Khan

*Figure 4.1* Kyagalanyi Field Station in Gibuzale, Sironko District

1995). Both small producers and casual workers face persisting inequalities in informal institutions that are shaped by dominant social norms and practices. However, the liberalization of agriculture in Uganda has caused extensive organizational changes in cooperatives, and disadvantaged groups among organized small producers utilize new opportunities to generate processes of socio-economic change, thereby directly affecting their access to resources at the local level. Against the background of weakly developed labor organizations in

Uganda's highly informal labor market, such processes do not seem to be repeated among wage workers.[2] Furthermore, cooperative members enjoy significantly improved access to skills training, compared to wage workers. This result is also confirmed for non-agricultural wage workers in higher-skilled labor market sectors, who face poor working conditions, insufficient skills development opportunities and high job insecurity.

This study draws predominantly on two schools of thought, New Institutional Economics (NIE) and, to a greater extent, on historical political economy approaches to institutional change. NIE illuminates major aspects of the role of institutions in economic development and growth, although it fails to explain how distributional conflicts and relations of inequality shape institutions and subsequently affect the process of economic development (*see*, for example, North 1990a; Ostrom 1990; Nelson 1994; Aoki 2001; Bowles 2004; World Bank 1997; Stiglitz 1998). Its main argument concentrates on the function of institutions to promote an efficient allocation of resources by reducing uncertainty, risk, and transaction costs in processes of economic interaction. The recent historical analysis of institutional development by North et al. (2009) illuminates the interlinkages between institutions on the one hand, and political stability, social order, and economic growth on the other. Their main proposition, as relevant for this research, regards the role of institutions and organizations in the development of open-access societies, which offer improved access to information, rights, and resources to large sections of society.

Based on neoclassical economic thinking, NIE essentially focuses on efficiency in resource allocation, while distributional issues are addressed only because extreme inequality may cause instability and obstruct growth. Although North *et al.* (2009) recognize the positive effects of greater equality in access to resources on social order and economic growth, NIE remains generally weak in explaining the role of inequality in economic exchange and how it affects development outcomes at the micro- as well as the macro-level. In contrast, historical political economy approaches provide an in-depth analysis of the reproduction of institutionalized inequality and the development of distributional patterns under historically specific institutional arrangements (*see*, for example, Robinson 2002; Chang 2002; Chang & Evans 2005; Bowles & Gintis 1988, 1993; Rebitzer 1993). Following these insights, this study expands the analytical focus on the role of institutions in enforcing and reproducing existing power structures, which generally promotes the historically specific interests of elites, rather than universally applicable notions of efficiency in resource allocation (*see* for example, Leftwich 2007 on the role of power and distributional issues within institutional development processes, and Rebitzer 1993 for a political economy approach to the analysis of labor markets).

The political economy approach to institutional development provides a useful analytical framework for understanding social and economic development outcomes among small producers and casual workers in Uganda. Institutions, including those internal to organizations, are examined as the outcomes of historically specific struggles between elite interests (Tilly 1998; Di John &

Putzel 2009; Bowles et al. 2005; Foucault 2003, 1976; Bourdieu and Passeron 1977; Bourdieu 1990). This enables a better understanding of how inequalities are reproduced or transformed in the context of cooperatives and casual labor relations. Cooperatives reflect existing power structures that shape relations of inequalities in disaggregated rural communities, although some organizations also offer opportunities for disadvantaged groups to generate socio-economic change. How far cooperatives improve the capacity of disadvantaged groups to better defend their interests depends on internal and external institutions that regulate social interaction and economic exchange between members, political elites, and other economic actors. These institutions go beyond formal organizational rules, agricultural development policies, and vertical integration strategies of multinational coffee buyers. Rather, they include dominant social norms and practices that are utilized, reproduced, and transformed by contending social groups in decentralized and historically specific processes. Similarly, informal institutions play an important role in structuring labor relations in Uganda, and a political economy perspective on the social regulation of the labor market illuminates barriers for improving working conditions and labor supply quality.

Following a political economy perspective, this study examines how formal and informal institutions underlying smallholder agricultural production and marketing on the one hand, and Uganda's largely informal labor market on the other, affect the capacities of disadvantaged groups to defend their interests. Although initial access to resources significantly influences the representation of social groups in institutions, some forms of collective action emerge as an essential means to enforce subsequent changes in distributional patterns. On the basis of formal economic organization in cooperatives, some disadvantaged groups of small producers in the coffee sector, most notably women, have significantly improved their access to resources, such as land, cash income from export crop production, and skills training. However, other farmers, including cooperative members, remain trapped in highly exploitative economic relations. Casual wage workers generally endure dismal working conditions and low mobility within the labor market due to their lack of relevant skills. Given the highly discriminatory nature of the social regulation of labor market transactions, sporadic labor action seems to have a limited impact on improving their economic prospects.

## 4.1 New Institutional Economics: a critical reappraisal

This section outlines the central ideas of NIE, of the "pro-poor" growth literature (PPG hereafter) and of more heterodox approaches to institutional development as a starting point for exploring how institutions shape processes of social and economic development among small producers and casual wage workers. The present study focuses on the institutional arrangements that underlie structures of socio-economic organization at the local level. With regard to small producers, the discussion concentrates on the *internal* institutions of agrarian cooperatives, but also examines their economic and political environment or broader institutional framework. Both formal and informal institutional structures of cooperatives are analyzed: the formal rules that are, in theory, legally enforceable by the state, and the informal institutions or norms that shape the distribution of power and access to resources within the organization. With regard to casual labor, in the coffee sector and beyond, the discussion focuses largely on informal institutions or, to put it differently, on the dominant social norms and practices that regulate Uganda's labor market, because effective state regulation based on formal institutions is largely absent.

The definition of institutions used here follows that established by NIE, which may be summarized as a set of recognizable rules that structure social and economic interaction by providing information on how individuals or groups are expected to behave in particular situations (*see*, for example, Knight 1992; North 1990a; Ostrom 1990). The distinction between formal and informal institutions is rather blurred, and discussions over the existence of this distinction in political science and in economics have often referred to differences in the underlying mechanisms of institutional creation, rather than providing distinct structural and functional definitions (Shepsle 1989; Langlois 1986). What can be noted is that formal institutions are *intentionally* created, although they are often designed on the foundation of informal institutions or rules, either to stabilize or to change the latter, or in some cases to regulate social interaction in the absence of informal institutional arrangements (Knight 1992, p. 171). Invariably, formal institutions are based on rules that may be reinforced by external enforcement mechanisms that are generally, and more or less directly, controlled by the state.

Informal institutions, on the other hand, are generally understood as having emerged *unintentionally* as social conventions or norms, compliance with which is not enforced by law or by the state. However, it remains unclear how much of the development of informal institutions is unintentional, or, put differently, it is likely that distributional inequalities and power asymmetries allow some actors to influence the development of informal as well as formal institutions. As Knight (*ibid.*, p. 172) argued, 'Even though the process of spontaneous emergence is decentralized and the resulting product is unintentional, they [informal institutions] do not prevent this framework from reflecting the main cleavages of interest and power in a society'. It is thus not surprising that informal institutions may also be enforced by the threat of sanctions imposed by other actors in the event of non-compliance (*ibid.*, p. 54). As dominant social norms and practices that are based upon general consent and upheld by large sections of society, compliance with informal institutions may be perceived as obligatory in similar ways as with formal institutions.

The distinction drawn above between informal and formal institutions indicates close interlinkages between institutions, both formal and informal, organizations, and beliefs on the one hand, and power, politics, and relations of inequality or exploitation on the other. Thus, institutional arrangements are likely to reflect existing distributional patterns and the conflicting interests of different social groups or classes that were involved in their intentional creation or spontaneous emergence. This may be less apparent in an intentionally created, formal institution, if the objective was the balancing of power or the redistribution of resources between contending social groups, but it may be more apparent, if the institution aims at protecting the privileged access to resources enjoyed by a particular elite. Furthermore, the internal institutional arrangements that structure organizations, and the beliefs underlying particular social norms and practices, may reflect existing power asymmetries more or less directly. As is discussed in more detail in section two of this chapter, following Tilly's (1998) notion of 'durable inequality', but also in Chapters 5 and 6 with reference to the empirical data presented there, institutions and organizations are likely to contribute to the reproduction of existing inequalities, but they may also offer opportunities for human agency to generate social change.

To conclude, this study analyzes both formal and informal institutions. Because of the weak development of formal labor market institutions, the labor market data concentrate on the informal rules or social norms and practices that regulate casual employment relations. With regard to small producers, the analysis focuses on formal and informal institutional arrangements *within* cooperatives, as well as on the wider institutional framework that enables or impedes the development of agrarian cooperatives in Uganda. These include rural development policies and the behavior of both political elites and powerful economic actors within the coffee sector, such as multinational commodity buyers. In this sense, the discussion follows the definition of institutions outlined by the NIE literature, as representing both the rules and the 'players of the game' (Nelson 1994). On the one hand, institutions provide the formal and informal rules that make up the regulatory framework for organizations or individual economic actors, while on the other hand, organizations entail internal institutional structures that are embedded in a wider institutional framework themselves.

### *The New Institutional Economics*

As norms, rules and moral codes that structure social interaction, institutions shape forms of socio-economic organization in the context of the labor market as well as within agricultural production and marketing. Labor represents a '*pseudo-commodity*' which is embedded in social relations that reach well beyond the terms and conditions of commodity exchange (Storper & Walker 1989). Both the price of labor and the processes by which the level of wages is determined depend not only on the impersonal forces of demand and supply, but also on a range of interdependent factors, including workers' individual skills and efforts, perceptions of fairness, and the dominant social norms and practices pertaining to wage-cutting (Solow 1990). The nature of labor relations, therefore, depends on the distribution of power between contending social groups who engage in bargaining processes structured by formal and informal rules and norms about, among other factors, the nature and value of labor, the social and economic cost of defection in case of wage-cutting, and the social obligations of workers and employers to share the costs and benefits accrued in times of growth and recession. Following Solow's (1990) view, which reflects older institutionalist perceptions of labor economics, this study analyses the labor market in Uganda as a social institution structured by, and *de facto* inseparable from, historically specific norms of behavior.[3]

Agrarian cooperatives, similar to trade unions, are member-based organizations with clearly defined boundaries and a set of objectives that are generally shared by all participants. In this sense, cooperatives are a different type of phenomenon from labor markets, which consist of much larger numbers of actors with shared, distinct, and conflicting sets of objectives. However, the relations of social and economic exchange within small producers' organizations are partly regulated by informal institutions that are in similar ways shaped by dominant social norms and practices than the informal institutional arrangements that structure labor market transactions, in particular if the latter take place in a highly informal labor market. Thus, small producers and casual wage workers are subject to comparable socioeconomic conditions, and the present analysis aims to take into account the major interlinkages. These conditions are characterized by historically specific, institutionalized inequalities that are to some extent based on and shaped by the same division of class, gender, and ethnicity.

Furthermore, cooperatives, like trade unions, have internal institutional structures that regulate relations of social and economic exchange. Simultaneously, they also represent economic actors or 'players of the game' within a broader institutional framework. Thus, the effects of cooperatives on the ability of disadvantaged groups to better defend their interests depend to a significant extent on their internal institutional structures, because they shape the distribution of power and access to resources among members, and the nature of relations between members, other economic actors, and the state. However, external institutions directly or indirectly regulate the development of cooperatives and influence their performance in important ways.[4] Against this background, small producers' organizations are analyzed, in this study, as social institutions that are embedded in, and influenced by, a wider political and socio-economic institutional framework.

NIE, a term first used by Williamson (1975) to distinguish the development of transaction-cost economics from older institutionalism (as originated in Veblen 1899, 1919 and Commons 1931), addresses the role of institutions that structure economic exchange on the basis of historically specific, political, and cultural factors. By recognizing the role of social norms for market-based exchange, NIE extended the original neoclassical model of the market as an analytical starting point (North 1981; Khan 1995). The basic assumption underlying neoclassical thinking – that the exchange of (supposedly homogeneous) goods is based on the atomistic interaction of maximizing individuals endowed with perfect information – is rejected, because it fails to hold empirically. Instead, NIE provides an analysis of the behavioral patterns of economic actors that recognizes the historically specific institutional structures in which they originate and develop (Coase 1992; North 1990a; Nelson & Sampat 2001; World Bank 2003).

Despite this historically sensitive approach, NIE retains a narrow perspective on the role of power and relations of inequality, and how they shape the structure of interaction between economic actors. The essential argument promoted by NIE concentrates on the function of institutions to reduce the transaction costs of economic exchange, but it fails to address the social and economic costs caused by relations of inequality in distributional patterns. Thus, the NIE literature emphasizes that by providing a set of norms to regulate social interaction, institutions create a favorable environment for the realization of cooperative solutions to economic development problems (Ostrom, 1990). As 'a set of rules of the game that define and limit the choice set', institutions provide solutions to problems of coordination and exchange (North 1990a, p. 383). Because different individuals and groups have conflicting interests, cooperation is necessary to accrue benefits beyond particular (often small and elitist) interest groups and thus improve welfare levels. Because the threat of free-riding and the cost of coordination may limit cooperation or impair its outcomes, a framework of rules is needed to discipline social relations. Institutions provide such a framework, and because they exist independently of the individuals who maintain them, they enable cooperation between large groups and beyond individual life-spans (North et al. 2009). This creates stable social structures that promote accumulation and growth and are *potentially*, albeit not necessarily, open to large sections of society (*ibid*.).

The following discussion illuminates the relevance and limitations, for the purpose of this study, of the main strands of NIE that have been most influential in development studies literature. The comparative historical school focuses on the emergence of institutions, recognizing that institutional change is guided by path dependency (North 1990a; Alston 1996; Greif 1993, 1998). Institutions are understood as endogenously emerging equilibrium outcomes, reached through strategic interaction of optimizing economic agents in a situation of multiple possible equilibria (Gagliardi 2008; Aoki 2001). The second strand of the NIE literature analyzes the rationale of institutional arrangements, in particular formal and informal contracts, in terms of the strategic interaction of economic agents under conditions of imperfect information (Bardhan 1989; Nabli & Nugent 1989; Hoff et al. 1993).

The limitations identified with regard to both approaches refer to the application of strict methodological individualism[5] to explain the emergence of social norms and institutions, an exclusive focus on efficiency leaving aside distributional issues, and a relatively weak theory of the state. As Bowles and Gintis (1993) showed, the role of distributional conflicts in a situation of unequal bargaining power is crucial for understanding the emergence and persistence of labor market institutions. Equally, with regard to agricultural production and marketing, it is crucial to ask who controls not only the relevant organizations, that is, the cooperatives that organize marketing and other services, but also the institutions that regulate their activities. Thus, an analysis of the factors which shape the economic performance of the laboring classes needs to be firmly situated in the context of social and political processes and structured relations underlying patterns of production, trade, and labor relations.

For the empirical study of institutional arrangements in developing economies, which are commonly characterized by high transaction costs, NIE's recognition of information problems (as a particular type of transaction costs) is a useful analytical starting point. The historical perspective developed mainly by North (1990b) analyzes how institutions affect economic exchange by influencing transaction costs. It ascertains that institutions, as the 'rules of the game', guide social interaction and reduce uncertainty (and thus transaction costs) by defining available choices and structuring incentives for economic agents (*ibid.*). The approach integrates the concept of path dependency[6] into the analysis of institutional change by assuming that under conditions of imperfect information, individuals behave according to subjective, but culturally derived and relatively change-averse, 'mental models' of reality, leading to increasing returns of compliance with institutional arrangements (*ibid.*). The recognition that institutional development is conditioned by existing and preceding social and economic structures postulates a historically sensitive analysis.

The comparative institutional approach, applied in close convergence with North's historical perspective, is focused on the emergence of self-enforcing institutions linking interdependent political, social, economic, and organizational domains (Aoki 2001). Based on a concept of institutions as endogenously evolved equilibrium outcomes under constraining conditions, it uses evolutionary and repeated game theory models to analyze the emergence, development, and internalization of institutional structures. The evolutionary approach, analyzing institutions as forms of self-enforcing norms and conventions (Aoki 2001; Sugden 1989), has produced a number of empirical studies focusing on the interdependence of firms' organization and governance structures with wider institutional structures, such as those of the labor market (for example, Greif 1998; Aoki 1994). The repeated game approach, similarly assuming that compliance with social norms is based on the rational beliefs of self-interested individuals (Aoki 2001), has been applied to analyze the significance of institutions in their particular social, political, and cultural contexts (Greif 1998).

The imperfect information approach explains the emergence of formal and informal institutions in terms of strategic interaction between optimizing individuals under conditions of imperfect information (Bardhan 1989). Institutional arrangements are understood as a response to missing or imperfect markets, due to their role of reducing uncertainty and helping to overcome information problems (Arnott & Stiglitz 1991). As in transaction cost economics, imperfect information theory assumes an agency problem as the analytical starting point, which leads to market failure unless incentive mechanisms to overcome existing information problems are put in place (Nabli & Nugent 1989; Bardhan 1989; Hoff et al. 1993; Platteau & Seki 2000). Applied to processes of interlocking transactions in labor, credit, and land markets, this approach has been used to explain the economic rationale underlying agrarian institutions and organizational structures in peasant economies (Braverman & Stiglitz 1982a, b; Braverman & Guasch 1986; Bardhan 1989).

However, the application of imperfect information theory to the study of agrarian labor relations in developing countries has been rightly criticized for its assumption that capitalism is invariably connected with the emergence of free wage labor (Brass 2002). With reference to Cotlear, Bardhan and Platteau, Brass argued:

> In all these neo-classical economic analyses of agrarian relations [...] coercion is equated with economic inefficiency and thus constitutes evidence of a backward agriculture, while any working arrangements connected with capitalism are by contrast perceived as non-coercive, and thus freely entered by the workers concerned. (2002, p. 460)

As the debates on modes of production in India and Latin America in the 1960s and 1970s have shown, this is not the case (for Latin America *see*, for example, Frank 1967; Laclau 1971; for India *see*, for example, Thorner 1982).

Similarly, Acemoglu *et al.*'s (2002) historical account of the changes in income distribution between countries colonized by European powers has been criticized for generalizing the effects of specific sets of institutions on economic development across the colonial world (Bandyophaday & Green 2012; Olsson 2004; Prezeworski 2004). In their 'Reversal of Fortune' thesis, Acemoglu *et al.* argue that by introducing institutions that encouraged investment in poor regions, the colonial powers laid the foundations for a reversal of relative incomes between formerly rich and poor countries during the late eighteenth and early nineteenth centuries. Extractive strategies were most likely to be pursued in relatively prosperous areas, while in others, the introduction of institutions to secure private property was more likely. As a result, relatively poor countries were able to industrialize and generate wealth on the basis of 'good institutions', while those countries that had formed the richest civilizations 500 years ago were left behind.

A critical analysis of Acemoglu *et al.*'s data sets on urbanization and population density, which they used to estimate relative wealth across time and geographical distance, confirms the Reversal thesis for some countries but not for others (Bandyopaday & Green 2010). Thus, the 'Neo-Europes' (Canada, the United States, New Zealand, and Australia) were able to generate sustained economic growth at least partially on the basis of institutional structures introduced by the colonial powers, but other countries that were relatively poor at the time of colonization failed to do so (*ibid.*; Prezeworski 2004; Olsson 2004). The critique of the Reversal thesis illuminates the weaknesses of using a single analytical framework for the development of institutions in historically specific social structures.

Furthermore, the assumption that formal institutions, such as legal structures and norms, predominantly determine the behavioral patterns that shape development processes disregards the diverse ways in which rules and regulations are enacted according to the interests of conflicting social groups. As Benda-Beckmann (1989) has shown in an anthropological analysis of law in development theory and practice, neither the introduction of relatively formalized, so-called modern law, nor the persistence of customary law can convincingly be associated with unambiguous effects on social and economic development processes. Instead, the enactment of both state law and customary law is shaped by social norms and practices and as a result, the effects of particular institutions on development processes differ depending on historically and often locally specific social structures (*ibid.*). Relations of power and inequality among heterogeneous social groups therefore need to be considered to understand the nature of institutional development processes, because they strongly influence how rules and regulations are enacted, reproduced, or resisted to.

This leads to a broader critique of NIE on the grounds that alongside factors such as information asymmetries and the presence of uncertainty and transaction costs, the existence of relations of inequality and exploitation needs to be addressed. The extraction of surplus value from others represents a recurrent part of economic exchange that occurs in different historical contexts, but is invariably based on relations of inequality.[7] Its effects on accumulation, growth, and poverty reduction, therefore, need to be better understood. The discussion of political economy approaches to the analysis of institutions in section two of this chapter provides a useful analytical framework for thinking about how relations of inequality affect processes of social and economic development. In particular, Tilly's (1998) analysis of inequality illuminates why it is so persistent, resilient, and durable across different historical contexts. Based on the conceptualization of social phenomena in binary pairs being transferable to diverse social and cultural contexts, inequality serves essential organizational functions that make it a fundamental element of any society (*ibid.*). One of the major mechanisms that sustain inequality is exploitation – as is illuminated by the persistence of poverty among casual workers in Uganda's labor market (for a discussion of empirical material, *see* Chapter 2). Before presenting a more detailed discussion of institutionalized inequality, this section concludes by summarizing the major shortcomings of NIE, as relevant to the present study.

First, NIE fails to treat power and inequality as decisive factors in shaping institutions.[8] The analysis of institutions as a means of reducing transaction costs in social interaction ignores the impact of relations of inequality on the structure of institutions and, in turn, on economic development outcomes (*see*, for example, North 1990b). The concentration on efficiency in resource allocation implies a simplistic concept of economic development based on accumulation and growth as the single most important factors, while distributional issues are treated as a by-product. The exclusive focus on allocative efficiency as a means to achieve economic development, including improved welfare levels, is reminiscent of the widely accepted argument of the inverted U-relationship, which suggests that with rising income levels in times of growth, (income) inequality will necessarily reduce in the long-term, after an initial increase (for example,

Robinson 1976; for a critical review, *see* Cramer 2000). However, the relationship between inequality and economic development is far from being unilinear, and although a rise in one may impede the other, the lack of equality and equity in access to resources has occurred alongside the development of stable social structures as a means for sustained accumulation and growth (Tilly 1998; Chang 2002; Cramer 2000). Thus, the role of power and relations of inequality in institutional development processes needs to be addressed in its specific historical context to illuminate the trajectories of social and economic development.

Second, NIE's attempt to bring back history into the analysis of economic development by recognizing the historically contingent nature and development of institutions remains incomplete. On the one hand, the concept of institutions as a response to missing or imperfect markets provides some insights for understanding the structure of labor markets in developing economies. North's historical perspective on how institutions emerge and why they persist draws on empirical insights, and in conjunction with the imperfect information theory (as suggested by Aoki 2001), this approach illuminates the interdependence between particular institutions and organizations and their wider social, political, and cultural environment. On the other hand, NIE essentially concentrates on ahistorical concepts of asymmetric information, moral hazard, and risks as the major conditions of economic exchange, and on allocative efficiency as the single most important factor for economic development. As a result, the understanding of how particular institutional structures are created and reproduced remains partial, because interlinkages between distributional patterns and economic development outcomes for particular social groups are insufficiently illuminated.

In the context of this study, the failure of NIE to address the role of power and inequality in the development of institutions can be linked to the prevailing assumption of a homogeneous rural population. Thus, in a (value-free) world in which the function of institutions to reduce transaction costs in social interaction leads to socially beneficial economic development on the basis of allocative efficiency, the population is expected to benefit evenly – at least eventually – from growth.[9] This presupposes that all social groups ultimately access the resources unleashed by economic growth, even though a time delay clearly indicates that some groups are more privileged than others. Against this background, the notion of equality among "the poor" immediately becomes an inevitable assumption and logical conclusion, because recognizing the existence of inequality and exploitation in disaggregated rural communities would demonstrate the existence of power asymmetries as a fundamental part of institutional arrangements and *vice versa*. Thus, the notion that value-free efficiency may serve as an adequate condition for beneficial economic development creates erroneous images of social reality. In contrast, following Sayer (2009), the present study suggests that a critical rather than merely reflective social science analysis should include both an exploration of the contradictory beliefs and interests underlying social interaction, and an evaluation of what is right and what is wrong about social processes.

As a concluding remark, it should be noted that NIE's basic premise of methodological individualism limits an understanding of the role of power and relations of inequality for the development of institutions. Based on the notion that individual choice is guided by norms and conventions, NIE recognizes the social determination of preferences to some extent. However, an analytical inconsistency exists between this recognition, which essentially accepts the endogenous qualities of the development of preferences, and the premise of preferences as an exogenous variable (Costabile 1995; Lukes 2006 [1973]). If individual preferences develop in reciprocity with the strategies of the wider social environment, the latter will influence how the former shape institutional development. Finally, the concept of constrained optimization underlying methodological individualism assumes non-hierarchical conditions of exchange between rational individuals (Bowles & Gintis 1993). As a result, the analytical starting point of NIE precludes a comprehensive understanding of how social coercion and control affect the outcomes of social interaction.

## 4.2 Institutional development as elite bargains

The discussion in the previous section has shown that despite its important contribution to understanding the role of institutions for economic development, NIE fails to explain how conflicting interests are negotiated and how claims are enforced within formal and informal institutions. As noted at the beginning of this chapter, sociologists and economists have pointed out that elite interests dominate institutional development. In his particularly apt and well-known analysis of how elite interests are protected by a codification of violence in institutions, including laws, social norms and language, Foucault (1976, p. 17–18) argued for the need to 'awaken beneath the form of institutions and legislations the forgotten past of real struggles, of masked victories or defeats, the blood that has dried on the codes of law'.[10] NIE's limited concept of the state as a self-restricted enforcer of contracts and property rights, based on the public choice theorist's model of the rentier or predatory state, assumes that (self-)restriction by the powerful suffices as a condition for socially beneficial economic development (Bardhan 2000). This ignores the role of elite interests in institutions underlying economic development processes. As Bardhan noted, 'the political stumbling blocks to beneficial institutional change in many poor countries may have more to do with distributive conflicts and asymmetries in bargaining power' that impede self-restriction by powerful groups (*ibid.*, p. 13).

Historical political economy approaches to the analysis of institutions attribute a central role to relations power between social groups or classes and the negotiation processes underlying distributional patterns in access to resources. The relations between state and society, also called the 'social contract', are based on political settlements that reflect the outcomes of struggles between *contending* social groups or classes, rather than a *common understanding* of elites (Di John & Putzel 2009, following Khan 1995 and 2001). Based on this perspective, the present study understands institutions or sets of institutions such as labor markets as 'arenas of contested exchange' (Bowles & Gintis 1993). The notion of the contested exchange relationship describes endogenous enforcement strategies between exchange parties in the absence of third-party enforcement, thereby integrating the concept of power into the analysis of economic exchange.[11] Thus, the persistence of socially sub-optimal institutions is explained on the basis of the unequal distribution of power between contending social groups and classes. The formation of organizations to pool resources among disadvantaged groups may create opportunities to address these inequalities, but existing inequalities within the internal institutional structures of organizations may allow for the persistence of exploitation, not only within the organization but also in its wider social and economic environment. As Doner *et al.* (2005, p. 329) have noted with regard to Northeast and Southeast Asia, 'economic institutions ultimately arise from the rough-and-tumble of elite politics, not from the choices by private parties to enhance mutual welfare'.

With its focus on conflicting elite interests, the distinction between inclusive and exclusive political settlements explains the interlinkages between institutional development, state fragility or resilience, and economic development outcomes (Di John & Putzel 2009, p. 7). Inclusive political settlements recognize and protect the shared economic interests of elites and are thus likely to be durable and efficient in strengthening state resilience, which is defined as 'control over coercive power, administrative authority and popular allegiance' (*ibid.*, p. 15; *see also* Acemoglu et al. 2005). This increases the developmental capacity of the state and may therefore lead to social policies that advance welfare levels in a given society. Political settlements that exclude the interests of major elites and thereby sever economic relations with influential social groups or classes are likely to reduce state resilience and impede economic development, thereby making further redistributive processes less likely. Whether social policies aimed at greater economic equality are designed and implemented depends on the actual distribution of rights and entitlements between contending social groups, or on the outcomes of political settlements, rather than the level of participation in its negotiation (*ibid.* p. 5). In this sense, 'authors examining political settlements from the perspective of historical political economy offer a more robust explanation of institutional change and development than new institutional economics on which much of the policy community's thinking about good governance rests' (*ibid.*, p. 6).

The notion of institutions as the outcomes of elite bargains was brought into mainstream thinking on development by the pro-poor growth and inclusive development debate (*see*, for example, Leftwich 2007; Harriss 2006). The PPG literature started to address the dominant role of elite interests in institutional development in an attempt to identify how social policies may effectively promote a more equitable distribution of the benefits of growth (*see*, for example, Jütting 2003; Leftwich & Sen 2010; Dorward et al. 2004). The focus of PPG on the development of pro-poor institutions is based on the recognition that institutional design shapes the political settlements underlying development outcomes, because institutions provide the rules and norms for negotiating these settlements. Emphasizing the importance of distributional issues for shaping pro-poor institutions, Leftwich (2007, p. 4) noted that 'what emerges is that the politics of development is intimately and unavoidably associated with the development of politics'.

The PPG literature stopped short of generating a critical debate on the interlinkages between institutional structures of 'durable inequality' (Tilly 1998) and economic development outcomes. What it has contributed to, however, is that the role of institutions in economic development has become a central focus of international development assistance over the past twenty years (*see*, for example, Natsios 2010; Jütting 2003; IMF 2005; World Bank 2003; Gagliardi 2008; Nelson & Sampat 2001; Bastiaensen et al. 2005). In response to the persistence of widespread rural poverty and high levels of inequality in low-income countries, despite periods of sustained economic growth, the PPG literature has emphasized the benefits of active state intervention for creating institutions to support agricultural market development (Dorward et al. 2004, 2005; Mahdi 2010; Wiggins et al. 2010). Overall, the need for institutional change as a means to better protect the interests of disadvantaged groups within economic development processes has been widely recognized, but re-distributional issues have been addressed cautiously at best (*see*, for example, Grootaert et al. 1995; OPPG 2005).[12] Thus, the PPG literature represents an important but insufficient step towards re-politicizing the international debate on development (Leftwich 2007).

### *The institutionalization of inequality*

This section analyzes how economic inequality is institutionalized in the context of wider social, cultural, and political relations and how it affects the socio-economic development outcomes of disadvantaged groups. The discussion is based specifically on Tilly's (1998) concept of 'durable inequality', and more generally on an historical political economy approach to the analysis of institutions which structure economic exchange. In Chapter 5, the processes of socio-economic change and reproduction that are generated in the context of institutions that structure the organization of small producers are examined in detail. This section only uses a few empirical examples, taken from the analysis of labor markets, to underline the points made in the following discussion.

Subsequently, a discussion of economic organization examines the scope and limitations of collective action as an instrument of social change in the interests of disadvantaged groups. Drawing on political economy approaches, the focus of development initiatives, both national and international, on so-called 'grass-roots' or community-based organizations (CBOs) as well as self-help groups is scrutinized. As Pattenden (2010) has argued on the basis of data from India, such organizations often have short-term positive effects on parts of the rural population, but they are likely to foreclose opportunities for structural changes in distributional patterns. Following Brass (2007b), a critical review of the concept of civil society, as utilized within the international development debate, illuminates how it displaces a discussion on distributional outcomes among contending social groups and classes with a focus on participation.[13] Trade unions and cooperatives, on the other hand, directly address the lack of bargaining power of workers and small producers *vis-à-vis* stronger economic actors and the state. The weak performance, throughout Africa, of trade unions and agrarian cooperatives has contributed to a widespread reduction or dismissal of public-sector support in the context of structural adjustment. However, it is argued that the shift towards supporting CBOs and self-help groups also reflects an intellectual and political climate that emphasizes the cost of state interventions, but fails to acknowledge its benefits for rural economic development.

Across different, historically specific institutional contexts, relations of inequality and exploitation shape the terms and conditions of economic exchange. Understanding the reproduction of social and economic inequality should be central to the debate on economic development: on the one hand because its reduction is a valuable goal in itself and on the other because the relationship between inequality and growth is still not fully understood. Tilly's (1998, p. 6) concept of durable inequalities, that is, those 'that last from one social interaction to the next... that persist over whole careers, lifetimes, and organizational histories", illuminates how inequality is created, operationalized, and reproduced within formal and informal institutional structures. Tilly describes the creation of binary social classifications, such as male/female or Christian/Muslim, on the basis of bounded categories, such as gender, ethnicity, or religion. In contrast, continuous categories such as wealth or physical appearance entail more fluid and context-specific characterizations, such as rich/poor or beautiful/ugly. Binary classifications that depend on bounded categories can be easily reproduced and maintained in any social setting, thereby breaking down any group into 'oneself' and the 'other'. As Tilly puts it, the boundaries defined by such categories 'do crucial organizational work', because they are associated with particular characteristics, thereby legitimating, more or less directly, the definition of rights and entitlements (*ibid.* p. 6).

The central role played by particular, socially defined categories in Uganda's labor market provides clear evidence for the existence of durable inequalities on the basis of bounded pairs in the context of labor exchange. Thus, bounded social categories are used to associate labor market participants with personal abilities and entitlements that directly determine – and often limit – their labor market opportunities. The fieldwork conducted in Uganda's rural, agricultural as well as urban, non-agricultural labor markets showed that the types of jobs available to workers are to a large extent defined by their gender, while ethnic categories also play a role. The gendered division of labor is closely associated with inequalities in wage levels and other aspects of working conditions, such as break times and the provision of low-cost appliances to improve health and safety standards. Furthermore, the data gathered indicate that bounded categories defined on concepts of ethnicity are crucial for creating labor market segments and shaping individual employment opportunities in important ways.

The Ugandan data also confirm Tilly's suggestion that socially defined boundaries are naturalized over time. The term 'naturalization' as used by Tilly refers to the concept of symbolic violence, which was originally defined by Bourdieu (1997) as the internalized legitimation of inequality and hierarchy. The concept illuminates how domination is exercised with the (unknowing) consent of the dominated, who understand their social, economic, and political environment through categories and symbols that simultaneously define their oppression (Bourdieu & Wacquant 1992). Thus, characteristics that are ascribed to social groups on the basis of bounded social categories are perceived as the 'results of variation in individual talent or effort' (Tilly 1998, p. 6). In this way, gender-based inequalities tend to be reproduced, as individuals internalize relevant perceptions of bounded categories because they form part of their broader social environment, and the cost of opposing them may be high. As a result, even those who are disadvantaged by particular social boundaries are likely to contribute to their reproduction.

The process of naturalization is crucial for the durability of inequalities in Tilly's sense. The dominant perceptions of the abilities as well as the entitlements of labor market participants in Uganda are naturalized by virtue of being embedded in 'traditions' or knowledge that is rarely or no longer questioned. As Hobsbawm (1983) showed in his discussion on the invention of traditions, the latter may be perceived as self-evident and 'true' because the historically specific circumstances of their emergence have been reinterpreted in a discourse that is dominated by elite interests. The particular bounded categories that are associated with labor market participants transfer information about job seekers to potential employers and ease transaction costs within recruitment processes in mutually reinforcing ways. On the one hand, they guide employers' selections of applicants, while on other they shape job seekers' expectations and influence their job searching behavior. Existing hierarchies and relations of inequality associated with dominant bounded categories are, therefore, reproduced by all players, including those who suffer from exploitation in the resulting relations of economic exchange. As Tilly emphasizes, the durable inequalities introduced through particular organizational forms represent the main mechanism for exploitation (*ibid.*, p. 15).

One of the major functions of symbolic violence as defined above is to normalize and enforce structural violence (*see*, for example, Bourgois 2002, on power and neoliberal, cold-war politics in El Salvador). The latter is defined as forms of political and economic organization that impose conditions of distress, including poverty and abusive working conditions, and are expressed in exploitative conditions of economic and labor exchange (Bourgois 2001). Labor market conditions throughout the developing world reflect the operation of structural violence, and an analysis of institutionalized inequalities underlying the regulation of labor market transactions should be understood from this perspective. In an analysis of labor market conditions in developing countries, Khan (2001) showed that disguised underemployment is common, with a high occurrence of work sharing and income sharing permitted by a weak institutional framework.[14] International statistics on income levels for Uganda and other low-income countries further show a weak correlation between employment and poverty reduction, with a large share of workers depending on poverty wages. These figures reinforce Breman's argument, based on data from South Gujarat, India, that only a tiny and decreasing proportion of workers in highly informal labor markets benefit from the regularity, stability, security, and dignity that ensure modest welfare levels (Breman 1994, 2001).

In Uganda, many rural and urban labor market participants face low returns to labor and high levels of job insecurity. The data presented in Chapter 5 indicate that virtually all waged employment in Eastern Uganda's agricultural sector is casual, with a severe lack of job security. A similar situation seems to prevail throughout the country for skilled, non-agricultural workers in the urban labor market. Given the insecure nature of employment relationships, there is a high level of fluctuation at the workplace and the motivation of workers tends to be low, as is confirmed by the survey in Uganda's non-agricultural labor market (*see* Chapter 5). As a result, productivity levels are on average low, a situation that is further worsened by the low quality of labor.

Given that Uganda's labor markets are largely regulated by informal institutions, a note is appropriate on how the distinction between formal and informal institutions, as defined in the above section of this chapter, relates to the reproduction of inequalities. Bounded categories, such as gender or ethnicity, are likely to structure labor exchange anywhere, but they are particularly relevant in highly informal labor markets.[15] In Uganda, ascribed group attributes are a major source of information for recruitment processes, while in a more formal institutional setting, individual skills and competencies are likely to gain importance if standardized measurement systems are available. Thus, the naturalization of inequalities may be perceived as less severe in formal institutions, in particular if these are subject to democratic control mechanisms aimed at promoting greater economic equality. In this context, hierarchies and relations of inequality are more likely to be perceived as such and may lead the generation of support for disadvantaged groups to challenge exploitation.

However, the development of formal as well as informal institutions is embedded in dominant social norms and practices that often reflect existing inequalities. As a result, both formal and informal institutions may incorporate existing inequalities in implicit ways. An example is the reproduction of inequalities within formal education systems which, although free of charge, may cater to the interests of particular social groups in multiple and intricate ways (*see*, for example, Bourdieu & Passeron 1977; Bourdieu 1990, 1997). Also, formal labor market institutions, such as social dialogue processes, often reflect gender- or ethnicity-based inequalities that are reproduced in trade unions and/or the wider society. While no definite conclusion can be drawn here on the relevance of the formal/informal distinction for the reproduction of inequalities, *formal* institutional settings, especially in open-access societies, tend to allow for greater social mobility of non-elites due to a functional legal framework of reference that includes, at least to some extent, the interests of non-elites (North et al. 2009). In Uganda's highly informal labor market, this wider framework of reference is largely dysfunctional, and the reproduction of distributional patterns takes place largely on the basis of bounded social categories.

## 4.3 Collective action and inclusive institutional change

The NIE literature generally assumes that grievances caused by market failures serve as a major incentive for the formation of collective action. Subsequently, NIE focuses on problems of group coherence and how the free-rider problem can be overcome (*see*, for example, Olson 1965; Ostrom 1990). The literature essentially suggests two main factors for the success of cooperative solutions to resource allocation problems: common interests of a clearly defined group of beneficiaries as well as strong leadership that ensures the existence of clearly communicated rules and the implementation of effective sanctions. However, the definition of common interests may be less straightforward and universally applicable than is assumed within NIE. Incentives to organize may include a spectrum of non-material interests that are 'typically rooted in a common sense of identity, aided by a common ideology, and assisted by lack of internal differentiation within the community of actors' (Munoz et al. 2007, p. 1930). Following this perspective, the present study aims to transcend a narrow definition of incentives for collective action based on methodological individualism to capture a broader range of relational factors that shape historically specific forms of collective action.

Furthermore, strong leadership plays an important, but also an ambiguous role in the development and impact of collective action, because it may be used (or abused) to pursue objectives that divert from the original interests underlying a particular manifestation of collective action, such as labor or small producers' organizations.[16] On the one hand, it is likely to strengthen organizations by generating order and promoting efficiency, but on the other hand, strong leadership and the associated hierarchies are instrumental for the creation and reproduction of inequalities, which may lead to internal conflict (Heyer et al. 2002). Thus, the operation of power and relations of inequality within manifestations of collective action, and their effects on the capacity of organizations and social movements to act as an effective means for disadvantaged groups to defend their interests, is a major focus of the present analysis of small producers' organizations. The examination of cooperatives in Uganda's coffee sector, as discussed in Chapter 5, aims to illuminate issues of power and inequality both within organizational (management) structures and within the relations between cooperatives (or their actors) and the wider socio-economic and political environment, including the state.

The focus on both the *internal* institutional structures of organizations and their relations with the wider environment, in particular the state, is essential for understanding the role of collective action for social change. For an organization to be effective in representing members' interests against those of stronger economic actors, local elites, and the government, it needs to extend beyond primary organizational units or groups to enable 'trans-communal' coalitions (Tarrow 1998). Such coalitions are based on organizational structures that facilitate communication between actors across primary groups to allow the exchange and dissemination of ideas, while also ensuring some level of predictability and reliability regarding the behavioral patterns of actors and the major functions of organizational structures. Such organizations include labor unions and agrarian cooperatives with secondary and national-level organizational structures and functional channels of communication and representation between primary, secondary, and national levels. In contrast, CBOs and other self-help groups that are largely based on face-to-face communication tend to have a restricted or no direct impact on shaping the development of institutions that determine the terms and conditions of economic exchange beyond the local level.

The relational perspective on the development and impact of collective action which has been outlined above essentially follows the approach to analyzing political struggles that was developed by the authors McAdam, Tarrow, and Tilly in various publications (*see*, for example, Tilly 2004a; Tarrow 1998; McAdam et al. 2001). In a nutshell, they concentrate on the nature and dynamics of contentious politics to explain recurrent mechanisms and processes within different forms of claim-centered collective action, including social movements and member-based organizations. Their program of study emphasizes the importance of relations between actors and the wider socio-economic and political environment, in particular the state. Thus, the motivation, nature, development, and impact of different manifestations of collective action are analyzed in relation to the dynamic development of the wider institutional framework and their underlying political settlements which determine state-society relations. For an analysis of the relations between actors (or members of organizations) and the state, Tilly's (2004a) concept of 'repertoires of contestation' is particularly useful because it illuminates how learned cultural creations or 'repertoires', such as rhetoric or behavioral models, are used to shape institutional development processes within the politics of everyday social interaction.

The capacity of disadvantaged groups to organize in order to increase their bargaining power against that of stronger economic actors and the state is crucial for the development of institutions that promote and protect a more equal distribution of the benefits of economic growth. The knowledge and resources that are pooled and accumulated in relevant organizations, such as trade unions and cooperatives, enable an improved representation of interests of weak economic actors within relevant institutional development processes, such as the regulation of product and labor markets, but also the informal regulation of access to resources at the local level, such as access to cash income from crop sales, to primary processing infrastructure and storage facilities, and to markets under conditions of high information asymmetries. In the case of small producers' organizations, the vicious circle of low output quality and volume, low profits, and low investment levels, which is engendered by an initial lack of skills, capital, and other resources, may thus be disrupted. Before discussing the objectives and historical experience of agrarian cooperatives, with a particular focus on Africa, in the following section, the capacity of different forms of so-called grassroots or member-based organizations as an instrument for rural poverty reduction is scrutinized more generally.

As indicated above, the capacity of member-based organizations to engender social change processes depends to a significant extent on the existence of a favorable institutional framework that protects the basic functions of such organizations. This explains the analytical focus on relations between organizations (or their members) and the state, because in order to engender structural change or have any impact on the terms and conditions of economic exchange, organizations depend on the existence of legal institutions that enable the implementation of horizontal and vertical structures of cooperation and representation. Thus, an effective state that is capable of maintaining an enabling (in the above sense) institutional environment is necessary for these organizations to function remotely well.

At the same time, the relationship between organizations and institutions is of a two-way nature: on the one hand, institutions enable organizations to function, and on the other, organizations shape institutional development processes by representing particular interests and exerting political pressure within existing institutional structures. A further aspect of the dependency of organizations on institutions in order to achieve their stated objectives relates to the likelihood of an organization being able to provide a foothold for the reproduction of existing inequalities. As will be shown with regard to coffee sector cooperatives in Chapter 5, inequalities in access to resources and participation in decision-making processes may be reproduced through organizational structures. A broader institutional framework, made up of legal, political, and economic institutions, is necessary to impose rules aimed at enforcing the democratic principles stated by particular socio-economic organizations. In the absence of this broader frame of reference, the reproduction of inequalities may happen within any organizational structure, even if the latter is considered to be 'bottom-up', as elites may capture key positions at local, regional, and national levels and divert resources to objectives contrary to some or all members' interests. This may happen in more or less open contradiction to the stated organizational purposes, as is discussed in more detail in Chapter 5.

### *Civil society as a conceptual framework of collective action*

The increasing focus on inclusive institutional change within the international debate on development has been accompanied by the rise of participatory and rights-based approaches to social and economic development. These are generally expressed in the framework of civil society as a tool to counterbalance and engage with the state, but often without challenging underlying considerations about property relations, the functioning of markets, and the relations of power and control underlying the state itself (for example, Tripp & Te Velde 2006; Newell & Wheeler 2006; Gray 1992; Green 1993, 1996; Giddens 2001, 1994; Uphof 1996).[17] Thus, debates that focus on rights to democratic participation and well-being as a path to social and economic development have often failed to sufficiently recognize the role of power relations in law enforcement by assuming that different social groups and classes have equal access to legal institutions and the rights and entitlements associated with them.

The emphasis on participation within civil society centered approaches to development can be misleading, because it suggests that the inclusion and protection of the interests of disadvantaged groups and classes within institutional arrangements can be measured by the mere extent of their *involvement* in relevant bargaining processes (Di John & Putzel 2009, p. 5).[18] Rather than the level of participation, the *outcomes* of bargaining processes in terms of the distribution of rights and entitlements, as well as the extent of their enforcement, are essential for social and economic development processes, because they shape distributional patterns, thereby enabling structural change in the long run (*ibid.*). The concept of civil society makes a valuable and much-needed contribution to a more comprehensive understanding of different forms of collective action and how these could be operationalized, but it should be applied carefully to avoid the impression that the presence of civil society actors at the negotiating table is sufficient to assume a democratization of policy-making and state institution-forming processes.

Furthermore, civil society-centered approaches to inclusive development have often treated CBOs as organizations that are effective promoters of transformative social and economic change, both at the community level and within the wider institutional framework. This perception should be critically reviewed, because it relies on an image of local communities as largely homogeneous and essentially progressive social units and ignores the extent of inequalities that also exist among rural communities of small producers. In addition, it fails to acknowledge the structural limitations to the influence of disadvantaged groups in institutional development processes that remain dominated by elites. As Fraser (2005) has argued, the integration of civil society participation as an element of policy instruments aimed at poverty reduction may in fact increase rather than decrease the level of control exerted by donors, international NGOs, and the International Finance Institutions over local development processes in Africa. This is because these groups, although representing an 'uneasy coalition', share an agenda of securing consent to liberal political and economic structures, without necessarily scrutinizing their effects on disaggregated local communities (*ibid.*). Similarly, Golooba-Mutebi & Hickey (2010) argue that community-based responses to chronic poverty, promoted in the context of 'inclusive liberalism', essentially represent an abrogation of political responsibility.

To conclude, civil society-centered approaches do not necessarily address the political and economic conditions for structural change, most notably the need for redistributive policies that counterbalance initial inequalities in access to resources. As Brass (2007b, p. 586) noted, the concept of civil society that has come to play a central role within the international debate on development has sometimes reflected conservative and neoliberal perceptions of state-society relations.[19] The concept of civil society as networks, groups, and associations defined in separation from (or in opposition to) the state is valuable, because it illuminates the fact that social groups organize to defend their interests. In addition, the distribution of power within state-society relations needs to addressed, because the latter is decisive for shaping institutional arrangements. Thus, as a framework for thinking about the political and economic empowerment of resource-poor groups, the concept of civil society is necessary but ultimately insufficient, because it focuses on participation in development processes, instead of their outcomes in terms of distributional patterns within and between social groups and classes.

The above discussion calls for a critical use of civil society-centered approaches. Many civil society organizations aim explicitly at increasing the economic and political bargaining power of resource-poor groups vis-à-vis stronger economic actors and the state. Their objectives go beyond involvement-focused participation and poorly-defined notions of empowerment. Instead, such institutions pursue significant influence over policy design and implementation processes in order to advance a redistributive agenda. Similarly, agrarian cooperatives seek to increase the economic and political bargaining power of small producers by pooling resources and uniting the economic strategies of large numbers of people who generally belong to the poorest sections of society.[20] These claims, made by those who set up, subsidize and manage cooperatives (or trade unions, for that matter), are realized with varying degrees of sincerity and commitment, as the discussion of the African experience of cooperatives in the next chapter shows. Thus, civil society organizations as well as small producers' organizations may affect structural change, but their capacity to do so depends on the nature of their relations with the state, and on the distribution of power within internal institutional structures.

## Notes

1 Additional evidence from the non-agricultural labor market is used to explore how the social regulation of labor market transactions affects the quality of employment and labor supply in higher-skilled jobs.

2 As discussed in Chapter 2, the data from Uganda's coffee sector show that casual workers engage in sporadic labor action to press for improved working conditions. There is no evidence of these informal and temporary organizational structures turning into more formal and permanent forms of economic organization.

3 Solow (1990) showed how social norms prevent downward wage flexibility, thereby maintaining unemployment, but also protect workers by enforcing a wage floor that is determined by socially defined concepts of fairness and decent living standards, rather than simply by the impersonal forces of demand and supply. Solow's view is followed here because labor market models based exclusively on supply and demand do not capture the ways in which labor exchange is structured

in socially and historically specific ways. Theoretical approaches that better explain the empirical reality of labor exchange include the Cambridge school of segmented labor market theory (*see*, for example, Rubery 1978; Rubery and Humphries 1984).

4 Such external institutions include laws on trade in agricultural commodities, rural development policies, and the existing rules and practices regarding the democratic representation of different interests at the local and national government level. Some of the major effects of such external institutions are discussed in Chapter 6.

5 Both the historical comparative and the imperfect information approaches are based on methodological individualism, which explains social and economic phenomena through 'our understanding of individual actions directed towards other people and guided by their expected behaviour' (Hayek 1944, p. 8 in Costabile 1995, p. 607).

6 See David (1985) and Arthur (1989) for an original discussion of the concept of path dependency within economics.

7 See Tilly (1999) for a discussion of exploitation as an inherent part of economic exchange.

8 *See*, for example, Stiglitz's (1993) and Williamson's (1993) reactions to Bowles and Gintis's (1993) assertion that inequalities in the distribution of power determine the structure of economic exchange in important ways. However, some notable exceptions include Bardhan (1989) and Knight (1992), who have pointed to the persistence of vested interests and the problem of inducing institutional change in a situation of inequality, in terms of the capacity for coordination, between different social groups.

9 There is no doubt that they do. However, it is suggested here that institutions do more than that: they contribute to the reproduction of existing power relations and thereby shape distributional patterns in complex, dynamic, and historically specific ways.

10 See also Foucault (2003) for a discussion of the notion that politics is war continued by other means.

11 Going beyond the endogenous enforcement problem of creating incentives for the optimization of resource allocation under conditions of moral hazard and adverse selection, Bowles and Gintis (1993) take the disciplinary problems arising from the contested nature of exchange relations as their analytical starting point. Based on the assumption that labor market institutions are not simply allocative, but provide enforcement mechanisms for exchange parties with contradicting interests, they argue that the threat of termination of the exchange relationship leads to the payment of an enforcement rent, which, exceeding the value of the exchange partner's next best alternative, is paid as a 'contingent renewal strategy'. As a result, economic agents are not indifferent between their current transaction and their next best alternative, leading to non-clearing markets.

12 For a critical discussion of the need to re-incorporate income distribution into the mainstream of economic analysis, albeit without a focus on developing countries, *see* Atkinson (1997).

13 The importance of civil society for strengthening democratic representation is recognized. The critique of the concept presented here refers to its sometimes-selective utilization within parts of the international development and aid sector, which concentrates on the creation of a favorable institutional environment for private sector activities to promote economic development, but fails to sufficiently address the role of the state and of state-society relations to enable long-term structural change.

14 'Work sharing' refers to workforce expansion without significant increase in total output, while 'income sharing' refers to unchanged total income distributed among an expanded workforce.

15 For empirical studies of how inequality is reproduced in informal as well as formal institutional structures that regulate labor exchange, *see*, for example, Harriss-White (2006) and McKeever (1998).

16 In addition to assessing leadership in terms of its strengths and weaknesses with regard to functional efficiency, a critical social science analysis should also be capable of evaluating what is right or wrong about particular social phenomena on the basis of moral and ethical aspects.

17 Gray (1992) and Green (1993, 1996) advocate the concept of civil society as a framework for managing access to resources on the basis of local communities, but neglect the importance of divisions of class and gender in the everyday politics of local resource control. Tripp and Te Velde (2006) and Newell and Wheeler (2006) advocate a rights-based development path, while Giddens (2001, 1994) proposes civil society as an apparently non-political 'Third Way' towards social and economic development. These approaches are problematic, because they imply, to a greater or lesser extent, that the introduction of laws and the development of social norms promoting individual rights and democratic structures may eventually substitute for addressing inequalities in distributional patterns.

18 Di John and Putzel (2009) refer to the level of inclusion or exclusion of social groups' interests in a political settlement, pointing out that the *outcomes* of bargaining processes in terms of the distribution of rights and entitlements are decisive, rather than the level of participation.

19 Brass describes a conservative and neoliberal strategy to protect individual property rights as an attempt to generate the support of workers and peasants within the context of a strong capitalist state. The political left, he argues, wants to capture the state as an instrument to realize policies of redistribution to fulfill the demands of those for whom 'redistribution of landed property and other economic resources were indeed central to any notion of democracy' (Brass 2007b, p. 586).

20 Before structural adjustment reforms, agrarian cooperatives often included the collectivization of landed property, as was the case in cooperatives established in the 1960s and 1970s in the USSR, China, North Vietnam, Eastern Europe, Latin America, and parts of Africa (Tanzania and Ethiopia). However, the economic performance of most of these enterprises was weak and agrarian cooperatives today are largely limited to joint storage, marketing, and sometimes joint processing of crops.

## References

ACEMOGLU, D., JOHNSON, S. & AND ROBINSON, J. A. 2002, 'Reversal of Fortune: Geography and Institutions in the Making of the Modern World Income Distribution', *American Economic Association Papers and proceedings, May 2006*, 117, 1231–1294.

ALSTON, L. J. 1996, 'Empirical work in institutional economics: an overview', *Empirical studies in institutional change*, 25–30.

AOKI, M. 2001, *Toward a comparative institutional analysis*, MIT Press, Cambridge, MA.

AOKI, M. 1994, 'The Contingent Governance of Teams: Analysis of Institutional Complementarity', *International Economic Review*, 35, 657–676.

ARNOTT, R. & STIGLITZ, J. E. 1991, 'Moral Hazard and Nonmarket Institutions: Dysfunctional Crowding Out of Peer Monitoring?', *The American Economic Review*, 81, 179–190.

ARTHUR, W. B. 1989, 'Competing technologies, increasing returns, and lock-in by historical Events', *Economic Journal*, 99, 116–131.

ATKINSON, A. B. 1997, 'Bringing Inequality in from the Cold', *Economic Journal*, 107 (441), 297–321.

BANDYOPADHYAY, S. & GREEN, E. 2010, 'The Reversal of Fortune Thesis Reconsidered', STICERD, London School of Economics and Political Sciences (LSE).

BARDHAN, P. K. 2000, 'Understanding Underdevelopment: Challenges for Institutional Economics from the Point of View of Poor Countries', *Journal of Institutional and Theoretical Economics (JITE) / Zeitschrift für die gesamte Staatswissenschaft*, 156, 216–235.

BARDHAN, P. K. 1989, *The Economic theory of agrarian institutions*, Clarendon Press, Oxford, England.

BASTIAENSEN, J., HERDT, T. D. & D'EXELLE, B. 2005, 'Poverty reduction as a local institutional process', *World Development*, 33, 979–993.

BENDA-BECKMANN, F. 1989, 'Scape-goat and magic charm: law in development theory and practice', *Journal of Legal Pluralism and Unofficial Law*, 129.

BOURDIEU, P. 1997, *The Forms of Capital*, Oxford University Press.

BOURDIEU, P. 1990, *The logic of practice*, Stanford University Press.

BOURDIEU, P. & PASSERON, J.C. 1977, 'Reproduction in education, culture and society', *Trans.Nice*, Sage, London.

BOURDIEU, P. & WACQUANT, L. J. D. 1992, *An invitation to reflexive sociology*, University of Chicago press.

BOURGOIS, P. 2002, 'The violence of moral binaries: Response to Leigh Binford', *Ethnography*, 3, 221–231.

BOURGOIS, P. 2001, 'The power of violence in war and peace: Post-Cold War lessons from El Salvador', *Ethnography*, 2, 5–34.

BOWLES, S. 2004, *Microeconomics: behavior, institutions, and evolution*, Russell Sage Foundation, New York; Princeton, N.J.

BOWLES, S. & GINTIS, H. 1993, 'The Revenge of Homo Economicus: Contested Exchange and the Revival of Political Economy', *The Journal of Economic Perspectives*, 7, 83–102.

BOWLES, S. & GINTIS, H. 1988, 'Contested Exchange: Political Economy and Modern Economic Theory', *The American Economic Review*, 78, 145–150.

BOWLES, S., GINTIS, H. & OSBORNE GROVES, M. 2005, *Unequal chances: family background and economic success*, Princeton University Press.

BRASS, T. 2007b, "A world which is not yet': Peasants, civil society and the state', *The Journal of Peasant Studies*, 34, 582–664.

BRASS, T. 2002, 'Rural labour in agrarian transitions: The semi-feudal thesis revisited', *Journal of Contemporary Asia*, 32, 456–473.

BRAVERMAN, A. & GUASCH, J.L. 1986, 'Rural credit markets and institutions in developing countries: lessons for policy analysis from practice and modern theory', *World Development*, 14, 1253–1267.

BRAVERMAN, A. & STIGLITZ, J. 1982a, 'Sharecropping and the Interlinking of Agrarian Markets', *The American Economic Review*, 72(4), 695–715.

BRAVERMAN, A. & STIGLITZ, J. 1982b, 'Moral hazard, incentive flexibility and risk: cost sharing arrangements under sharecropping', Research Memorandum No. 298, Princeton University.

BREMAN, J. 2001, 'An Informalised Labour System: End of Labour Market Dualism', *Economic and Political Weekly*, 36, 4804–4821.

BREMAN, J. 1994, *Wage hunters and gatherers: search for work in the urban and rural economy of South Gujarat*, Oxford University Press.

CHANG, H. J. 2002, 'Breaking the mould: an institutionalist political economy alternative to the neo-liberal theory of the market and the state', *Cambridge Journal of Economics*, 26, 539–559.

CHANG, H. J. & EVANS, P. 2005, *The role of institutions in economic change. Re-imagining Growth. Towards a Renewal of Development Theory*, Zed Books, London.

COASE, R. H. 1992, 'The Institutional Structure of Production', *The American Economic Review*, 82, 713–719.
COMMONS, G. R. 1931, 'Institutional economics', *The American Economic Review*, 21, 648–657.
COSTABILE, L. 1995, 'Institutions, social custom and efficiency wage models: alternative approaches', *Cambridge Journal of Economics*, 19, 605–623.
CRAMER, C. 2000, 'Inequality, Development and Economic Correctness', SOAS Department of Economics and the School of Oriental and African Studies, London.
DAVID, P. A. 1985, 'Clio and the Economics of QWERTY', *American Economic Review*, 75 (2), 332–337.
DI JOHN, J. & PUTZEL, J. 2009, 'Political Settlements Issues Paper', Governance and Social Development Resource Centre (GSDRC), University of Birmingham.
DONER, R. F., RITCHIE, B. K. & SLATER, D. 2005, 'Systemic Vulnerability and the Origins of developmental States: Northeast and Southeast Asia in Comparative Perspective', *International Organisation*, 59, 327–361.
DORWARD, A., KYDD, J., MORRISON, J. & POULTON, C. 2005, 'Institutions, Markets and Economic Co-ordination: Linking Development Policy to Theory and Praxis', *Development and Change*, 36, 1–25.
DORWARD, A., KYDD, J., MORRISON, J. & UREY, I. 2004, 'A Policy Agenda for Pro-Poor Agricultural Growth', *World Development*, 32, 73–89.
FOUCAULT, M. 1976, 'War in the Filigree of Peace: Course Summary (Autumn 1976)', *Oxford Literary Review*, 1, 17–18.
FOUCAULT, M., BERTANI, M., FONTANA, A., EWALD, F. & MACEY, D. 2003, *Society must be defended: lectures at the Collège de France, 1975–76*, Picador, New York.
FRANK, A. G. 1967, *Capitalism and Underdevelopment in Latin America*, Monthly Review Press, New York.
FRASER, A. 2005, 'Poverty reduction strategy papers: Now who calls the Shots?', *Review of African Political Economy*, 32, 317–340.
GAGLIARDI, F. 2008, 'Institutions and economic change: A critical survey of the new institutional approaches and empirical evidence', *The Journal of Socio-Economics*, 37, 416–443.
GIDDENS, A. 2001, *The Global Third Way Debate*, Polity Press, Cambridge.
GIDDENS, A. 1994, *Beyond Left and Right: The Future of Radical Politics*, Stanford University Press, Stanford, CA.
GOLOOBA-MUTEBI, F. & HICKEY, S. 2010, 'Governing Chronic Poverty under Inclusive Liberalism: The Case of the Northern Uganda Social Action Fund', *Journal of Development Studies*, 46, 1216–1239.
GRAY, J. 1992, *The Moral Foundations of Market Institutions*, Institute of Economic Affairs, London.
GREEN, D. 1993, *Reinventing Civil Society*, Institute of Economic Affairs, London.
GREEN, D. 1996, *Community Without Politics: A Market Approach to Welfare Reform*, Institute of Economic Affairs, London.
GREIF, A. 1998, 'Historical and Comparative Institutional Analysis', *The American Economic Review*, 88, 80–84.
GREIF, A. 1993, 'Contract Enforceability and Economic Institutions in Early Trade: The Maghribi Traders' Coalition', *The American Economic Review*, 83, 525–548.
GROOTAERT, C., KANBUR, R. & OH, G. T. 1995, The dynamics of poverty: why some people escape from poverty and others don't - an African case study, World Bank, Washington D.C.

HARRISS, J. 2006, 'Notes on a Historical Institutionalist Approach to the IPPG Agenda', University of Manchester, Manchester.

HARRISS-WHITE, B. 2006, 'Poverty and capitalism', *Economic and Political Weekly*.

HAYEK, F. A. 1944, *The Road to Serfdom*, Chicago University Press, Chicago.

HEYER, J., STEWART, F. & THORP, R. 2002, *Group behaviour and development: Is the market destroying cooperation?*, Oxford University Press, Oxford.

HOBSBAWM, E. J. 1983, 'Introduction: Inventing Traditions', In: HOBSBAWM, E. J. & RANGER, T. (eds.) *The Invention of Tradition*, Cambridge University Press, Cambridge.

HOFF, K., BRAVERMAN, A. & STIGLITZ, J. E. 1993, *The Economics of Rural Organization. Theory, Practice, and Policy*, Oxford University Press, Oxford.

IMF 2005, 'Chapter 3: Building Institutions', International Monetary Fund, Washington D.C.

JÜTTING, J. 2003, 'Institutions and development: a critical review', *Research programme on social institutions and dialogue*, OECD, Paris.

KHAN, A. R. 2001, 'Employment policies for poverty reduction', *Issues in Employment and Poverty*, Recovery and Reconstruction Department, International Labour Office, Geneva.

KHAN, M. 1995, 'State Failure in Weak States: A Critique of New Institutionalist Explanations', In: HARRIS, J., HUNTER, J. & LEWIS, C. (eds.) *The New Institutional Economics and Third World Development*, Routledge, London.

KNIGHT, J. 1992, *Institutions and social conflict*, Cambridge University Press, Cambridge, England; New York, N.Y.

LACLAU, E. 1971, 'Feudalism and Capitalism in Latin America', *New Left Review*, 0, 19–38.

LANGLOIS, R. N. 1986, *Economics as a Process. Essays in the New Institutional Economics*, Cambridge University Press, Cambridge.

LEFTWICH, A. 2007, 'The Political Approach to Institutional Formation, Maintenance and Change', University of Manchester, Manchester.

LEFTWICH, A. & SEN, K. 2010, 'Beyond Institutions. Institutions and organizations in the politics and economics of poverty reduction - a thematic synthesis of research evidence', *Research Programme Consortium on Improving Institutions for Pro-Poor Growth (IPPG)*, University of Manchester, Manchester.

LUKES, S. 2006, *Individualism*, ECPR Press, Essex.

MAHDI, S. 2010, 'The Impact of Regulatory and Institutional Arrangements on Agricultural Markets and Poverty: A case study of Tanzania's Coffee Market', University of Manchester, Manchester.

MCADAM, D., TARROW, S. & TILLY, C. 2001, *The Dynamics of Contention*, Cambridge University Press, Cambridge.

MCKEEVER, M. 1998, 'Reproduced Inequality: Participation and Success in the South African Informal Economy', *Social Forces*, 76, 1209–1241.

MUÑOZ, I., PAREDES, M. & THORP, R. 2007, 'Group Inequalities and the Nature and Power of Collective Action: Case Studies from Peru', *World Development*, 35, 1929–1946.

NABLI, M. K. & NUGENT, J. B. 1989, *The new institutional economics and development: theory and applications to Tunisia*, North-Holland, Amsterdam.

NATSIOS, A. 2010, 'The Clash of the Counter-bureaucracy and Development', *The Clash of the Counter-bureaucracy and Development*, Centre for Global Development.

NELSON, R. R. 1994, 'The co-evolution of technology. Industrial structure and supporting institutions', *Industrial and Corporate Change*, 3, 47–63.

NELSON, R. R. & SAMPAT, B. N. 2001, 'Making sense of institutions as a factor shaping economic performance', *Journal of Economic Behavior and Organization*, 1, 54.

NEWELL, P. & WHEELER, J. 2006, *Rights, Resources and the Politics of Accountability*, Zed Books, London.

NORTH, D. C. 1990a, *Institutions, institutional change and economic performance*, Cambridge University Press, Cambridge.

NORTH, D. C. 1990b, 'A Transaction Costs Theory of Politics', *Journal of Theoretical Politics*, 2, 355–367.

NORTH, D. C. 1981, *Structure and change in economic history*, W.W. Norton, New York.

NORTH, D. C., WALLIS, J. J. & WEINGAST, B. R. 2009, *Violence and Social Orders: A Conceptual Framework for Interpreting Recorded Human History*, Cambridge University Press, New York.

OLSON, M. 1965, *The Logic of Collective Action: Public Goods and the Theory of Groups*, Harvard University Press, Cambridge, MA.

OLSSON, O. 2004, 'Unbundling Ex-Colonies: A Comment on Acemoglu, Johnson, and Robinson', 2001, Göteborg University.

OPPG 2005, 'Pro-Poor Growth in the 1990s: Lessons and Insights from 14 Countries', World Bank, Washington D.C.

OSTROM, E. 1990, *Governing the commons: the evolution of institutions for collective action*, Cambridge University Press, Cambridge.

PATTENDEN, J. 2010, 'A neoliberalisation of civil society? Self-help groups and the labouring class poor in rural South India', *Journal of Peasant Studies*, 37, 485–512.

PLATTEAU, J. P. & SEKI, E. 2000, 'Community arrangements to overcome market failures: pooling groups in Japanese fisheries', In: AOKI, M. & HAYAMI, Y. (eds.) *Communities and Markets in Economic Development*, Oxford University Press, Oxford.

PRZEWORSKI, P. 2004, 'Geography vs. Institutions Revisited: Were Fortunes Reversed?', Mimeo, New York University.

REBITZER, J. B. 1993, 'Radical Political Economy and the Economics of Labor Markets', *Journal of Economic Literature*, 31, 1394–1434.

ROBINSON, J. A. 2002, 'States and Power in Africa by Jeffrey I Herbst: A Review Essay', *Journal of Economic Literature*, XL, 510–519.

ROBINSON, S. 1976, 'A Note on the U-Hypothesis', *American Economic Review*, 66, 437–440.

SAYER, A. 2009, 'Who's Afraid of Critical Social Science?', *Current Sociology*, 57, 767–786.

SHEPSLE, K. A. 1989, 'Studying Institutions: Some Lessons from the Rational Choice Approach', *Journal of Theoretical Politics*, 1, 131–147.

SOLOW, R. M. 1990, *The labor market as a social institution*, Basil Blackwell, Oxford.

STIGLITZ, J. E. 1998, *More instruments and broader goals: moving toward the post-Washington consensus*, World Institute for Development Economics Research, United Nations University, Helinski.

STORPER, M. & WALKER, R. 1989, *The capitalist imperative: territory, technology and industrial growth*, Basil Blackwell, Oxford.

SUGDEN, R. 1989, 'Spontaneous Order', *Journal of Economic Perspectives*, 3, 85–97.

TARROW, S. 1998, *Power in movement: Social movements and contentious politics*, Cambridge University Press, Cambridge.

TILLY, C. 2004a, *Social movements: 1768–2004*, Paradigm, London.

TILLY, C. 1998, *Durable inequality*, University of California Press, Ltd., Berkeley and Los Angeles, California.

THORNER, A. 1982, 'Semi-Feudalism or Capitalism? Contemporary Debate on Classes and Modes of Production in India', *Economic and Political Weekly*, XVII, 49–52.

TRIPP, R. & TE VELDE, W. 2006, 'Civil Society and Economic Growth', *International Journal of Technology and Globalisation*, 3.

UPHOFF, N. 1996, 'Learning from Gal Oya: Possibilities for Participatory Development and Post-Newtonian Social Science', *Intermediate Technology Publication*.

VEBLEN, T. 1899, *The theory of the leisure class: an economic study of institutions*, Routledge / Thoemmes Press, London.

WIGGINS, S., KIRSTEN, J. & LLAMBÍ, L. 2010, 'The Future of Small Farms', *World Development*, 38, 1341–1348.

WILLIAMSON, O. E. 1975, *Markets and hierarchies: analysis and antitrust implications. A study in the economics of internal organization*, Free Press, New York.

WORLD BANK 2003, *World Development Report 2003: Sustainable Development in a Dynamic World: Transforming Institutions, Growth, and Quality of Life*, World Bank, New York.

WORLD BANK 1997, *World Development Report: The State in a Changing World*, World Bank, New York.

# 5 The socioeconomic effects of Uganda's coffee cooperatives

This chapter assesses the ability of cooperatives in Uganda's coffee sector to directly improve the welfare levels of small producers. The socioeconomic effects of cooperatives vary depending on internal organizational characteristics and external political and economic determinants. The following analysis focuses on internal factors by exploring the development of democratic organizational structures, and those structures' effects on rural inequality, productivity, and quality improvements. Particular attention is paid to the role of women in cooperatives, because women remain underrepresented as members and leaders in organizations across the country and indeed across Africa. The unequal distribution of power in cooperatives is partly caused and reinforced by widespread gender-based inequality in land ownership. The resulting power asymmetry has ethical and economic consequences, because women not only contribute a large share of agricultural labor, but are also bearers of valuable bodies of knowledge on production processes and, through their role as producers and traders of cash crops for local markets, on marketing.

The chapter presents evidence from a survey among 330 small coffee producers and coffee wage workers, thirteen semi-structured interviews with small producers, nine semi-structured interviews with representatives of NGOs and donors active in rural and agricultural development, twenty semi-structured interviews with representatives of cooperatives and Uganda's umbrella organization UCA, sixteen semi-structured interviews with representatives of local and national government, eighteen focus group discussions with small producers as well as participant observation on small farms, in cooperative warehouses, village-based primary-processing sites, and processing factories[1]. Additional semi-structured interviews were conducted with coffee-buying companies (for a discussion, see Chapter 6). The survey, the semi-structured interviews with producers, and the focus group discussions also covered coffee producers who were not members of a cooperative.

The group of four member-based organizations selected as case studies represents the types of organizations that dominate the cooperative landscape in Uganda today and also includes Uganda's umbrella organization of cooperatives.

*Figure 5.1* NUCAFE farmer in Kaptokwoi Village, Kapchorwa District

There is a small, community-based cooperative called *United Organic Coffee Producers* (UOCG), the medium-sized *Gumutindo Cooperative Enterprise* (hereafter referred to as Gumutindo), the country-wide operating *National Union of Coffee Agro-Businesses and Farm Enterprises* (NUCAFE), and also the country-wide active umbrella organization *Uganda Cooperative Alliance* (UCA). UOCG, Gumutindo, and NUCAFE specialize in coffee, while UCA works across economic sectors. The three cooperatives were founded

*Figure 5.2* NUCAFE coffee nursery in Kaptokwoi Village, Kapchorwa District

after the liberalization of Uganda's agricultural sector, while UCA, founded in 1961, has undergone significant organizational changes since the 1990s.[2] All four organizations provide training and advisory and marketing services to their members, who are organized in primary cooperatives, but only UOCG and Gumutindo trade (and export) coffee, while UCA and NUCAFE focus on capacity building and input delivery. UCA's duties additionally involve advocacy as well as building and strengthening micro-finance capacities to improve members' access to capital.

The ability of a cooperative to contribute to poverty reduction depends on its effectiveness in representing members' interests, based on the nature of its organizational structures and the existence of democratic control mechanisms, and also on its success in generating faster rates of growth of output and productivity, which may vary with internal organizational characteristics and external determinants. This chapter concentrates on internal factors by exploring how internal organizational characteristics shape a cooperative's contribution to the reduction of inequalities in dis-aggregated rural communities and to the improvement of members' living standards. An examination of the quantity and quality of training activities provided by cooperatives illustrates the extent to which member-based organizations can effectively transfer skills to disadvantaged sections of the population in poorly-served rural areas. The focus on training sheds light on the socio-economic effects of a major activity of cooperatives, because all of the member-based organizations included in the case studies provide training, as opposed to financial services or political representation at the national level.

An analysis of some of the major external factors that determine a cooperative's economic viability is presented in Chapter 6. These include domestic political and economic constraints on the functionality and expansion of cooperatives that are created or intensified by the design of agricultural development and investment policies. For example, some of Uganda's strategies of agricultural subsidies have strengthened elite interests for tightened political control over the rural electorate by supporting "model farmers" rather than small producer organizations that are inclusive and capable of representing their members' interests vis-à-vis large commodity buyers and the state. Furthermore, widespread rural poverty and a lack of a social security system that can safeguard small producers in the face of increasingly frequent external shocks – such droughts, floods, and other extreme weather events – weaken the ability of cooperatives to maintain members in competition with domestic and transnational buyers. Due to a poor transport, storage and communication infrastructure, few buyers can afford to buy at the farm gate, leaving local traders and a small number of TNCs that buy unprocessed cherries or washed (primary-processed) coffee directly from small producers. The nature of business relations with producers varies, but some TNCs seem to follow a pragmatically progressive approach to secure adequate quality levels and stable volumes. However, corporate strategies for vertical integration seem to lock small producers at the source of the value chain, as they forego opportunities for vertical diversification.[3]

This first section of this chapter provides an outline of Uganda's coffee sector as a case study with strong relevance for rural economic development in sub-Saharan Africa. Coffee is a major export crop in Uganda, as well as in more than a dozen countries across region, and cooperatives play a key role in improving smallholder coffee production and in organizing marketing activities in these countries. The section introduces the socio-cultural and economic characteristics of Eastern Uganda – the country's major production area of Arabica coffee and the main research area for coffee sector research for this book – and outlines the key organizational characteristics of the four cooperatives where qualitative data was collected.

The second section examines the socio-economic effects of cooperatives in the form of changes in class- and gender-based inequalities as well as improvements of members' living standards as compared with non-organized producers.[4] The data presented further illuminate the organizational mechanisms that are in place in the four case study cooperatives to ensure the representation of members' interests within the organization and *vis-à-vis* other economic actors and the state. As noted above, this discussion aims to shed light on the internal organizational conditions under which cooperatives may contribute to more equal socio-economic outcomes.

This section also explores the capacities of cooperatives to act as training providers. Producers depend on access to good-quality training to increase productivity and output quality.[5] Furthermore, they need more and better skills to articulate their demands to the state, most notably regarding extension services and rural infrastructure development. Lastly, the increasing dependence of rural households on wage employment indicates the need for transferable skills to improve their labor market prospects. While cooperatives cannot substitute for general and vocational education and training, they may strengthen small producers' capacities to develop viable income generation strategies in a changing economic environment.

In the third section, particular attention is paid to gender inequalities within cooperatives, because women still represent a small proportion of cooperative members in the coffee sector, even though they have long contributed a significant share, if not the majority, of agricultural labor in smallholder farming. Against this background, the creation of women's primary cooperatives in parts of Eastern Uganda's coffee-growing area indicates a potentially powerful step towards women's economic, social, and political empowerment.

The analysis reveals significant differences between small (community-based), medium-sized, and national organizations. Overall, the existence of a larger organizational frame of reference, in combination with direct channels of communication between members and higher levels of management, seems to be essential to prevent a closing of ranks between local elites and the cooperative management, but it is unlikely to exist in community-based organizations.[6] In large organizations, however, close relations between the management and national political elites may increase the gap between organizational strategies at the top and the reality of members' needs, which ultimately impedes the functionality of democratic organizational structures.

## 5.1 Mt. Elgon: social and economic features of a coffee growing area

The main fieldwork area consists of five districts in Eastern Uganda, located on and around the fertile slopes of Mt. Elgon at the border with Kenya[7]. Along with Nebbi district in the northwest and Bundibuyo and Kasese districts in the southwest, the area is one of Uganda's three production areas of washed Arabica coffee. Four of the five districts, namely Mbale, Manafwa, Bududa, and Sironko, make up the former district of Bugisu, which is home to the Bagisu people (La Fontaine 1959). Their language Lugisu, also called Masaaba, was spoken by 1,120,000 people in Uganda (2002 census) and represents the most widespread language in the four districts (Lewis et al. 2009). As a Narrow Bantu language, it belongs to the same linguistic lineage as Luganda, the language of the Baganda people of southern Uganda, including the capital city Kampala (*ibid.*). Although the lexical similarity of Lugisu and Luganda is low, the Bagisu generally emphasize that they find Luganda easy to learn and throughout the Lugisu-speaking area, it can be used as a means of communication (*ibid.*).

In Uganda, the ability to speak Luganda is socially and economically significant, because it is widely used by members of the elites. Alongside English, the official state language, Luganda remains the chief language of communication in national government institutions as well as in large companies and major media outlets, all of which are concentrated in Kampala. In this regard, Kapchorwa, the fifth of the districts that make up the fieldwork area, stands out. Among the Sebei (also called Sabin) people, who represent the vast majority of the district's population, Luganda is less widely spoken (Ladefoged et al. 1972). This not only constrains communication with government institutions, but also the ability to read and understand some of the largest national newspapers and radio programs. The Sebei language, also called Kupsabiny or Sabiny, is spoken by only 181,000 people in Uganda (2002 census). As a Nilo-Saharan language, it belongs to a different linguistic lineage than Luganda and Lugisu, and most Sebei people rely on basic knowledge of a mixture of languages and dialects to communicate with their Bagisu neighbors.[8] English is also less widely spoken in Kapchorwa than in the Bugisu area, indicating lower levels of formal schooling, given that the language of instruction in Uganda's formal schooling system is English from the primary level onwards.

In addition to its linguistic singularity, Kapchorwa is possibly the most remote of the five districts around the Ugandan side of Mt. Elgon. Historically the poorest population group around Mt. Elgon, the Sebei today continue to face particular constraints on economic opportunities. Because a significant part of the district is located within Mt Elgon National Park, it is accessible only on foot and restrictions on agricultural activities are applied by the national government. From Kapchorwa town, there is neither a paved road to the nearby Kenyan border nor towards northern Uganda, although a well-maintained, paved road connects to Sironko district. This road is vital for the economic activities of the Sebei, because it provides a connection to Mbale municipality, where the majority of manufactured products that are available in the fieldwork area arrive on trucks and are sold on to traders serving more remote areas. Furthermore, Mbale municipality is home to the largest regional markets for agricultural products, including export cash crops, and to Eastern Uganda's agro-processing industry. While Sironko as well as the areas that today make up Manafwa and Bududa districts have a long history of economic exchange with Mbale, Kapchorwa has remained somewhat isolated since its establishment as a separate district from the Bugisu area in 1962 (Bunker 1987).

Between the Bagisu and the Sebei, as between other ethnic groups in Uganda, there is a history of ethnic and religious divisions, which are closely related to social and economic development processes (Saul 1976; Young 1976). In Bugisu, the identification of political elites with religious leaders from Protestant and Catholic churches was an important factor of their success in organizing support among Bagisu farmers from the early 20th century onwards (Bunker 1987). The higher prevalence of Islam as well as traditional religions among the Sebei is likely to have reinforced the exclusion of Sebei people from equal access to political and economic power. In the late 1950s, the Bagisu arguably intensified their economic dominance over the Sebei through the Bugisu Cooperative Union (BCU), which was largely run by Bagisu leaders and controlled the marketing of coffee in the entire Mt Elgon area (Bunker 1987). The increasing marginalization of the Sebei resulted in an escalation of existing conflictual relations, in which ethnic identity played an important role. Against this background, the Sebei established the district of Kapchorwa and a separate Sebei coffee cooperative in the early 1960s (*ibid*).

The cultural and economic differences between Sebei and Bagisu persist today, but the expression of conflictual relations in terms of ethnicity has become less common. The fieldwork of the present study confirmed that religious and political leaders at the community level in Eastern Uganda tend to emphasize neighborly cooperation rather than historical relations of antagonism. However, the qualitative research also showed that intermarriage between the Sebei and the Bagisu continues to be exceptional. Furthermore, discriminating cultural stereotypes often surface in descriptions of the neighboring group.

The persistence of these divisions should not obscure similarities between the Sebei and Bagisu regarding social and economic inequalities *within* communities. Thus, gender inequalities are pronounced and widespread within both groups, and they are institutionalized in labor markets, conjugal relations, and inheritance systems. As some studies have shown, high gender wage differentials, even after accounting for education attainment, age, work experience, and employment sector, point to the discrimination against women across ethnic groups (Kagundu and Pavlova 2007; Sebagalla 2007). Similarly, the high prevalence of domestic violence, which is linked to cultural norms as well as alcohol abuse, represents a serious problem throughout Uganda, rather than being limited to particular social or ethnic groups (Office of the Prime Minister 2009)[9]. Lastly, Uganda's various customary legal systems reinforce inequalities in the gendered distribution of resources, most notably land, across ethnic groups (Women's Land Link Africa 2010). Throughout Uganda, land owned by men is mostly acquired through inheritance, whereas most women have purchased the land they own (Office of the Prime Minister 2009).

The present fieldwork confirmed that the above-described gender inequalities in formal institutions are visible in equal measure among the Sebei and the Bagisu[10]. Both societies are patrilineal, and women move to the husband's village upon marriage, where they generally receive a new name (La Fontaine 1962). During the fieldwork, women emphasized that these names signify their status as a 'newcomer' and some explained that when they moved to their husbands' villages, their access to informal support networks deteriorated significantly.[11] Against the background of institutionalized discrimination against women, the disruption of women's access to such networks is likely to contribute to the reinforcement of existing inequalities.

### *Coffee as a driver of economic development on Mt. Elgon and in Uganda at large*

As the major export crop cultivated on the slopes of Mt. Elgon, coffee is vital to the economy in Eastern Uganda. Because of the national economic significance of the coffee sector in Uganda at large, the Mt. Elgon region is worth studying for its wider relevance to the country's economic development. In particular, it provides an opportunity to study some dimensions of the linkages between agricultural exports and local welfare dynamics, because large numbers of people depend on coffee as a source of income. Coffee is Uganda's most important export cash crop and a major generator of foreign exchange revenues. Although its contribution to export earnings decreased considerably since the late 1990s in response to a slump in world market prices, coffee is still central to the national economy and to people's livelihoods (Ponte & Kawuma 2003; UBOS 2010. Lower prices and the spread of the coffee wilt disease negatively affected earnings during the early 2000s, but in 2005, coffee was still the primary source of income for about 2.5 million people or 10 percent of the total population (Ribbink et al. 2005, p. 23).[12] Based on growing export volumes in recent years, it has been estimated that this number is increasing again (*ibid.*; ICO accessed September 2011 and 2017; UCDA accessed March 2009 and September 2017).

The coffee sector is also a major and perhaps the single most important source of wage employment in the fieldwork area. The processing factory which is run by Kyagalanyi, a large multinational company, in Mbale municipality and the smaller processing operations of the formerly monopolistic cooperative Bugisu Cooperative Union (BCU) are by far the largest single employers, and there are smaller, domestic factories engaged in individual coffee processing services that employ significant numbers of workers in the town and the surrounding areas.[13] As the largest agricultural sub-sector in Eastern Uganda in terms of transaction volumes, coffee presumably creates more employment in ancillary industries, such as transport, storage, and infrastructure development, than other economic sectors. Thus, Kyagalanyi is building new processing field stations in various locations on the slopes of Mt. Elgon, including feeder roads and expanded storage facilities. Foreign buyers who do not process any coffee in the region have built large warehouses and employ significant numbers of workers for sorting the coffee beans before they are transported to Kampala.

Coffee cooperatives have long formed part of the social, political, and economic fabric of society in Eastern Uganda, and although the region's coffee market is dominated by two TNCs,[14] cooperatives remain highly relevant today (Bunker 1987, 1983; Kyamulesire 1988; Kyazze 2010). The liberalization of Uganda's coffee sector in 1990/91, and the associated increase in competition from foreign buyers and the radical cut-back of public sector support led to the collapse or significant reduction of trade by the formerly monopolistic cooperatives. However, the assumption that "the cooperative has almost disappeared" (Ponte 2002, p. 266) has not been confirmed by the present study. Throughout Africa, including Uganda, new cooperatives have been created within the coffee as well as other agricultural sub-sectors, and as a result of their dynamic development, interest among scholars and policy makers has increased since the mid-2000s (*see*, for example, Wanyama et al. 2009; Pollet 2009; Develtere et al. 2008; and for Uganda, *see* Kyazze 2010; Boesen et al. 2004).

As briefly outlined above, the four organizations chosen as case studies for the coffee sector analysis in Eastern Uganda include a small, community-based cooperative, one coffee organization with countrywide outreach, the National Union of Coffee Agro-businesses and Farm Enterprises (NUCAFE) and the Uganda Cooperative Alliance (UCA), the national umbrella organization that has extended its activities to the primary and secondary cooperative levels.[15] In addition, it includes one of the few economically sustainable, medium-sized agrarian cooperatives in post-liberalization Uganda that is internationally competitive: the Gumutindo Cooperative Enterprise (another one being 'Good African Coffee' in western Uganda). Gumutindo has members throughout the fieldwork area and, as an exporter of roasted beans, competes with international commodity buyers and roasters. The combination of small producers' organizations that operate in the fieldwork area chosen for this book represents one case of each of the major types of cooperatives that operate in Uganda's coffee sector today, which increases the comparability of data discussed. The next section outlines the major characteristics of the four case organizations.

### *Four cooperative case studies*

The selection of case studies reflects the main types of organizations which are today operative at the primary and secondary levels in Eastern Uganda's coffee sector. At the time of the fieldwork, neither of the two formerly monopolistic cooperatives, the Bugisu Cooperative Union (BCU) or the Sabin Elgon Cooperative Union (SECU), provided services to farmers. Both cooperatives had performed weakly in the 1970s and 1980s, under the influence of increasing state control (Bunker 1987, 1983).[16] In the years following the liberalization of Uganda's coffee sector in 1990/1991, they reduced their trade volumes under the economic pressures created by increasing competition with foreign buyers and the drastic cut-back of public sector support. In 2002, BCU ceased to trade coffee, but it slowly started to buy again in 2009, although most primary cooperatives remained dormant and the organization was buying coffee almost exclusively from local middlemen rather than from farmers. Therefore, BCU was inactive *with regard to its original cooperative functions*, most notably the provision of training and marketing services to small producers. SECU, the smaller of the two cooperatives, was not buying coffee at the time of the fieldwork and its processing factory in Kapchorwa town had been non-functional for several years.

The Uganda Cooperative Alliance (UCA), founded in 1961, is the largest of the four case-study organizations. Following liberalization, the UCA transitioned from the apex organization it had originally served as to an umbrella organization that serves not only secondary and tertiary level cooperatives but also primary societies and SACCOS (Kapiriri 2008; Nannyonjo 2013; Okello & Ahikire 2013). In response to the collapse of cooperative unions under the pressures of liberalization reforms, the organization continuously expanded its activities by establishing so-called Area Cooperative Enterprises (ACE) at the secondary level (UCA website accessed March 13, 2018). These provide training and marketing services to primary cooperatives, just as a cooperative union does, by employing extension workers financed through members' contributions (UCA 2015). Thus, although UCA does not include primary organizations on their list of members (www.uca.co.ug), small producers identify as UCA members through their membership in ACEs, with no difference between UCA and "regular" cooperative unions.

The simultaneous engagement of UCA at the primary society and the national level is noteworthy, because it can help to keep political advocacy at the national level effective and relevant. In early 2018, the UCA was working to extend its advocacy capacities through an Advocacy Strategy Development project that is supported by several domestic civil society organizations, and the International Co-Operative Alliance (ICA). The data discussed in this chapter is particularly insightful on UCA's primary-level activities, which the organization is especially active in Eastern Uganda's coffee sector, as compared to other regions and also sectors. It maintains one of its eight regional offices in Mbale and in contrast to some of its other regional offices, the Mbale division is functional and actually employs as many extension workers as stated on its website (field visits and interviews), who work with ACEs throughout the region.

The second case study, also a large organization with country-wide operations, is the National Union of Coffee Agro-businesses and Farm Enterprises (NUCAFE). This cooperative union is the largest active member-based organization in Eastern Uganda's coffee sector. It was founded in 1995, after the liberalization of the coffee sector, and has since registered members in nineteen districts from all major coffee growing areas of Uganda. NUCAFE's administrative structure is equivalent to that of any cooperative union in Uganda, with a national board which is granted authority by the Members' General Assembly, a national secretariat and regional offices with extension workers (also called business managers) who attend to primary cooperatives (NUCAFE 2015). NUCAFE's main objectives are identical to those of all coffee as well as other agrarian cooperatives in Uganda, namely that "coffee farmers profitably own their coffee along the value chain for their sustainable livelihoods" and that they are "empowered to enhance their households' incomes" on the basis of economic organization (UCDA, accessed March 2009). NUCAFE's system of operation is based on its *Farmer Ownership Model* (FOM), designed to help small producers in the coffee sector to adopt a business view of farming and to organize them to assume as many roles in the supply chain as possible (*ibid.*).

NUCAFE's activities include the provision of advisory and training programs, and the construction and maintenance of storage facilities. Furthermore, the organization has invested in the wider social and economic infrastructure in order to improve the conditions for production and marketing, including the construction of feeder roads, the purchase of transport vehicles and the establishment of rural health stations. However, the union has grown faster than its capacities to provide adequate services to new members. At the time of the fieldwork, NUCAFE representatives at the national level estimated that less than half of the organization's members were actually served. Thus, throughout the fieldwork area, with the exception of Kapchorwa district, insufficient numbers of extension workers posed significant challenges to the provision of services. Furthermore, the lack of staff at the secondary level, which is in direct contact with members, increases the potential gap between the highly-educated management staff in Kampala and the members at the farm level.

The third case study is Gumutindo Coffee Cooperative Enterprise (called Gumutindo hereafter), a cooperative which specializes in the fair-trade and organic niche markets. It was founded in 1998 as a joint project of BCU and Twin Trading, a UK-based dealer in fair-trade products. In 2003, after BCU's business had collapsed a year earlier, Gumutindo's members, then part of BCU, founded Gumutindo, which means "excellent quality" in the local Lugisu language, as an exporter of Arabica coffee, which is registered independently of BCU and Twin Trading. During the first data collection phase for this book in 2009, Gumutindo was an economically viable enterprise which operated independently of both organizations, but Twin Trading continued to be one of its major clients. The cooperative has grown rapidly since its creation, from a total of 3,034 members in 2007 to more than 7,000 members in 2010, a number that has remained stable since. In 2016, all registered primary cooperatives seemed to be active, that is, they sell at least some of their coffee through the cooperative. The cooperative was certified as a fair-trade producer in 2004. At the time of writing in 2011, all of its coffee was sold as fair-trade and 90 percent was certified as organic. Similar to NUCAFE, Gumutindo also reinvests some of its profits in local infrastructure projects, including feeder roads, rural health stations, and school buildings, in addition to the provision of training and marketing services.

The fourth case study is a small, community-based organization called United Organic Coffee Growers (UOCG), which operates in Sironko district, with an estimated 100 members located in six neighboring villages. The villages are within walking distance of one another and all the members know each other personally, at least superficially. UOCG was founded in 2007 as a community-based organization and subsequently registered as a cooperative union in the same year (UOCG 2007). The founders of UOCG were coffee growers and members of the local elites, according to the size of land ownership and access to non-land resources. They perceive the organization as a form of social community as well as an economic enterprise.

The structure of UOCG is equivalent to that of the larger cooperative unions, with primary societies of about 25 members each. However, due to its small size, the members of the board at the top management level seem to have a particularly strong influence on decision-making processes within the primary cooperatives. For example, during the time of the fieldwork, decisions regarding production and marketing strategies were taken in meetings between the leaders of primary cooperatives and the board members, rather than being discussed with members first. In larger cooperative unions, secondary-level field- or service-workers are likely to hold relevant meetings with primary-level managers, who in turn meet with members, before a decision is taken at the top-level management. However, within UOCG, the only extension worker is also the organization's chairman, who is a founder and board member. During the time of the fieldwork in 2009, the composition of board members had not changed since its inauguration and there were no regulations in place for the turnover of power (UOCG 2007).

## 5.2 Access to cooperatives and the benefits of membership

On the basis of the survey and the qualitative research results, this section examines how the four above-described cooperatives in Eastern Uganda's coffee sector addressed existing class-based inequalities among small producers and contributed to improving members' living standards. The evidence presented illuminates existing socio-economic barriers to participation in cooperatives, as well as the potentially conflicting effects of cooperatives within disaggregated rural communities. An analysis of the nature and functionality of internal structures established by each cooperative to represent its members' interests explores the different organizational responses to economic development challenges within a changing socio-economic and political environment.

Data from throughout the Global South have shown that even organizations designed to promote social and economic equality frequently provide footholds for the reproduction of inequalities. In Peru, Brass (2007) examined how better-off farmers, rather than an overpowering state bureaucracy, misused cooperatives as a vehicle of accumulation during the 1970s. Referring to Honduras, Castillo and Carter (2004) argued that the social norms of reciprocal and altruistic transfers that were reinforced by endogenous social interactions among poor households after a hurricane produced social safety nets that favored a subset of relatively privileged households. Similar studies have warned against naive expectations of general welfare improvements on the basis of social networks or organizations, such as those of wage workers or small producers, which promote concepts of reciprocity and mutual assistance (for example, Udry & Conley 2004 on Ghana; Lee 2010; Pattenden 2010; Banerjee 2009).

The data from Eastern Uganda confirm this point, but indicate important differences between organizations. First, the effects of cooperatives on inequalities vary depending on internal organizational characteristics, such as formal rules and informal institutional mechanisms, which regulate access to membership and to resources within the organization. Second, the impact of cooperatives depends on the nature of interrelations between internal organizational characteristics and existing structures of socio-economic organization at the household, farm, and community level. Dominant social norms and practices which structure the wider social and economic environment might thereby support or impede the achievement of organizational objectives.

Thus, the ability of a cooperative to reduce existing inequalities and improve the living standards of all its members depends not only on its formal and informal rules and mechanisms, but also on how these interact with historically specific forms of socio-economic organization. A cooperative's organizational frame of reference necessarily accommodates some of the dominant norms and practices that regulate economic relations in an historically specific context. Thereby, it generally contributes to processes of social reproduction, but it may also provide the conditions for progressive social change. The social agency of members and leaders at the local level is crucial for determining whether this process takes a progressive or a reactionary direction. At the same time, the present data indicate that favorable conditions for the generation of social change seem to entail an organizational frame of reference that is large and flexible enough to allow for the introduction of new ideas and concepts, while also providing an approachable structure for action at the local level.

The aggregate effects of a cooperative on the economic prospects of members are closely related to its ability to promote greater equality in economic relations, including access to material and social resources.[17] In the context of poor and disaggregated rural communities, the development of organizational structures that reduce socio-economic inequalities is likely to make a significant contribution to poverty reduction. In Eastern Uganda's coffee sector, the simultaneous effects on existing inequalities among small producers and on members' living standards achieved, to a greater or lesser extent, by

Gumutindo, UCA, and NUCAFE indicate that medium-sized and large cooperatives may achieve both a contribution to poverty reduction and more equal socio-economic outcomes. In contrast, the reproduction of gender- and class-based inequalities within the small, community-based organization UOCG is closely related to the organization's failure to significantly improve the living standards of its members.

### *A socio-economic profile of cooperative members*

Who are the members of cooperatives in Eastern Uganda's coffee sector? The coffee sector survey showed that cooperative members tend to have higher levels of formal education and slightly larger land holdings than small producers who are not organized in cooperatives ('non-organized' henceforth), indicating that the poorest small producers may be excluded from membership (for detailed figures on land ownership and indicators of living standards). Thus, 77 percent of cooperative members were educated up to primary level or below, with 38 percent holding a primary school certificate and 8 percent having no formal schooling at all. Among non-organized producers, the education of 84 percent did not extend beyond the primary level, including 29 percent who held a primary school certificate and 16 percent without any formal schooling (See Table 5.1). The size of land available for cultivation equally differed.[18] Among cooperative members, 50 percent cultivated between one and five acres and 15 percent cultivated between five and ten acres. These figures compare with 42 percent of non-organized producers with one to five acres and only 5 percent with five to ten acres, while a large group (29 percent) cultivated only up to one acre. However, these land size figures are estimations and should be used with caution.[19]

*Table 5.1* Formal educational attainment of small producers (%)

| *Organizational status and type* | *Non-organized producers* | *Cooperative members* | *NUCAFE, UCA* | *Gum-utindo* | *UOCG* |
|---|---|---|---|---|---|
| No schooling | 15.8 | 7.9 | 4.6 | 10.7 | 20.0 |
| Below elementary (P7) | 39.5 | 30.7 | 29.2 | 28.6 | 20.0 |
| Elementary (P7) | 28.9 | 38.1 | 39.2 | 42.9 | 45.0 |
| Lower secondary (S4) | 7.9 | 11.2 | 13.8 | 3.6 | 10.0 |
| Upper Secondary (S6) | 2.6 | 2.3 | .8 | 10.7 | 5.0 |
| Technical certificate/ teacher diploma | 5.3 | 5.1 | 6.2 | 3.6 | 0.00 |
| Currently in elementary | | .9 | 1.5 | | |
| Currently in secondary | | 1.9 | 3.1 | | |
| Currently in university | | 1.9 | 1.5 | | |

The identification of a possible bias of cooperatives towards better-off households should not obscure the fact that poverty is widespread among rural households in general, including both cooperative members and non-organized producers. Thus, the survey data on formal education, like Uganda's national statistics, indicated enrollment and graduation figures, but failed to capture the *quality* of schooling. The GoU introduced free primary and secondary education in 1997 and 2007 respectively, but widespread implementation challenges have led to serious inadequacies in the quality of schooling, in particular in rural areas (Chapman 2010). These shortcomings are likely to affect organized *and* non-organized small producers, as few households in the fieldwork area can afford private formal education. The poor quality of state schools in rural areas indicates that formal education among cooperative members, albeit higher than that of non-organized producers, is unlikely to be comparable to equivalent education levels in urban areas.

Furthermore, the likelihood of depending on wage-work as well as non-agricultural self-employment in addition to farming is high among small producers in general. A large proportion of cooperative members (54.4 percent) and non-organized producers (44.7 percent) had additional jobs outside farming (*see* Table 5.2), and a quarter of both groups (25 percent and 26 percent respectively) carried out wage jobs. The vast majority of these jobs were casual and low-skilled, most often seasonal, off-farm agricultural work, but some individuals also carried out casual work outside agriculture.[20] More organized than non-organized producers were likely to own a business outside farming (30 percent compared to 18 percent), but the vast majority of these businesses were micro-enterprises with limited growth potential.[21]

Other variables applied in the coffee sector survey indicated slightly higher living standards of organized producers, although the differences were small, and the most significant differences were *between* different types of cooperatives and *within* individual organizations. Thus, the average household size was somewhat higher for organized (8) than for non-organized producers (7), and cooperative members tended to have more dependents per household. Among cooperative members, 66 percent ate meat once or more than once each week, compared with 61 percent among non-organized small producers. However, a comparison between the living standards of organized and non-organized producers invariably brushes over substantial differences that exist *within* both groups. The present data

*Table 5.2* Dependence on additional jobs among small producers (%)

| *Organizational status and type* | *Non-organized producers* | *Cooperative members* | *NUCAFE, UCA* | *Gumutindo* | *UOCG* |
|---|---|---|---|---|---|
| Yes, has additional job | 44.7 | 54.4 | 45.4 | 71.4 | 50.0 |
| No, does not have add. job | 55.3 | 45.6 | 54.6 | 28.6 | 50.0 |

certainly indicate differences between members of different types of cooperatives. Furthermore, differences in living standards were substantial among members of individual cooperatives, most notably within the small, community-based UOCG.

The survey indicated higher levels of poverty among members of the small, community-based cooperative UOCG, as compared with members of the three other organizations. Thus, the dependence on casual wage-work in addition to farming was relatively high among UOCG members (35 percent), but significantly lower for producers organized with NUCAFE or UCA (22 percent). The figure for Gumutindo was highest, with 39 percent involved in wage-work, but the sample included a larger proportion of non-agricultural wage workers compared with the other samples. Thus, the higher dependence on wage-work may in this case indicate better-off, rather than particularly poor, households, because agricultural wages tend to be particularly low (UBOS 2010).

Regarding the likelihood of eating meat frequently, UOCG members seemed to be the most deprived, while members of Gumutindo, and to an even greater extent NUCAFE and UCA, were likely to be able to afford meat regularly. Regarding the likelihood of owning a non-agricultural business, the data equally point to higher living standards among NUCAFE and UCA, followed by Gumutindo and then UOCG members. Thus, NUCAFE and UCA members were most likely to run such a business (24 percent), followed by Gumutindo (21 percent), while UOCG members (15 percent) were the least likely to do so. To reiterate, these businesses tend to be micro-enterprises with limited growth potential; however, according to the coffee sector survey, they tend to produce more reliable incomes than wage-work and were therefore singled out as a preferred economic activity by respondents.

The qualitative data further indicate that class-based divisions among members of individual cooperatives seem to be more severe within UOCG than within other organizations. Inequalities in material wealth and access to services certainly exist between cooperative members across all four organizations, but some of the most extreme disparities were visible within UOCG. The quality of housing in the fieldwork area was generally low, as most people lived in non-fortified houses with mud floors and thatched roofs, but a closer look reveals that some have better sanitation facilities, more space per inhabitant and are located closer to the nearest road. Furthermore, most of the larger villages include a few brick-built houses with concrete floors and metal roofs. Among UOCG members, the quality of housing among the vast majority of members was at the low end of living standards within Eastern Uganda: mud huts with poor sanitation facilities, situated a long walk away from the nearest (unpaved) road. The housing quality of primary- and top-level cooperative leaders, on the other hand, was high measured against regional standards, and the apparent gap between members and producers with leadership functions was nowhere more apparent.

Furthermore, differences in social status seem to be particularly significant within UOCG. Cooperative meetings were held in front of the house of one of the cooperative leaders, which happened to be the wealthiest household in the area. Inside the house, board meetings were held by the cooperative leaders. In contrast, primary cooperatives registered with Gumutindo, UCA, and NUCAFE generally held their meetings in a public space, rather than one dominated by more powerful and better-off community members. Unsurprisingly, the UOCG meetings are characterized by the top-down transfer of information and by the campaigns of leaders in favor of or against particular production- and marketing-related decisions to be taken by the organization. Members, on the other hand, often remain quiet and there is little discussion compared to the group meetings of Gumutindo, UCA, and NUCAFE. Similarly, members of these three organizations were likely to actively participate in the focus group interviews, given that the discussion groups were single-gender, whereas no interactive group discussions were possible with UOCG members.[22]

The respective samples of UOCG and Gumutindo members covered by the coffee sector survey were small, and quantitative results on internal divisions *within* these samples are therefore not emphasized here.[23] However, the quantitative figures support the qualitative findings, indicating that the interpretations presented above and made from informal observations, semi-structured interviews, and focus groups discussions are also reflected in quantifiable indicators. Thus, the largest internal differences in schooling levels are found in the sample of UOCG members, which included the highest proportion of respondents without any schooling and the highest proportion of respondents with primary school certificates. According to the survey, 20 percent of UCOG members were without any formal schooling, followed by Gumutindo (10 percent) and members of the large organizations NUCAFE and UCA (5 percent), while 39 percent of NUCAFE and UCA members, 43 percent of Gumutindo, and 45 percent of UOCG members were educated up to primary school level (*see* Table 5.1). Land holdings equally confirm the existence of pronounced inequalities within UOCG, with 10 percent of members cultivating less than 0.5 acres and 15 percent cultivating more than 10 acres. Within Gumutindo, the proportion of members with particularly small or large land holdings was 7 percent and 4 percent respectively. For UCA and NUCAFE, these figures were 5 percent for particularly small and 6 percent for particularly large land holdings.

Overall, the data show that the majority of small producers in Eastern Uganda's coffee sector are poor, with small land holdings, low levels of formal education and housing conditions that fail to provide basic health and safety standards. Furthermore, roughly half depended on generating income in addition to farming and a quarter carry out mainly low-paid, casual wage-work, indicating that many small producers cannot live off farming alone. Nevertheless, the heterogeneity among those considered poor is significant, and there were noteworthy socio-economic differences among small producers in Eastern

Uganda. While cooperative members tended to be slightly better off than non-organized producers, a comparison of living standards between the different types of cooperative indicated that a simple division between organized and non-organized producers does not hold. Rather, members of *some* cooperatives, most notably the medium-sized and larger organizations, tended to benefit from higher living standards compared with members of small, community-based organizations and non-organized producers. Increased poverty levels among members of community-based organizations coincided with increased internal inequalities, that is, among members of individual organizations, which were most significant within UOCG.

Thus, the mere existence of joint processing and marketing structures based on cooperative principles may say little about an organization's socio-economic effects at the local level. According to members and leaders of UOCG, the organization had increased the output and quality levels of its members within two years since its foundation in 2007, an assessment which was confirmed by the general manager of a domestic coffee roasting company which has bought UOCG's coffee from the start. However, the cooperative's effectiveness in increasing output and apparently also productivity levels (according to cooperative leaders), as well as improving quality, is insufficiently reflected in the living standards of members. Poverty and inequality among UOCG members remained high compared with those prevalent among members of other cooperatives. Unsurprisingly, the survey results indicate that members of UOCG were least likely to think that they have benefited from cooperative membership. Thus, only 40 percent of UOCG members associated their membership with improvements in living standards, compared with 86 percent of Gumutindo members and 72 percent of producers who were organized with UCA and NUCAFE (*see* Table 5.3). In the next section, a discussion of the differences in organizational responses to class-based divisions within disaggregated rural communities sheds more light on possible reasons for these diverse results.

### *The social and economic benefits of membership*

At first sight, members of cooperatives generally seem to enjoy direct economic benefits. In Eastern Uganda's coffee sector, there is a noticeable difference of around 10 percent between the prices which cooperatives pay and those

*Table 5.3* Improvements in living standards achieved through cooperative membership, by type of organization (%)

| *Type of cooperative* | *Cooperative members (all)* | *NUCAFE and UCA members* | *Gumutindo members* | *UOCG members* |
|---|---|---|---|---|
| Yes | 71.6 | 71.5 | 88.9 | 40.0 |
| No | 28.4 | 28.5 | 11.1 | 60.0 |

offered by local middlemen and foreign buyers.[24] A further advantage is the method of payment. Cooperatives make a single payment to producers, after selling the bulked coffee of a primary cooperative at once. By receiving a bigger lump sum, producers are able to make investments into increased production levels, which most households would otherwise not be able to make. Against this background, it is not surprising that the majority of organized producers directly associated improvements in living standards with their membership of cooperatives.

However, an in-depth analysis of social and economic relations within primary cooperatives reveals complex linkages of dependency and exploitation under the surface of the joint marketing structures that are often coated in a terminology of sharing and solidarity. Thus, within the three larger organizations, the proportion of members in the fieldwork area who actually sold most of their coffee through the cooperative was only around 40 to 50 percent.[25] The proportion of cooperative members' coffee production that is sold through the cooperative is likely to be much higher, because some of the better-off cooperative members buy coffee from poorer members when these are in need of immediate cash and have to defect from their bulk selling commitments because they lack access to credits or alternative sources of income to bridge the period until the cooperative pays. In many cases, the defecting members deliver their coffee to the primary cooperative store to disguise the sales arrangement made with the wealthier members. As a result, the amount of coffee sold by the cooperative may match its expected volume, although some members have failed to benefit from the higher prices achieved through bulk selling.

Michael Wepondi, a producer from Bududa district, described this process as such:

> Some powerful farmers in the groups buy the coffee of poorer group members, either because they twist them into accepting or the poorer member becomes too desperate to wait to take it [the coffee] to the group. It is them, the powerful farmers, who really enjoy the group and they are very active members. (Michael Wepondi, producer from Bududa district)

The problem described above indicates that the economic viability of a cooperative may not be matched neatly to its ability to contribute to poverty reduction. Rather, the effects of a cooperative on the living standards of its members should be analyzed from the perspective of inequality, scrutinizing the interlinkages between internal organizational structures and the reproduction of existing inequalities within the wider social and economic environment. The following discussion aims to do this, using the examples of the four cooperatives discussed above.

Each organization under scrutiny has developed different organizational structures to address existing inequalities and improve its members' living standards. In Eastern Uganda's coffee sector, asking a small producer why she has not joined a cooperative may produce the simple response that she is "too poor to organize". Joining a cooperative invariably involves costs. Members have to be able to withhold produce for bulk sales, which necessitates some level of savings. The ability to save often depends on participation in saving and credit groups that are based at least partially on financial contributions by members. The requirement to plan economic activities in accordance with those of the primary cooperatives represents a serious challenge for many asset-poor households. Robert Bumatofu, a small producer who is not organized, explained: "If we sell together, we get better prices. But when I have pressing needs, and the middleman is near me, how can I wait for the cooperative to pay me?"

However, another small producer might assert that joining a cooperative has helped her to overcome a vicious circle of short-term economic strategies that are focused on immediate needs, but are likely to create more distress in the future. Mary Mahame, a member of a primary cooperative that sells predominantly to Gumutindo, explained:

> We unite against poverty. As a group, we have more *budwera* [social cohesion]. When I have pressing needs, I borrow money from the circle [saving and credit group]... If I fear that my husband will spend the money, I leave it with the circle until I pay the bills. If he takes out money, everyone knows, so there is more motivation to do things properly.

Overall, Gumutindo members, but also producers who are registered with UCA and NUCAFE, emphasized that joining a cooperative helped them to respond to economic needs more strategically, thereby increasing returns in the longer term.

The differences between producers' accounts raise the question of how, if at all, cooperatives address inequalities within rural communities and to what extent disadvantaged groups are able to benefit as a result. The qualitative data indicate significant differences in the support structures offered to disadvantaged groups by individual organizations. The most apparent way is the provision of micro-finance services for members, to cover registration fees as well as possible further contributions and to support members in times of heightened cash needs.[26] In Cheema village, Kapchorwa district, some of the producers with the smallest landholdings recorded during the fieldwork (below 0.5 acres) explained that becoming a member of the Kayanet group, a primary cooperative registered with NUCAFE, had helped them to increase their income from coffee. They were able to join because Kayanet's saving group provides small credits to cover registration fees while deferring additional contributions demanded from members for joint investments until after the first payments for bulk sales are made. However, the ability of this saving group to provide loans to bridge the time during which coffee is stored for bulk sales is limited. Thus, the cooperative extension agents in Kapchorwa district not only promote the establishment of saving groups but also try to facilitate access for NUCAFE primary groups to one of the savings and credit cooperatives, also called village banks, established by UCA and/or the government.

Similarly, Gumutindo's primary cooperatives or groups[27] facilitate members' access to micro-finance services. As Yowana Nandudu, a member of the Busamaga primary cooperative of Gumutindo, explained:

> When I couldn't pay my registration fee, the circle [saving group] provided a credit, even though I had not yet joined the cooperative, which means I had not yet contributed. In fact, the circle is part of our activities and everyone [of the primary cooperative] is a member.

UCA ideally provides access to credits to all its members, on the basis of its Savings and Credit Cooperatives (SACCO), although considerable challenges exist. After Uganda's Cooperative Bank was dismantled in 1999 as a consequence of neoliberal reforms, the UCA reintroduced financing to cooperatives through village bank programs, started to strengthen SACCOs through its Microfinance Department (Leonard 2012). Thus, the UCA sub-regional offices directly support the formation of SACCOs at the community level and provide trainings to members (*ibid.*). UCA audits SACCOs to ensure they are adhering to micro-finance and cooperative bylaws and principles and it connects SACCOs to producer and marketing cooperatives in their area. Lastly, it provides advocacy services for SACCOs and domestic and international levels to improve the political environment that SACCOs and other cooperatives operate in (*ibid.*)

The Ministry of Finance and Economic Planning (MoFPED) subsidizes the SACCO program (and has increased its support in recent years), but this has, for years, been criticized as disruptive government interference by the UCA, because the GoU's SACCO-related activities largely fail to respect the cooperative principle of autonomy (*see*, for example, Nannyonjo 2013). Despite public support, implementation-related shortcomings of the SACCO system remain pronounced. Many village banks have limited operational capacities due to a lack of capital as well as adequately trained and supervised staff. Some UCA members reported that their SACCO lacked funds or was temporarily closed due to cases of mismanagement and a lack of new staff. Village banks exist throughout the fieldwork area, although many sub-counties and thus numerous villages remain without access to ongoing services. At the time of the fieldwork, all of the functioning institutions were located in larger and relatively wealthy villages in the vicinity of a town or trading center and generally close to a paved road. However, despite these implementation-related shortcomings, UCA has succeeded in building a country-wide network for the provision of rural micro-finance services.

At the time of the fieldwork, UOCG offered no institutionalized support to improve access to rural financial services among its members. The survey results confirm this, illustrating significant differences between organizations regarding members' access to credits. As indicated above by producers' accounts, Gumutindo, UCA, and NUCAFE members are more likely to have access to credits than UOCG members. Thus, only 5 percent of the latter had access to credit during the previous year, compared with 18 percent of UCA and NUCAFE members and 21 percent of Gumutindo members (*see* Table 5.4).

A further dimension of a cooperative's ability to contribute to poverty reduction is the way in which it relates to existing structures of socio-economic organization in disaggregated rural communities. Thus, the effects of a cooperative on gender- and wealth-based inequalities within local communities is also shaped by its level of reliance on existing structures of socio-economic organization at the local level. To some extent, formal organizational structures always reflect existing socio-economic and political structures, because they are neither conceptualized nor implemented in a state of *tabula rasa*. However, NUCAFE, UCA, and Gumutindo make explicit efforts to build up new structures of economic organization at the local level, which are guided by ideas and concepts of equality in the division of labor within the household, the farm, and the cooperative. Also, access to leadership positions in new primary cooperatives is regulated by quotas to ensure a greater participation of women in decision-making processes, and votes are encouraged to facilitate a rotation of power.

Although shortcomings in the implementation of such regulations are widespread, in particular with regard to votes and the fulfilment of women's quotas, it is noteworthy that cooperative extension workers openly and continuously addressed issues of equality – or the lack thereof – in the division of labor and access to resources at the local level. Furthermore, some of the extension workers and cooperative staff at regional offices emphasized the existence of pronounced inequalities within existing informal group structures, as well as BCU's primary cooperatives. Thus, informal support groups tend to be single-sex clusters of particularly poor *or* better-off individuals, while BCU's primary cooperatives – most of them dormant at the time of the fieldwork – are almost exclusively run by male producers with above-average landholdings. According to extension workers of UCA, NUCAFE, and Gumutindo, their organizations try to avoid a heavy reliance on existing group structures, and members throughout the fieldwork area emphasized the difference between their cooperatives and informal groups as well as BCU's primary societies.

*Table 5.4* Small producers' access to credit, by organizational status and type (%)

| *Organizational status and type* | *Non-organized producers* | *Cooperative members* | *NUCAFE and UCA members* | *Gumutindo members* | *UOCG members* |
|---|---|---|---|---|---|
| Access to credit | 5.3 | 18.1 | 17.7 | 21.4 | 5.0 |
| No access to credit | 94.7 | 81.9 | 82.3 | 78.6 | 95.0 |

Participant observation in the fieldwork area indicated that the organizational structures of UOCG most closely reflected existing divisions of gender and class; however, throughout the fieldwork area, local elites tended to be better represented within the primary cooperative management than particularly poor households. Existing inequalities based on divisions of wealth and gender are therefore likely to be reproduced to some extent in all organizations, but most significantly within this small, community-based cooperative. Given the lack of organizational structures and institutional mechanisms to promote more egalitarian socio-economic outcomes, this trend is likely to be intensified as the organization accumulates more resources.

This section has brought forward the following main points: cooperatives show a slight bias towards better-off producers, but the differences in initial access to resources, such as land holdings and levels of formal education, tend to be small. Instead, differences in living standards may be as great between members of different cooperatives as between organized and non-organized producers. Thus, members of medium-sized and larger cooperatives tend to be significantly better-off than the majority of producers in small, community-based organizations, whose living standards are more comparable to those of non-organized producers. Furthermore, class-based divisions within community-based organizations seem to mirror existing inequalities closely, while in larger cooperatives, however, concerted efforts to reduce existing inequalities have created opportunities for change which are, to some extent, being realized. Thus, within UOCG, better-off members are likely to benefit disproportionately, while within Gumutindo, UCA, and NUCAFE, members are likely to share in the benefits more equally.

If these significant differences between organizations are considered, it can be said that cooperatives, *under certain conditions*, clearly benefit their members. Interviews with domestic coffee buyers indicated that the wet-processed (or washed) coffee sold by cooperatives is of higher quality than that sold by non-organized small producers, largely because of improved skills and better technical equipment, but the data presented above also indicate that the living standard of the poorest members, and therefore inequalities among members, are not necessarily reduced.[28] At the same time, positive effects for all members include better access to credits and a higher ability to save income generated from coffee. Therefore, there is a large probability that organized small producers associate improvements in living standards directly with membership of a cooperative.

The qualitative data confirm these results, but also illuminate the extent to which these positive effects depend on the nature of internal organizational structures and the ways in which they relate to major aspects of socio-economic organization at the local level. The following discussion of the representation of members' interests in different cooperatives sheds some more light on the conditions under which these organizations are likely to benefit disadvantaged as well as more privileged groups of members.

### *Access to training for organized and non-organized small producers*

Throughout Africa, the provision of training services in rural areas is highly insufficient, both in quantity and quality. A number of factors reduce the economic viability of private for-profit provision, such as the poor quality of the transport, energy, and communication infrastructure; low population density; and the limited purchasing power of those in need of training (Adams 2010). Furthermore, regulatory frameworks to ensure the quality of non-formal training tend to be inadequate or missing and there is limited robust evidence on the outcomes of existing programs (Betcherman et al. 2007). In Uganda, non-formal training so far remains entirely unregulated and the available evidence suggests that both private and public providers largely fail to offer consistent quality standards.[29] The urban bias of Uganda's formal technical and vocational education and training (TVET) system further means that there are few vocational training institutes in rural areas to which non-formal training programs could be linked to create synergy effects: for example, by sharing training materials and facilities and making joint use of trained staff.

Some studies have argued that public farmer field schools (FFS) in Kenya and Tanzania significantly contribute to increased incomes and agricultural productivity of small producers (Davis, et. al 2010). The available data indicate more limited effects in Uganda, mainly in the form of improved crop productivity of female growers (*ibid.*). One factor that limits the effectiveness of FFSs in Uganda may be the provision of competing public services, most notably by NAADS (*ibid.*). Another important factor, indicated by the data from Uganda that is presented below, is the limited coverage of public providers such as NAADS and FFSs. Thus, Eastern Uganda had no functional FFSs in the fieldwork area. Furthermore, growers frequently insist that better-off farmers benefit disproportionately from training provided by NAADS.[30] Similarly, Davis *et al.* (2010) note for East Africa at large that farmers with medium-size land holdings benefit most from FFSs, and that those closer to urban areas are more likely to attend training. Thus, although the survey results from Eastern Uganda indicate that public providers are an important provider of non-formal training, their contribution to improved skills levels among disadvantaged rural groups is likely to be limited.

A variety of local and foreign NGOs also provide non-formal training in Eastern Uganda, but the available data on their coverage and socio-economic impact are too incomplete to enable general conclusions to be drawn.[31] However, some remarks on existing constraints to their services are offered below. First, the quantity of NGO services seems to be far less than the amount of press coverage in Western media and the documentation of programs by donors might indicate. In the fieldwork area, most training is provided by cooperatives and public training providers. After these, the survey results for small producers and wage workers point to companies and to family or clan members rather than to NGOs as likely sources of training (*see* Table 5.6).[32]

*Table 5.5* Access to training of organized/ non-organized producers by gender (%)

| *Organizational status and gender* | *Non-organized producers* | *Female non-organized producers* | *Cooperative members* | *Female cooperative members* |
|---|---|---|---|---|
| Yes, access to training | 50.0 | 45.5 | 83.7 | 81.1 |
| No access to training | 50.0 | 54.5 | 16.3 | 18.9 |

Second, the quality of NGOs' services varies significantly, given the wide range of organizations involved in rural training. As the coordinator of a country-wide skills development program which focuses on rural areas explained, in addition to the lack of state regulation, weak linkages between not-for-profit providers are a major barrier to ensuring consistent quality levels. Thus, the only NGO network for rural training within the fieldwork area focuses on adult literacy, and there is no coordination of services with NGOs providing agricultural and/or business training.

Against this background, cooperatives emerge as important rural training providers. The coffee sector survey from Eastern Uganda shows that access to non-formal training improves significantly with membership of cooperatives: 84 percent of cooperative members had received training, mostly for agricultural skills, compared with 50 percent of non-organized growers (*see* Table 5.5). Access figures are similar for women: 81 percent of female cooperative members had received training, compared with 46 percent of non-organized female growers (*ibid.*).

In addition to the training provided by cooperatives, cooperative members are also more likely to receive training from public sector providers and NGOs, while non-organized growers are more likely to be trained by family and clan members (*see* Table 5.6). The improved access of cooperative members to training from public and private not-for-profit providers points to their greater 'visibility', compared with not formally organized individuals. Overall, the

*Table 5.6* Producers' access to training, by type of training provider (%)

| *Training provider accessed* | *Non-organized producers* | *Cooperative members* |
|---|---|---|
| **NGO** | none | 4.7 |
| **Cooperative or union** | 2.6 | 27.4 |
| **Private training institute** | none | 2.3 |
| **Public provider** | 18.4 | 27.0 |
| **Company** | 13.2 | 14.4 |
| **Religious institution (church/mosque)** | none | 1.4 |
| **Family or clan** | 18.4 | 6.5 |
| **Not applicable** | 47.4 | 16.3 |

*Table 5.7* Type of training accessed by producers (%)

| *Type of training accessed* | *Cooperative members* | *Non-organized producers* |
|---|---|---|
| **Literacy and numeracy training** | 5.6 | 0.0 |
| **Agricultural training** | 74.0 | 39.5 |
| **Non-agri. technical training** | 1.9 | 2.6 |
| **Business training** | .9 | 0.0 |
| **Other** | 1.9 | 7.9 |
| **Not applicable** | 15.8 | 50.0 |

survey indicates that cooperative membership increases access to training by various providers, although it should be recalled that cooperative members tend to have slightly higher schooling levels, which is likely to improve their willingness to invest in training.

The positive effects of cooperative membership on access to training are noteworthy, but further research is necessary to assess the benefits of cooperatives' trainings beyond agricultural production. The data from Eastern Uganda's coffee sector show that most training provided to farmers-cum-wageworkers concentrates on agriculture (*see* Table 5.7). The focus on agricultural skills applies to all rural training providers, including cooperatives, public institutions, and NGOs. Thus, small producers and wageworkers throughout the fieldwork area largely reported of attending agricultural trainings although interest in improving skills for other, non-agricultural employment was frequently mentioned during informal conversations and interviews.

Despite the limited coverage of occupational fields covered by cooperatives' trainings, the qualitative data indicate a high relevance of their agricultural trainings to small producers' needs, especially compared with the agricultural trainings of other providers. As economic actors within the agricultural sector, cooperative staff is constantly exposed to the changing conditions of production and marketing, and thus knowledgeable about growers' training needs. Indeed, growers throughout the fieldwork area confirmed that the agricultural training provided by cooperatives is far more relevant to their needs than that provided by NGOs. As Joseph Wobweni, who sells his coffee to Gumutindo's Busamaga growers' society, explained, "I attended seminars of various NGOs to acquire new farming skills, but for many, I don't use them. Some seminars were exactly the same as the previous one by another organization."

Similar complaints concerning the insufficient relevance of agricultural training were voiced about the services provided by NAADS. Sophie Musani, a member of Kwoti primary cooperative, which sells predominantly to UCA, described her experience with NAADS as follows:

> They taught us how to use new fertilizers and sprayers, but how can we use them if no-one has sprayers? When we learnt about the storage and receipt system, it was the same. Few people in our group are good with counting or even reading. How can we use that system when it is not clear if those storing our coffee are cheating us?

These two short examples reflect what growers throughout the fieldwork area repeatedly emphasized: the agricultural training provided by NGOs and also by NAADS frequently fails to respond to current training needs. While the large variety of NGOs within Eastern Uganda makes an assessment of the relevance of their services exceedingly difficult, interviews with officers of NAADS in Sironko and Mbale districts indicated that NAADS's training programs are developed without the guidance of local training needs assessments. Furthermore, NAADS representatives confirmed that the organization generally uses existing organizational structures within rural communities to identify demonstration farms as a focus of training activities (*ibid.*). While this approach contributes to a reproduction of existing inequalities, as members of the local elites are likely to be selected as focal points for the provision of training, it also supports the adaptation of training contents to the skill needs of better-off rather than disadvantaged groups. As a result, the socio-economic benefits of such training may be skewed towards the wealthier strata of small producers.

Overall, the data presented paint a relatively positive picture of cooperatives as agricultural training providers. In particular the quality and relevance of their trainings stand out in comparison with NGOs as well as public providers. However, the survey results indicate that the range of skills transferred by all rural providers in the fieldwork area remains narrow. As indicated above, the vast majority of small producers – cooperative members and non-organized growers – mainly received agricultural skills training (*see* Table 5.7). While a small proportion of cooperative members (6 percent) had access to numeracy and literacy training, very few received non-agricultural technical training, and the provision of business training was negligible (*ibid.*). This illustrates that the emphasis of the Government of Uganda's rural development agenda on commercial farming development is insufficiently realized at the local level, because growers' agricultural *production* skills are upgraded, but transferable and entrepreneurial skills receive little attention. Although cooperative members experience slightly improved access to some types of non-agricultural training compared to non-organized small producers, this is largely attributed to the positive spillover effects of being organized, rather than to the trainings provided by cooperatives themselves.

*Within* the field of agricultural training, however, cooperatives stand out as providers of broader transferable skills, which can contribute to improving the economic prospects of farmers-cum-wageworkers beyond agriculture. Thus, the qualitative data, which provide a more nuanced picture of actual training contents, indicate that NUCAFE, UCA, and Gumutindo implement extensive training activities focused on generating progressive change within the broader socio-economic organization of agricultural production and marketing. What is perceived simply as "agricultural training" by growers and categorized as such within the questionnaire-based survey, actually covers transferable skills to improve the economic effectiveness and equality achieved within production- and marketing-related decision-making processes at the household and primary cooperative level.

An example is the educational project implemented by NUCAFE, which focuses on "enhancing equity in decision making in coffee farming households in Uganda" and aims to transfer communication, organizational, and business skill from a gender perspective[33] (NUCAFE 2009c). Similarly, UCA and Gumutindo address gender equity as a crucial factor for achieving improved socio-economic outcomes, including economic viability, at the household and farm level (UCA 2009b). Furthermore, all three organizations include basic economic and political knowledge in their training by teaching about domestic and international value chain development within the coffee sector. The training thereby supports the development of improved entrepreneurial strategies by moving beyond numeracy and accounting skills to enhancing participants' knowledge about their own position, opportunities, and constraints as producers of export crops.

The organizational set-up of cooperatives entails a high potential for these organizations to transfer relevant skills to small producers. Their network of organizational units at the local level is extensive, thereby offering the possibility for reaching disadvantaged groups in poor rural areas – even though the much lower membership numbers of women in all cooperatives indicate that organizational structures at the grassroots level do not necessarily promote equality in socio-economic outcomes, as will be shown in the next section of this chapter. However, compared with other private as well as public providers of non-formal training, cooperatives have a significant potential to reach disadvantaged groups and provide training that responds to the changing production- and marketing-related skills needs of growers. Although the major focus of cooperative training necessarily lies in agricultural skills, entrepreneurial and other transferable skills are increasingly forming part of the training activities in larger cooperatives.

Given the increasing dependence of rural households on wage-work in addition to farming, such an expanded approach to the skills needs of small producers holds the potential to enhance skill levels among rural laboring classes beyond the narrow confines of agricultural production. While the training provided by cooperatives can substitute neither for non-agricultural technical and vocational training nor for further general education, it may help to equip growers-cum-wageworkers with transferable skills for the labor market. The next section analyzes the effects of non-formal skills training on the socio-economic prospects and well-being of participants. While training benefits in terms of increased levels of agricultural productivity and quality play an important role, a particular focus is also put on the transformative impact of

*Table 5.8* Training effects for organized/non-organized coffee producers (%)

| *Effect of training* | *All producers* | *Non-organized producers* | *Cooperative members* |
|---|---|---|---|
| **Change of jobs** | 12.6 | 21.1 | 11.7 |
| **New business** | 33.2 | 26.3 | 34.3 |
| **Increased income** | 62.2 | 72.2 | 61.2 |

learning and the potential or real acquisition of transferable skills for labor market participation.

### *Effects of training provided by cooperatives*

The survey results indicate tangible economic benefits from training for both non-organized producers and cooperative members, although more research is needed to illuminate whether these benefits lead to sustainable improvements of people's lives (*see* Table 5.8).

Given that few jobs are available in the fieldwork area, it is not surprising that only 13 percent of growers changed jobs after they received training, but a third started a new business and 62 percent noted higher incomes as a direct result of training. The likelihood of increased incomes as a perceived result of training is high among cooperative members (61 percent) and non-organized producers (72 percent). This indicates that the education and skills levels among farmers-cum-wageworkers are generally low, so that any acquisition of additional skills – and the often-associated improvements in self-confidence – are likely to improve access to income sources. The higher prevalence of increased incomes among non-organized producers further indicates that the income effect of training tends to be more pronounced for poorer groups. The likelihood of starting a new business, on the contrary, is higher among cooperative members. The latter tend to be slightly better-off than non-organized producers and are thus more likely to afford the modest investments needed for self-employment.

For estimating the long-term effects of starting a new business, caution is paramount. Among cooperative members, 34 percent started a new business after receiving training, compared with 26 percent of non-organized producers. A major reason for this difference might be that cooperative members have better access to financial services and possibly also to informal support networks that can facilitate entrepreneurial activities. However, there is a lack of quantitative data on the survival rates of these businesses. Based on the generally high failure rates of micro-entrepreneurial activities throughout Uganda, their long-term effects on the economic prospects of disadvantaged groups remain uncertain at best (Ishengoma and Kappel 2008). Furthermore, the low level of differentiation in economic activities that was visible throughout the fieldwork area indicates that many businesses have limited growth potential. Thus, a large proportion of micro-businesses encountered during the fieldwork in Eastern Uganda consisted of small shops for daily necessities (such as soap, sugar, bread, and similar items) and of transport services. Although the demand for both types of services is significant in rural Uganda, relevant skills need to be complemented by financial investments to build up sustainable businesses.

As a result, the positive effects of training beyond agriculture as well as their sustainability over a longer period of time cannot be determined with certainty on the basis of the available data. However, the present study indicates that training has discernible effects on how farmers and wage workers in Eastern Uganda's coffee sector generate income, and the high interest in training among the rural population points to its role in improving social and economic prospects. The demand for training is expressed by a widespread willingness among participants to progress to additional training and to pay for it (*see* Table 5.9). Thus, 84 percent of cooperative members and 74 percent of non-organized producers are willing to pay for training services. As noted above, the qualitative data indicate that training provided by cooperatives is perceived as particularly useful, compared with some of the training provided by NGOs, while training provided by public sector organizations, most notably NAADS, often fails to reach growers with average or particularly small landholdings, or simply those outside the vicinity of towns and trading centers. Frequently described economic benefits of training are an improved quality of coffee, and higher yields as well as enhanced sharecropping techniques, which increases overall output levels through a better adjusted and smaller choice of crops. These effects directly increase earnings, but also enable higher incomes to be achieved from farming in the medium to long term, because small investments into agricultural inputs can be made (*ibid.*).

In addition to increased levels of output and quality, growers throughout the fieldwork area associated broader changes in their personal and socio-economic well-being with their participation in training programs. In most cases, these accounts referred either to cooperative training alone or to a combination of training from cooperatives and from other providers. Similar to the findings of Duveskog (2006) with regard to participants in Farmer Field Schools (FFS) in Kenya, respondents in Eastern Uganda generally described well-being in terms of the ability to generate a sufficient income to ensure a modest living standard, but also in terms of self-worth and a positive sense of purpose in life. These aspects are closely related, because an improved sense of purpose and self-worth

*Table 5.9* Proportion of producers willing to pay for training (%)

| *Willingness to pay* | *All producers* | *Non-organized producers* | *Cooperative members* |
|---|---|---|---|
| **Yes** | 82.8 | 73.7 | 84.0 |
| **No** | 17.2 | 24.3 | 16.0 |

is frequently emphasized as an essential condition of being motivated to work and of finding employment. In particular, those growers with below-average land holdings and incomes insisted that improving their self-confidence and acquiring a positive outlook on life was essential for them to develop a commitment to work. Thus, Sauda Arapkwonyi from Kayanet primary cooperative, registered with NUCAFE, explained:

> I have participated in several trainings for some time. They are provided by NUCAFE, and we also join up with other organizations [NGOs and NAADS]. We learn about different agricultural techniques, and also about how to share ideas, take decisions together and plan our work. These trainings are about how someone thinks. For me, they have helped me to get up in the morning and be active, because I can now expect to create some positive outcomes with my work.

Similar accounts were recorded throughout the fieldwork area. While particularly poor growers were more likely to emphasize positive effects on personal confidence and motivation in addition to economic benefits, there was a general tendency to take such a broad perspective on the perceived well-being outcomes of training. However, as with regard to the survival rate of micro-entrepreneurial activities, the longevity of these effects on personal well-being cannot be adequately assessed on the basis of the present data. Again, more research is needed to evaluate whether and in how far the changes described by respondents in Eastern Uganda contribute to long-lasting improvements in the economic prospects of disadvantaged social groups in rural areas.

Growers-cum-wageworkers certainly emphasized that an improved outlook on life and an associated strengthened commitment to work helped them to improve their outcomes from farming. Furthermore, training participants talked at length about how a greater emphasis on planning in combination with an improved sense of self-worth had improved their economic outcomes more generally. Thus, respondents explicitly connected participation in agricultural training to a heightened degree of success in non-agricultural self-employment activities on the basis of an improved personal capacity to be active and resourceful. Commonly used phrases were the ability to "be prepared" for new economic opportunities, the condition of "having plans", rather than being "aimless", and the ability to be "strong" or show resilience when faced with social and economic difficulties, such as disturbing demands on one's labor by more powerful household members or the occurrence of unexpected financial burdens.

These accounts indicate two things about the role of transferable skills in non-formal skills training for small producers: First, they form an essential part of the training provided largely by cooperatives – and to some extent by other non-formal providers – even if the training is apparently focused on agricultural skills. Second, the acquisition of transferable skills makes an important contribution to improving the welfare levels of participants. Against this background, the potential relevance of non-formal training in the agricultural sector for enhancing the skills of growers-cum-wageworkers for labor market participation emerges clearly, and cooperatives are a significant, if not the single most important, provider of such training. In Uganda, employers indicate a high demand for transferable skills, and emphasize that these are exceedingly hard to find.[34] Workers who lack transferable skills are not only less able to adapt to new working environments, it is also harder for employers to train them in new job-specific skills.

The discussion of cooperatives in the next section of this chapter will illustrate how cooperatives may provide footholds for the reproduction of existing inequalities within disaggregated rural communities. This is relevant for the provision of training, because both access to and the ability to utilize newly acquired skills, including the realization of new ideas concerning the division of labor, are largely determined by existing structures of socio-economic organization. The extent to which dominant social norms and practices underlying these structures of organization may contribute to the reproduction of existing inequalities by organizing the perceptual world into binary pairs based on kinship, gender, religion, or ethnicity has been aptly explained by Tilly (1998). The acquisition and utilization of skills is shaped by such processes of reproduction because it is embedded in the wider social and economic environment in which they take place. The effects of structural inequalities on gender disparities in educational outcomes have been analyzed by Kabeer (2003) using data from South Asia. Kabeer showed how women's educational outcomes are shaped by intra-household bargaining processes, pointing out the need to conceptualize the household in a way that takes into account the complex nature of bargaining power (*ibid.*). The latter includes individual economic resources, social norms that shape an individual's sense of self-worth, and external factors that determine an individual's opportunities to utilize skills and knowledge outside the household (*see also* McElroy 1990; Sen 1990).

While Kabeer's analysis relates largely to formal education, it also contributes to a better understanding of non-formal training outcomes, which are closely linked to the household and the wider work environment, including the farm, the cooperative, and the labor market. The rules, norms, and practices that structure the division of labor, the distribution of resources in the household, and the wider work environment, and the dominant conceptualizations of social relations form the institutional context in which the acquisition and utilization of skills take place. Thus, training programs need to continuously reflect upon, address, and challenge existing forms of socio-economic organization in order to generate progressive social changes and minimize the contribution made to the reproduction of inequalities. It is also in this sense that the failure of traditional educational approaches and methods to improve small producers' living standards should be understood (for a discussion of these approaches, *see*, for example, Anderson et al. 2006; Purcell & Anderson 1997).

On the one hand, approaches to training need to be learner-centered and problem-based, combining theoretical knowledge with learners' previous experience while taking advantage of local ways of knowing (Duveskog 2006). On the other hand, training programs need to challenge existing forms of knowledge to enable progressive social and economic development. This may create contradictions with powerful institutions. An example from Eastern Uganda is the divide between the authoritarian discourse of punishment and reward that dominates popular church sermons and the ideas of self-confidence and joint decision-making that are promoted by cooperative training programs.[35] The effects of such contradictions on training outcomes in the long-term have to be analyzed within their historically specific context, a task that goes beyond the scope of this study, but the importance of recognizing such contradictions as a limiting factor for the potential of training programs to generate socioeconomic change processes at the individual and local level are noted here.[36] The nature of interactions between contradicting ideas and values may be diverse and their effects far from self-evident. Thus, while cooperatives offer a sustainable means to improve access to transferable skills in rural areas, the integration and possible subordination of cooperatives within wider institutional structures should be considered.

## 5.3 Organizational structures of representation

Cooperatives have responded in different ways to the need for reliable and effective support of members' interests in the face of significant economic and political constraints. This section examines the establishment of effective representational structures and how these are being implemented at the local level. The reduction of public sector support to cooperatives, since the liberalization of the agricultural sector, has created intense economic pressures that represent serious challenges to cooperative growth. Most notably, the lack of social safety net – and the inability of especially smaller cooperatives to provide pre-payments – has increased the risks for small producers who want to participate in joint marketing strategies. However, the level of interest in cooperative membership remains high at the local level. Despite their criticism of cooperatives' weak performance in the past, small producers throughout the fieldwork area frequently emphasized that cooperative members have access to better prices as well as other tangible benefits, most notably agricultural and business training.[37]

The ability of a cooperative to deliver these benefits is linked to the level of transparency, or the lack of *buyaaye*, within the management, and to the establishment of mechanisms to support disadvantaged members in a competitive economic environment. Small producers weigh the risks associated with a commitment to bulk selling against the potential benefits, and households without sufficient additional income sources outside farming emphasize that sales to a TNC or a middleman are necessary fall back options, because they may be unable to wait for the deferred, albeit higher, earnings that are achieved by selling through a cooperative. In the past, BCU was able to make pre-payments through the Cooperative Bank, a bank that was owned jointly by Uganda's cooperative societies.[38] Since its closure in 1999, UCA has been building up its network of SACCOs with modest assistance from the government, but despite the noteworthy expansion of the program over the past decade, access to rural financial services remains limited (Goodwin-Groen et al. 2004).

Given the lack of pre-payments by the cooperative as well as insufficient availability of public sector supported financial services, members without additional sources of income have to bridge the time between harvest and the receipt of cooperative payments by taking loans from commercial banks. As a result, joining a cooperative represents a serious financial challenge for large numbers of small producers, which relates to producers' difficulties in accessing credits, but also to the risks associated with taking out a loan. As one member of a dormant BCU primary society, who now sells to Gumutindo, but also to middlemen, explained:

> Without cooperatives, it is harder for farmers to survive, because the middlemen and even Kyagalanyi [TNC] pay low prices. Yet, they pay immediately, while with the cooperative, you have to wait for the payment. What happens if the cooperative fails to pay you? (Milton Wettaka, BCU and Gumutindo member and local trader)

The introduction of a warehouse receipt system (WRS) in 2004 aimed to reduce producers' financial challenges by providing access to loans on the basis of certificates that are issued to both cooperatives and individuals. The system faced serious implementation challenges in its first years, which were related mainly to the poor quality of the physical system itself, long waiting times for loans and a lack of trust by small producers who had negative experiences with both traders and cooperatives in the past (Peoples 2006). A more recent assessment after the introduction of the e-WRS in 2015 (Katunze et al. 2016) as well as interviews with farmers in 2016 indicate that the system still fails to provide widespread access to credits. Key shortcomings include farmers' lack of knowledge of how the system operates, a frequent inability to meet volume demands, and a reluctance by banks to provide financing. Furthermore, levels of trust still seem to be low among farmers.

Overall, the major challenge to joining a cooperative, which was repeatedly pointed out by producers, is the need to engage in at least medium-term economic planning, even though many households consider themselves as too poor to forego opportunities for short-term gains from their labor. In the context of high economic risks in a liberalized, largely unregulated agricultural sector with a weak institutional framework that fails to ensure minimum living standards for disadvantaged groups, many producers fear the risks, however small, that are associated with any investment. The payment irregularities of

BCU in the past aggravate this, and many producers will quickly withdraw from a cooperative when under the impression of being "cheated." As one producer put it:

> During BCU times, sometimes the payments were late or never even reached us. But at the time, there was nothing you could do. You had to commit to bulk selling, even if the benefits failed to appear. Today, if payments are late or don't come at all, you sell to the middleman next time. (George Bifama, small producer)

Similarly, Peter Weduku, a producer from Bududa district, explained, "In BCU times, bad leaders could not be penalized, but today, if there are problems, you can just leave". Thus, while the belief in the potential benefits of cooperatives remains widespread, the willingness to tolerate organizational inefficiencies or the mismanagement of resources is low.

The behavior of producers in response to dissatisfaction with organizational performance reflects Hirschman's (1970) analysis of micro-level responses to deterioration in the rationality, efficiency and functioning of firms or member-based organizations. Hirschman suggested exit, voice, and loyalty as the three major categories of response that affect organizational development in significant ways. Thus, workers or members of organizations are likely to leave if they believe that the situation they face within an organization is unlikely to improve. They may also choose the 'voice option', defined as "any attempt at all to change rather than to escape from an objectionable state of affairs" (*ibid.*, p. 30). Workers or members who choose neither exit nor voice may remain loyal and "suffer in silence, confident that things will soon get better" (*ibid.*, p. 38). This option generally includes the rational expectation that "someone will act or something will happen to improve matters" (*ibid.*, p. 78–79). Therefore, loyalists may choose exit or voice at a later point in time if their situation fails to improve.

Among cooperative members in Eastern Uganda's coffee sector, exit is frequently practiced today. Furthermore, it is widely, albeit informally, discussed among members as an option if payment delays or other problems arise within a cooperative. Extension workers and managers of cooperatives take these expressions of dissatisfaction seriously because they indicate possible losses in expected output, thereby endangering the expansion and economic viability of the cooperative over time. Thus, Joan Kabayambi, project manager at Gumutindo, emphasized that the cooperative aims to continually inform members of organizational performance issues and to establish functioning communication channels within the organization to ensure that the management is able to detect and understand reasons for dissatisfaction in time.

As suggested by Hirschman (1970), both the exit and voice options may contribute to progressive organizational development by forcing, more or less strongly, the employer or the organizational management to re-think its behavior and explore ways to improve members' benefits within the organization. As opposed to exit, voice or interest articulation is likely to be a coordinated rather than merely an individual response to dissatisfaction. However, within Eastern Uganda's coffee sector, both options are likely to be an effective means to encourage progressive organizational change, because cooperatives face strong competition for buying steady volumes of good-quality coffee.

Overall, the data indicate that the competition between different buyers and exporters, including cooperatives, has put disadvantaged groups among producers in a stronger position to demand improved access to the benefits created by cooperatives. As is discussed in more detail below, larger organizations, which have less control over their members than the leadership of small, community-based organizations, have responded to these changing economic conditions by developing organizational structures that promote more equitable socio-economic outcomes. If the cooperative is able to ensure an improved representation of members' interests and to create benefits for more than a small part of its members, it is likely to significantly increase its productivity by reducing defection rates and attracting new members.

While the development of improved organizational structures is based on tangible economic reasons, it also reflects small producers' expectations regarding the ideas and objectives underlying formal economic organization. Thus, producers emphasize the advantages of 'shared ideas' as a basis for sound economic planning, and they stress that 'taking decisions together' has significantly improved their living standards, but also their quality of life more generally.[39] This contrasts sharply with the current structure of the domestic coffee market, which is seen to 'divide' communities along multiple lines, most notably into organized and non-organized producers, but also into those cooperative members who can afford to adhere to bulk-selling commitments and those who defect because of the need for immediate cash. Throughout the fieldwork area, small producers described the current era as a 'time of division'.[40] In this context, joint economic planning is perceived as being increasingly important, and producers stress that cooperatives are the single most important means to protect against high risks in today's economic environment.

Women in particular pointed out that cooperatives offer improved social as well as economic security. Thus, female producers frequently stressed that membership of a cooperative helps to reduce domestic violence and alcohol abuse and increases personal stability. Theoretically, any of the informal, so-called "self-help" groups, which are widespread in the fieldwork area, could serve as a means to protect (to some extent) against domestic violence and to strengthen members' self-confidence. However, informal groups frequently resemble weekly drinking parties and fail to offer any significant support.[41] Many producers, including women who have joined cooperatives and those who have not, wave aside inquiries about the presumed benefits of these groups and point to the lack of common economic objectives as a serious handicap. According to Loyce Nabukwasi, a non-organized small producer from Bunekesa village in Manafwa district:

> These [informal] groups are simply for drinking. Economically, they cannot help anyone but those who sell *busera* [42] [a locally brewed spirit]. If you do not have a common goal, like selling coffee or cassava, you have no sense of direction. For personal needs, they [self-help groups] also provide little, because the other members lack motivation to work hard. For me, I have not acquired a sense of purpose in these groups.

Overall, the perception is widespread that formal economic organization is potentially beneficial, while informal self-help groups are likely to provide little more than a shared pastime or may even promote "aimless" activities.

Contrary to what has been indicated in some of the literature on cooperatives, neither small producers nor other economic actors, such as local buyers or extension officers, regard the ideas and objectives underlying cooperatives as particularly akin to local cultural structures.[43] Instead, the need for establishing effective organizational structures, possibly in opposition to existing social and political hierarchies, is stressed. The Uganda data clearly disprove the notion that cooperatives somehow reflect African "communal" cultures. Thus, cooperatives are widely recognized as a means to generate social and economic benefits on the basis of principles that may or may not be supported by existing social and cultural concepts. As Kasula Tabisa, one small producer put it, "We organize to get higher prices and better access to markets. In some cases, big men help the group, but in other cases, they are opposed to it."

In a similar vein, Steve Banya, a domestic coffee buyer who also ran a cafe and popular sales outlet in central Kampala, stressed that:

> Cooperatives have worked for all kinds of farmers, no matter what culture. They are about reinvesting knowledge and profits [from coffee] into people's land in an organized way. But today, there is no holistic approach to cooperatives; many small groups exist and some are even tied to one person only, but the secondary level is weak.

### *Structures of representation in four different cooperatives*

Cooperatives have responded in different ways to the new challenges posed by a competitive environment, widespread poverty among the rural population, and a lack of government support.[44] In order to attract (and retain) members and to ensure economic viability, cooperatives have to provide reliable and effective support to risk-averse, highly vulnerable small producers. In some cooperatives, functional representational structures have been established to ensure members' control of vital organizational developments, while in others, different management levels and control functions are effectively collapsed into a single, often elite-driven organizational unit. These differences in representational structures contribute to diverse socio-economic outcomes for members, as the data presented in this chapter show. The four organizations – NUCAFE, UCA, Gumutindo, and UOCG – reflect the spectrum of organizational developments rather well. While their objectives are invariably alike, formal rules and regulations, as well as informal institutional structures, differ significantly (on organizational objectives, *see*, for example, NUCAFE 2009a; Fair-trade Foundation 2007; UOCG 2007).[45]

All four organizations employ a terminology of participation and inclusive development that emphasizes the improvement of small producers' economic prospects based on higher quality and increased rates of output and productivity. In addition to pooling economic resources, notions of social cohesion are promoted as a means for people at the 'grassroots' to respond to economic challenges. However, the four cooperatives differ significantly in their ability to address the economic challenges encountered by small producers. In particular within NUCAFE and UCA, there is an apparent gap – well-known from large agrarian cooperatives throughout the developing world – between the ideas and concepts developed by managers and advisers at the top level and the nature of exchange relations at the base. In both organizations, managers at the national and to some extent at the secondary level emphasized the task to promote small producers' to "move up the value chain," but activities at the primary cooperative level show that limited efforts are made to transfer relevant political and economic knowledge about the scope and limitations of small producers' economic opportunities within the domestic and international coffee markets.[46]

Thus, training and advisory services provided by NUCAFE and UCA concentrate on improving agricultural techniques and, to some extent, structures of socio-economic organization at the local level, but the political-economic conditions of export crop production and marketing are rarely addressed. Extension workers generally fail to discuss the nature of relations between small producers, buyers, and the state, despite a terminology of 'empowerment' and participation. Overall, the role of power underlying existing relations of economic exchange within the coffee sector is more likely to be addressed in organizational concepts at the management level than in direct interaction with producers. As a result, members have very limited knowledge of how the state could support small producers, apart from direct agricultural subsidies and technical training. In particular, there is no general awareness of opportunities for more and better public sector investment in rural infrastructure development to strengthen the competitiveness of cooperatives as opposed to TNCs, although small producers frequently complain that the government has ceased to provide 'guidance'.[47] Both UCA and NUCAFE oppose the, as one of UCA's extension workers in Mbale put it, "patronizing system of BCU, which has left farmers powerless", but the organizations' primary level activities so far display limited efforts to break existing structures of inequality and exploitation.

Small producers frequently emphasized that the technical (including agricultural) skills trainings provided by UCA and NUCAFE are generally more relevant than those provided by NGOs. Given the low levels of productivity and the widespread failure to ensure consistent quality levels in Uganda's coffee sector, the transfer of technical skills indeed represents a priority, compared with an improved understanding of the broader political and economic context. However, the gap between organizational objectives promoted at top management levels and the everyday reality at the base may hamper the ability of cooperatives to respond with any accuracy to producers' skills needs. A vivid example is NUCAFE's "Farmer Ownership Model," which concentrates on enabling members to sell graded coffee, but essentially ignores the fact that the majority of small producers lack the skills, technology, and capital to produce *washed* or primary-processed coffee. These producers are therefore unable to enter the milling process and to produce graded coffee. Some of these shortcomings are addressed by the training that is provided to primary cooperatives, but NUCAFE's top management and the major concepts and campaigns which it promotes pay little attention to this reality at the farm level.

The gap between the terminology of empowerment and participation employed at NUCAFE's and also UCA's top organizational level and the reality of the socio-economic challenges faced by producers is likely to lead to shortcomings of relevant activities at the primary cooperative level. However, both organizations have created formal organizational structures that connect members with the secondary and national levels, thereby providing institutionalized control mechanisms to protect the representation of members' interests. If the need arises for members to bypass primary cooperative leaders and local elites, who may act as gatekeepers of communication outside the community, members can address the cooperative management directly, either when extension workers visit individual farms or, in the case of UCA, at the regional field offices. In the case of NUCAFE, extension workers will also be cautioned by their supervisors – and may lose their jobs if members are unsatisfied and report irregularities.[48] As Daniel Nabende, an extension worker in Kapchorwa district, explained:

> Our work is performance based, and our market linkage fees [overheads for marketing services provided] are low, at 50 UGX per kilo. This means we cannot play around if the farmers are not satisfied. All members have to benefit from our services, because if too many go to the middleman, we cannot meet our targets.

Both organizations abstain from giving permanent contracts to extension workers at the secondary level, making their continued employment and promotion dependent on the satisfaction of members and the levels of output and productivity of primary cooperatives. The possible dissatisfaction of members is generally noticed at higher levels of management due to fluctuations in output of primary cooperatives associated with decreasing membership numbers in particular villages or parishes, or the splitting of existing groups into smaller ones.

Overall, both organizations have made noticeable efforts to develop organizational structures aimed at reducing the likelihood of a closing of ranks between local elites and cooperative managers. The implementation of relevant mechanisms, however, depends on frequently overstretched organizational capacities. In particular NUCAFE's membership numbers have grown rapidly, but the increase of extension workers to assess and attend to members' needs at the local level has seriously lagged behind (NUCAFE 2015; interviews with NUCAFE staff).[49] While the organization admits that less than 20 percent of its member associations (equivalent to primary cooperatives) are adequately served, extension workers at the secondary level pointed out that insufficient staff and funds also compromise the functioning of internal mechanisms to ensure the representation of members' interests. Thus, Fred Chemak, an extension worker at NUCAFE in Kapchorwa, explained that the regular holding of votes to ensure the turnover of power at the primary management level was difficult to supervise even in relative well-served areas such as Kapchorwa.

Similarly, UCA is still weakly developed at the secondary level, despite increasing numbers of Area Cooperative Enterprises (ACE).[50] Furthermore, there are considerable constraints on the ability of members to use ACEs as a platform to articulate their interests to higher organizational management levels. First, ACE leaders are likely to be local elites, characterized by above-average educational levels and larger land holdings than most members. As one UCA extension worker explained, the networking beyond a particular village, or even parish, which is necessary to gain influence within an ACE and increase one's chances of becoming its leader is exceedingly difficult to achieve for members with particularly low educational levels and/or social status.

Second, some of UCA's (and indeed NUCAFE's) extension workers are locals, or at least their parents or grandparents are, in the area in which they work and given their relatively high social status as full-time cooperative employees, they might sustain close personal relations with local elites, including primary cooperative leaders and ACE managers. Such relations can impair the representation of members' interests by increasing the existing social and cultural barriers which are encountered by members to voicing objections against cooperative leaders. If the organization fails to prevent a closing of ranks between cooperative leaders, local elites, and extension workers, those producers with a low social status, as well as their household members, are unlikely to complain about power abuse or malfunctioning organizational mechanisms. However, the cooperative extension workers who work at Mt. Elgon today tend to be young and relatively well-educated semi-urban or urban residents. They therefore have few commonalities with members of the rural elites, and they generally establish their social status among small producers to some extent in opposition to them.[51]

In the case of Gumutindo, a closing of ranks between primary cooperative leaders and local elites might also occur, but it is less likely because the organization has established representational structures that connect members as well as primary cooperative leaders to the secondary and top management levels, while also investing heavily in training services that are provided to members through extension workers, rather than primary cooperative leaders. Thus, the organizational design allows for members as well as primary cooperative leaders to be voted into committees that oversee outsourced management functions. During the time of the fieldwork, this mechanism was being implemented, thereby allowing members to represent their interests both directly and through primary cooperative leaders.

Compared with UCA and NUCAFE, Gumutindo has a relatively well-developed secondary structure, made up of extension workers who provide training and advisory services that extend beyond technical or agricultural skills to transfer basic knowledge of relevant political and economic issues. Both cooperative staff at the top management level and members emphasized that extension workers actively encourage the participation of *all* members in decision-making processes at the primary cooperative level. Participant observation before, during, and after cooperative meetings at the primary level confirmed these claims, in particular as compared to equivalent meetings with NUCAFE, UCA, and UOCG.

The broader socio-economic changes at the local level that were brought about by the collapse of the formerly monopolistic cooperatives create favorable conditions for the efforts made by UCA, NUCAFE, and Gumutindo to establish more democratic structures of organizations. Throughout the fieldwork area, members of the local elites used to dominate the local level management of BCU and of the Sabin Elgon Cooperative Union (SECU), thereby exerting considerable control over the only legal way to sell coffee to the national marketing board for export.[52] Today, in a competitive economic environment in which producers can sell export crops to different cooperatives, TNCs, and local middlemen, the ability of local elites to control producers' economic strategies is reduced, even though they are likely to continue to dominate the primary management level of cooperatives, at least to some extent. On the one hand, producers may join another cooperative if they have reason to expect greater benefits. On the other hand, they may officially remain members, but secretly sell some of their produce to TNCs or middlemen.[53] As a result, the local elites have lost some of their power, and joint strategies of cooperative managers and members of the local elites may not produce the same level of control or influence over members' economic decisions as in the past.

UOCG, the smallest of the organizations examined in this book, and the only one that is community-based, portrays a very different picture. With less than one hundred members and four primary cooperatives at the time of the fieldwork, UOCG's primary- and secondary-level management is identical, consisting of a small group of producers who hold the positions of primary cooperative leaders as well as board members. The board takes all decisions on production and marketing issues in consultation with the organization's general chairman, who is a local leader distinguished by his above-average education, in addition to work experience in Mbale and Kampala.[54] All the board members are relatively well-off *men*, with the exception of one woman, who is herself from a better-off family.[55] Although some primary cooperative leaders expressed concern for the well-being of *all* members, the differences in living standards between ordinary members and leaders are stark and reflect more general gender- and wealth-based inequalities within the community. Furthermore, members cannot replace board members through elections, and due to the significant differences in social status between members and leaders, it seems unlikely that any member of the management can be ousted from power by a gradual displacement process.

The lack of democratic structures of representation within UOCG is clear: no votes are conducted to elect the management or appoint direct representatives of members' interests at the top management level. Thus, those who have significant control of the cooperative's resources are not elected and no veto can be imposed by members against decisions over major organizational activities. Initially, all members have voluntarily joined the cooperative on the basis of shared economic interests, but there are no organizational structures in place to encourage, let alone enforce, the continued compliance of organizational activities with member interests.[56] The weak participation of disadvantaged groups within the cooperative's regular meetings reflects the lack of democratic organizational structures within UOCG. The attendance of women as well as men from particularly poor households is limited, and most of them remain silent during discussions. Furthermore, the flow of information within the organization is limited. During meetings, board members inform members about recent expenditures as well as profits, but many members lack sufficient literacy and numeracy skills to be able to understand the composition of the figures.

Within the discourse of poverty reduction that dominates the activities of UOCG, members are conceptualized as a homogeneously poor group, and the management fails to address potential inequalities in access to benefits created by the cooperative. In contrast, extension workers and managers in the three larger cooperatives acknowledged that organizational structures must be shaped deliberately to ensure that benefits are made accessible to all members. The management's motivation to realize more equitable socio-economic outcomes is linked directly to the organization's level of productivity and its economic viability, because discontented members will defect from bulk selling commitments and eventually leave the cooperative. Furthermore, if particularly poor members are not supported with loans or pre-payments, they may be practically forced to sell to middlemen. The threats of defection and exit are weaker within UOCG because, so far, other cooperatives are not active in the immediate vicinity and there is no field processing-station of an TNC nearby, making local middlemen the only obvious alternative. Therefore, social expectations to participate in the dominant cooperative seem to be relatively high.

To summarize, the three larger cooperatives provide a more progressive picture, albeit to different degrees. First, they have established direct channels of communication between the base and secondary or higher levels of the cooperative management. This allows members to disrupt a closing of ranks between primary cooperative leaders and members of the local elites, who are likely to be over-represented at the primary management level. Second, all three organizations explicitly address the role of class- and gender-based inequalities within agricultural production and marketing, both as part of training programs and in the context of everyday interaction.[57] Training in particular encourages progressive changes in the structure of socio-economic organization, most notably the division of labor within the household, the farm, and the primary cooperative. It can encourage the formation of new primary cooperatives, to avoid the reproduction of informal support groups that may be characterized by significant gender- and wealth-based divisions. By fostering egalitarian principles in the formation of new groups, the organizations contribute to the creation of conditions that minimize the reproduction of existing inequalities within formal organizational structures.

However, within UCA and NUCAFE, the weak development of organizational capacities at the secondary level is likely to compromise the generation of progressive social change at the local level. On the one hand, training and advisory services for primary cooperatives suffer from a lack of trained staff. While NUCAFE has developed an elaborate gender sensitization and training program, which has been implemented in Kapchorwa district, cooperative members in other areas that are supposedly served by NUCAFE reported that they have had no access to the program due to a lack of trainers and extension workers. On the other hand, weak organizational capacities at the secondary level impede the supervision of extension workers. As a result, formal institutional mechanisms aimed to ensure the representation of members' interests may be circumvented by primary cooperative leaders and extension workers. In the case of UCA, some extension workers maintain close personal relations with members of local elites who are in turn well represented within the management structures of primary cooperatives. Processes of organizational development at the local level may therefore be shaped on the basis of existing, informal structures of socio-economic organization, which increases the likelihood of reproducing existing inequalities.

Overall, major constraints on achieving the democratic representation of members' interests remain within cooperatives. The larger institutional framework that might ensure the proper implementation of an organization's rules and regulations is relatively weak: neither relevant government institutions nor UCA, in its function as a national umbrella organization of cooperatives, is capable of effectively carrying out supervisory functions.[58] As a result, footholds for the exploitation of poorer members are created or perpetuated because the existing relations of power and inequality at the local level may overrule the rights and entitlements ensured on the basis of the organization's formal institutional structure. While larger organizations have made visible efforts to improve the ability of members to bypass primary cooperative leaders if necessary, the interlinkages between higher levels of management and local elites within small, community-based organizations tend to be institutionalized. Thus, powerful community members generally appoint the cooperative management, creating a multitude of opportunities for the exploitation of disadvantaged groups within the cooperative, while potentially limiting access to the organization from outside a particular community.

## 5.4 Women's cooperatives: organizations for women's empowerment

Based on quantitative and qualitative data, this section examines the organized responses of some women farmers to gender inequalities in smallholder coffee production and marketing. Women are under-represented as cooperative members and leaders, even though they contribute a large share, if not the majority, of agricultural labor. Against this background, the creation of women's primary cooperatives indicates an important step towards the development of greater gender equality, including women farmers' improved access to land and non-land resources. Women-only primary cooperatives directly and explicitly address gender-based inequalities in control over income from coffee, leading some male farmers to aggressively denounce their existence. For example, David Wolufu, a UCA cooperative member, claimed, "These organizations came to make our women big-headed". Members of women's primary cooperatives describe the raison d'être of their groups in more factual terms:

> Coffee used to be a man's crop. Some call it black gold but it is more like male gold. With our group [women's primary cooperative], we now sell our coffee and we keep the money. After all, it is us who do a lot of digging in the fields. (Grace Mugobera, leader of a women's primary cooperative)

The discussion so far has shed light on the conditions under which cooperatives may effectively contribute to the reduction of inequalities and poverty in disaggregated rural communities. The latter are typically divided on the basis of an unequal distribution of material wealth, with the size of land holdings and access to additional, non-farming income as the major indicators of economic well-being. However, gender-based divisions are equally ubiquitous and women arguably form the largest rural population group that is disadvantaged in terms of access to land and non-land resources, such as extension services, credits, and wage employment.[59] Despite a far-reaching reform of land laws in 1998, women throughout rural Uganda still face severe difficulties in claiming their land rights, while limited access to non-land resources reduces their opportunities to invest in cash-crop production, even if land is available (Whitehead 2001).[60]

Socio-economic and cultural restrictions on access to non-land resources do not necessarily apply to all women, but certainly to those who are divorced, separated, widowed, or simply unmarried, as well as to women from households which contain few males. As the data from Eastern Uganda show, these women are particularly constrained in their ability to achieve higher living standards, both as individual economic actors and within cooperatives. Overall, women tend to be poorer than men, and they are over-represented among the poorest population sections within the fieldwork area, but with regard to non-land resources, inequalities based on wealth and social class are likely to override divisions of gender, at least to some extent. Thus, within primary cooperatives, the wife of a relatively wealthy and influential small producer is more likely to take up a leadership position than a particularly poor man. However, her economic power and social status is inextricably linked to her husband, a connection that can easily be severed within a patriarchal kinship system.[61]

Against this background, it is worthwhile to give special attention to the social agency of women as cooperative members and to explore how cooperatives have affected the development of female welfare levels in the context of changing economic and political conditions. The following section examines the ability of women to represent their interests within cooperatives in Eastern Uganda's coffee sector today. The discussion concentrates on how women who belong to particularly disadvantaged groups, as defined above, have responded to new economic opportunities in the context of significant changes in the institutional and organizational landscape of Uganda's liberalized agricultural sector. Before liberalization, the division of labor and access to resources within the then-monopolistic BCU was characterized by severe gender-based inequalities. Today, the socio-economic organization of coffee production and marketing continues to be characterized by gender discrimination, but some women have pressed for changes by forming women's primary cooperatives. Although not widespread, these cooperatives provide a palpable example of how women have improved their economic well-being by using the organizational structures of cooperatives to their advantage.[62]

The formation of women's primary cooperatives demonstrates some women's attempts to achieve better access to land and non-land resources on the basis of formal economic organization, and to gain control over the income generated from their contribution of labor in the production process. Their formation so far remains limited to a few localities, but they represent a remarkable development, because women's formal economic organization for the marketing of coffee (or indeed other export crops) is a novel phenomenon in Uganda. Village-based self-help groups are widespread among women throughout the developing world, but their effects on changes in distributional patterns is limited, and the feminization of such locally confined, informal organizations may even have disempowering effects in the long run (*see*, for example, Anand 2007; Chant 2008; Guerin & Palier 2005; Chen et al. 2005). In Uganda, the women's movement entails a variety of organizational structures that advocate change in agricultural production and the rural economy, but so far it has failed to produce permanent, formal economic organizations representing rural women in agriculture or the labor market (Tripp & Kwesiga 2002; Tripp 2001, 2004). By forming primary cooperatives in the context of larger organizations, some female producers in Eastern Uganda have formally organized their economic activities, while making use of existing cooperative structures to represent their interest *vis-à-vis* stronger economic actors, including male relatives, at the local level.

## *Women's position in Mt. Elgon coffee cooperatives: past and present*

> BCU was run by wealthy men. As for us [women], we remained in the village on payment days, and we could never be sure how much was paid for our coffee.
>
> (Allen Kinwende, producer in Sironko)

Although women contribute substantial amounts of labor to the production of unprocessed coffee, their power to influence marketing decisions is limited, and the income generated from coffee sales is generally controlled by men. The gendered division of labor within the coffee sector largely consigns tasks in the early stage of the production process, such as planting and pruning, to women, while men contribute more labor during primary-processing and marketing.[63] This effectively gives men control of a household's cash from coffee sales, but also of the machinery, such as hand-pulping machines, which is often shared within a community. The dominance of male producers in the marketing process is reflected in their position within Eastern Uganda's coffee cooperatives, all of them marketing and service, rather than production societies. By the late 2000s, all larger cooperatives in the fieldwork area had introduced quotas for women in leadership positions at the primary level, but women's membership, independently of their husbands or other male household members, is growing only slowly (NUCAFE 2009b, 2016; UCA 2009a, 2016; Gumutindo 2009, 2016). However, to what extent women are able to influence decision-making processes within cooperatives and benefit from their outcomes may be more accurately assessed by taking female producers' micro-level perspective, rather than looking at formal rules and cooperatives' databases alone.

Women's accounts of the time when all producers were organized with BCU point to the prevalence of severe discrimination against women within the cooperative that held a monopoly status in four of the five Mt. Elgon coffee-growing districts.[64] Similar narratives of women in Kapchorwa district, where the Sabin Cooperative Union (SECU) was the monopolistic organization for selling coffee to the national marketing board, indicate that gender inequalities were an integral part of coffee cooperatives. The idealization of the "old days" under BCU and SECU, expressed occasionally by male producers, is not shared by women. Older female producers stressed that their participation in decision-making processes was extremely limited even at the primary level. Yowana Nandudu, a producer in Sironko district, said, "Women rarely took part in meetings. Men still think it is a waste of time for women to join, but under BCU, our participation was never encouraged by group leaders."

Current extension workers of UCA and NUCAFE confirmed that leadership positions at all levels were almost invariably held by men. This means that women were present neither when coffee was delivered to cooperative warehouses nor when payments were made, because these tasks were handled exclusively by primary cooperative leaders. As a result, men were able to control information on the exact amount of coffee produced and the total amount paid for it.

Gender-based inequalities in cooperatives are still prevalent today, as indicated by persisting socio-economic barriers to membership, participation in decision-making processes, and access to leadership positions. Men continue to outnumber women as members of coffee cooperatives. While male producers generally state that their wives lack the time to become active members, female producers insist that they lack the money to pay the registration fees and to contribute to credit and saving groups. Patriarchal intra-household relations also produce constraints on women's participation in primary cooperative meetings. Thus, women's double burden of domestic and field work impedes their engagement in the public sphere and men frequently declare that women are "wasting their time" in such meetings.[65] Thus, assertions by extension workers on improvements regarding gender equality should be carefully weighed against women's own accounts. Fred Chemak, NUCAFE extension worker in Kapchorwa district, stressed:

> In the past [under BCU and SECU], coffee was owned by men. Women have always worked in the fields, but the men sold the coffee to the cooperative. Today, women are also leaders [of primary cooperatives], and they know for how much their coffee was sold.

While female producers unanimously emphasized that their access to and position in primary cooperatives has improved in comparison with "the old days" under BCU and SECU, their accounts of current inequalities indicate that women still struggle to secure equal participation within coffee cooperatives today.

Overall, a combination of gender inequalities in access to resources within the household and socio-economic constraints on women's mobility and participation in the public sphere continue to create barriers for women's equal participation. Thus, the difficulties in enforcing women's quotas for leadership positions at the primary level are partly caused by women's lower education and skill levels, by their discomfort at taking official positions, and by their

*Table 5.10* Perceived socioeconomic effects of cooperative membership, by gender (%)

| *Type of producer* | *Female cooperative members* | *Male and female cooperative members* | *Non-organized male and female producers* |
|---|---|---|---|
| Improved living standards attributed to membership | 73.7 | 71.6 | Not applicable |
| Has access to credit | 18.9 | 18.1 | 5.3 |
| Has savings from coffee (previous year) | 54.9 | 59.3 | 45.9 |

heavy work burden caused by multiple domestic responsibilities in addition to farming and wage-work. In some cases, women from wealthier households enjoy better access to leadership positions than particularly poor men, but most often class- and gender-based inequalities mutually reinforce each other, relegating women to the poorest, least influential section of rural society. Charles Wakoli, a non-organized farmer from Bududa district, explained: In the groups [primary cooperatives], everyone can take up a leadership position. But if you read and count poorly, how can you become the treasurer or secretary?

These inequalities reflect longstanding disparities between men's and women's access to resources throughout Uganda's rural society. Up to today, cooperative extension workers are invariably male, and female producers generally experience the cooperative as a predominantly male domain. In this context, Chamira Namusisi, project manager for an international NGO that provides agricultural skills training in Eastern Uganda, claimed: The problem in any agricultural activity is like this: The husband owns the land, the house, the crop, the money made from it and the labor of the wife. In fact, he owns the wife, too.

Given the nature of women's narratives, the quantitative data on women in cooperatives need to be used cautiously. The survey indicates that men and women benefit equally from cooperative membership, but this result may be compromised by the fact that female respondents are likely to compare the current welfare outcomes with the conditions which they faced in the past. Against this background, 74 percent of female members, compared with 72 percent of all organized producers, associated improved living standards with their membership in a cooperative (*see* Table 5.10). More specifically, 19 percent of organized women had access to credit during the previous year,

*Table 5.11* Female producers who attribute economic improvements to cooperative membership, by type of organization (%)

| *Type of organization* | *UCA and NUCAFE* | *Gumutindo* | *UOCG* |
|---|---|---|---|
| Yes, perceived improvements | 72.9 | 92.9 | 40.0 |
| No improvements perceived | 27.1 | 7.1 | 60.0 |

*Table 5.12* Female cooperative members with access to credit, by type of cooperative (%)

| *Type of organization* | *UCA and NUCAFE* | *Gumutindo* | *UOCG* |
|---|---|---|---|
| Yes, access to credit | 22.9 | 14.3 | 0.0 |
| No access to credit | 77.1 | 85.7 | 100.0 |

compared with 18 percent of all members and 5 percent of non-organized producers. At 53 percent, the ability to save money from coffee during the previous year was nearly as high for female cooperative members as for all members (59 percent), compared with 46 percent of non-organized producers (*see* Table 5.10). However, these figures fail to indicate the proportion of women who lack control over how a household's credits or savings are spent. Regarding differences in the ability of cooperatives to reduce gender inequalities, the survey results match the figures on inequalities based on material wealth and social class. Thus, organizations that implement, albeit imperfectly, institutional mechanisms to improve the representation of disadvantaged groups seem to have some positive effects on strengthening the position of women. The survey shows that 93 percent of women organized with Gumutindo and 73 percent of female members of UCA and NUCAFE associated improvements in living standards with their cooperative membership, compared with 40 percent of female UOCG members (*see* Table 5.11).

Similarly, 23 percent of women organized with UCA and NUCAFE and 14 percent of female Gumutindo members, but no female respondent organized with UOCG had access to credits during the previous year (*see* Table 5.12). Also, the ability to save money generated from coffee was high among women at UCA and NUCAFE (61 percent) as well as Gumutindo (67 percent), but at 40 percent it was significantly lower for UOCG's female members (*see* Table 5.13).

### *Women's primary cooperatives*

The formation of women's primary cooperatives in Eastern Uganda should be understood against the background of agricultural liberalization and the associated collapse of the monopolistic position of BCU in commodity exports.

*Table 5.13* Female cooperative members with savings from coffee production during the previous year, by type of cooperative (%)

| *Type of organization* | *UCA and NUCAFE* | *Gumutindo* | *UOCG* |
|---|---|---|---|
| Yes, able to save | 60.9 | 66.7 | 40.0 |
| No, not able to save | 39.1 | 33.3 | 60.0 |

The negative effects of policies associated with the Post-Washington Consensus on inequalities of gender – in addition to those of class and race – have been discussed extensively before (*see*, for example, Elson & Cagatay 2000; Kabeer 2008; Berik & Rodgers 2009; Seguino & Grown 2006). These studies have exposed and analyzed important global parallels in the effects of neoliberal macro-economic policies on inequalities within and between countries. At the same time, market-based reforms and the circumscription of the state's role in the context of historically specific structures of socio-economic organization have affected the economic opportunities of disadvantaged groups in different ways, depending on the nature of shifts in local power relations.

In Eastern Uganda's coffee sector, female small producers have benefited to a limited extent from the extensive ruptures in socio-economic relations which were caused by the collapse of BCU after the liberalization of agriculture. Power over the coffee trade had been firmly embedded within a cooperative that was, similar to cooperatives elsewhere, run almost exclusively by men. When most of BCU's primary societies became dormant, the degradation and partial disintegration of this exclusively male domain was associated with men's loss in social status and access to resources, at least at the local level. The ensuing power vacuum within rural communities, in combination with the development of organizations that provided more direct channels of communication between members and higher levels of management, created a new scope for disadvantaged groups to pursue their interests within cooperatives. In this context, some women have founded women's primary cooperatives in order to gain improved access to land and non-land resources.

In Kapchorwa district, a women producers' group or primary cooperative was founded in Cheema village as an offshoot of a "regular" primary cooperative that is registered with NUCAFE. It is managed by a married woman with average landholdings, but a relatively high level of education and training.[66] The membership is exclusively female, although men are invited to become members. However, no men had joined at the time of the fieldwork, because male members of "women's groups" apparently face ridicule from other men. Registered under the same name as the original, mixed-gender primary cooperative (which continues to exist as such), the Cheema women's cooperative developed on the basis of members' previous economic relations for the marketing of local cash crops. NUCAFE's marketing services were essential to gain access to the domestic market for export crops; however, members explained that their long-standing engagement in the sales of bananas, tomatoes, and maize in local markets provided them with the initial confidence to enter coffee marketing.

The cooperative represents an organizational response to gender-based discrimination within the household and within 'regular' cooperatives. The women emphasized that despite formal organizational rules to protect their rights as members, their access to cash income from coffee remained limited because they could neither become primary cooperative leaders, who handle the payments made for all members' coffee, nor secure equal access to cash income generated from coffee within the household. The formation of women's primary cooperatives therefore invalidates the notion of joint economic planning within "family farms," because members explicitly aim at gaining access to cash made from their own contribution of labor, as distinct from that of their husbands or other household members.[67] Thus, women in Eastern Uganda generally make their own money from the production of cash crops for local markets, but so far they have largely failed to secure access to money from coffee. As members of a women's primary cooperative, the female producers from Cheema designate their own coffee trees on the family farms and control the coffee produced from them until it is sold.

However, women's primary cooperatives invariably face challenges, most notably the resistance by male cooperative leaders as well as male household members and the associated constraints on women's time to pursue their own economic activities. Thus, the women from Cheema confirmed that they continue to contribute labor for the pruning and harvesting of their husbands' trees. As Dafin Nadungo explained:

> Even today, it is mostly the men who deal with the marketing and sometimes they keep the money for our coffee. In our group [women's primary cooperatives], each one receives all the money for her coffee. But it is hard, because we do a lot of digging in the fields of our husbands, too.

Members of another women's primary cooperative in Sironko, which sells mainly to Gumutindo's Busamaga Producers' society, pointed to similar challenges, but they also emphasized that they improved their living standards on the basis of the cash income from coffee. Furthermore, the cooperative's head asserted that they are becoming increasingly able to defend their interests within their households and the wider community.

Organizations such as NUCAFE and Gumutindo, but also UCA, provide organizational structures that allow women to realize socio-economic changes on the basis of new primary cooperatives. Within these organizations, disadvantaged women seem to be more likely to demand greater equality of access to resources than women in small, community-based cooperatives. This may be because these women, who experience intense pressure to secure a modest living standard for themselves and their dependents, have more space for social agency within the larger organizational frame of reference offered by cooperatives that provide access to training as well as institutional support structures outside the local community. Thus, Florence Nuwembe, a member of the Cheema women's cooperative, described how she had joined after having been encouraged by relevant training and advice provided by NUCAFE extension workers. She explained that not everyone in her social environment approves of these changes, but stressed the support they get from outside the community, both through training conducted in other locations and through the extension workers themselves.

The resistance of men to women's economic organization generally focuses on the improvements of women's position within "regular" primary cooperatives. Kusulu Titus, a producer in Gumutindo's primary cooperative in Bukalasi village in Bududa, explained his view:In the old days, the cooperative [BCU] was run by men, and it was them who received most of the money. Today men and women join our groups [primary cooperatives] and everyone can become a leader.

However, as indicated above, women's accounts of gender relations in cooperatives tell a different story. The achievements made by some female producers on the basis of women's cooperatives clearly illustrate the shortcomings regarding gender equality in cooperatives today, while also pointing out possible solutions. In Sironko, the women's primary cooperative has secured access to land, despite the inadequate enforcement of women's land rights. Based on the social recognition awarded to a registered primary cooperative, the women rent land for the production of coffee (and other cash crops) from wealthy (male) community members against a share in profits. These women have thereby improved their access to both land and non-land resources.

In the Mt. Elgon area, two registered women's primary cooperatives were identified during the first phase of data collection carried out for this book in 2009/10. By 2016, more than a dozen primary cooperative societies with female leadership, but often mixed-gender membership, was reported to be active in the region (interviews with farmers). Furthermore, informal women's groups for the production and marketing of cash crops destined for local markets continue to be widespread. Supported by the secondary organizational structures of existing (cash crop) cooperatives, they could form the basis for formal economic organization among women farmers-cum-wageworkers. While an assessment of the social, political, and economic viability of an expansion of women's primary cooperatives goes beyond the scope of this book, it is worth noting that the female producers' accounts presented in this chapter indicate considerable achievements in economic and social emancipation, which reflect Kabeer's (1999) comprehensive, processual understanding of women's empowerment. Thus, the three interrelated dimensions pointed out by Kabeer figure prominently: first, improvements in current and future access to resources; second, agency, in the form of decision-making and participation in negotiation processes; and third, achievements in well-being. All three aspects form part of the processes that this study has observed in the context of women's primary cooperatives.

## Notes

1 For an overview of qualitative data collected in Uganda, see Table 1.2 in Chapter 1.
2 As Uganda's umbrella organization of cooperatives, UCA continues to represent the interests of member organizations at the national level, but has expanded its activities to the primary and secondary level since the early 1990s.

3 For a discussion of domestic and international economic, political, and institutional constraints of vertical diversification as an industrialization strategy in agriculture-based economies, *see*, for example, Cramer (1999, 2003) or Owens and Wood (1997).

4 The term 'class' is used to refer to social class, rather than the distinction between property and labor in the strict Marxian sense. The broader concept of social class better captures the interrelated differences in material wealth and social status among small producers.

5 The quality of training was assessed as part of the coffee sector survey, using a set of indicators that included amongst others the range, relevance, and transferability of skills and the length and novelty of training programs. The follow-up semi-structured interviews allowed selected participants to include additional aspects of quality, such as practical orientation and responsiveness to changing socio-economic and environmental conditions.

6 Given their relatively smaller sizes, the secondary and top management levels of UOCG and Gumutindo are identical. In the case of NUCAFE and UCA, a national-level administration exists above the secondary level. The present discussion refers to members' relations to the secondary level; however, access to the latter generally improves the representation of members' interests at the top.

7 For the non-agricultural labor market survey, complementary data was generated in urban areas of southern, central, and northern regions of Uganda, but except for a small number of unstructured interviews in the vicinity of workplaces, no qualitative data was collected.

8 Swahili is fairly widespread in Kapchorwa, but it is also used by members of Uganda's armed forces and during the fieldwork for the present research, interview partners indicated this as a reason why they prefer to use other languages. Interviews in Kapchorwa were thus conducted by using a combination of Luganda, Lugisu, and English, while relying on Swahili only when necessary.

9 More than 50 percent of married women reported experiencing some form of domestic violence within the past 12 months (*ibid.*).

10 Female interview respondents from both groups provided examples with reference to the labor market, the domestic sphere, and land ownership.

11 Unstructured interviews with women throughout the fieldwork area were conducted to learn about the living and working conditions of women in the domestic sphere and at the farm level.

12 In 2003/4, export volumes went down to 1994/5 levels (Ponte & Kawuma 2003).

13 Employment estimates are based on interviews with local government officials and with representatives of employers and cooperatives, as well as on UBOS data (UBOS accessed March 2009 and September 2017).

14 These are Kyagalanyi Coffee Ltd., a daughter company of ED&F MAN, and Kawacom, the Ugandan branch of ECOM Agro-industrial Corporation Ltd.

15 Before liberalization, UCA functioned exclusively as an apex body at the national level. Today, its activities include the management of Area Cooperative Enterprises (ACEs) at the secondary level, which includes capacity building and input delivery services to primary societies, similar to the activities of producer and marketing cooperatives. UCA also retains its political advocacy and advisory functions at the national level.

16 During the 1970s and 1980s, the economic performance of monopolistic agrarian cooperatives was relatively weak throughout the developing world. For a discussion, *see* Hussi *et al.* (1993), Porvali (1993) and Deininger (1993).

17 The broad term 'social resources' is used to denote resources that may be used to satisfy economic needs beyond, but not unrelated to, material wealth, such as skills, information, social recognition, and security.

18 The vast majority of respondents stated that they cultivated virtually all available land. The size of land cultivated is therefore used as a general indicator of land ownership among small producers.

19 Figures given by respondents were cross-checked where possible with the databank of Kyagalanyi, a TNC that buys coffee directly from small producers in the field-work area. In addition, some plots were measured by the researcher. However, many figures could not be cross-checked, so small producers' estimates had to be taken as given.

20 There were some exceptions, such as school teachers and health workers who work in Mbale municipality, Kapchorwa town, or one of the trading centers (Sironko, Manafwa, Bududa), but cultivate coffee in their home villages on the basis of unpaid family labor and frequent absences in their wage jobs.

21 Most businesses were small kiosks selling sugar, soap, and other domestic utensils and serving half a dozen villages or so. Few businesses included noteworthy capital input, as in the case of bicycle or motorbike taxis.

22 A separation of focus groups according to gender and position within the cooperative was not possible for UOCG. Instead, cooperative leaders, both male and female, insisted on being present at all times and clearly influenced the ways in which members participated in the discussion.

23 The sample for UOCG included twenty cases. However, the total number of members was slightly below 100 at the time of the fieldwork, so the sample covered a fifth of the organization's membership. The sample of Gumutindo included 38 cases because it was reduced by several invalid questionnaires. However, the subsequent generation of qualitative data focused on balancing the resulting weaknesses of the relevant quantitative data.

24 Domestic companies as well as some TNCs buy through local middlemen, because maintaining direct relationships with producers is too costly due to the poor transport and communication infrastructure in rural Uganda.

25 These are estimations by cooperative members and non-organized farmers, given in the semi-structured interviews.

26 The membership fee usually amounts to the equivalent of between two and four US dollars, or about two days of casual agricultural wage labor.

27 Gumutindo has so-called primary societies, which comprise larger numbers of producers than UCA's, NUCAFE's, and UOCG's primary cooperatives, but Gumutindo's 'groups', as they are called by producers, are comparable to primary cooperatives in size and function.

28 The wet-processed coffee sold by non-organized small producers is generally produced under inferior conditions, including a poorly monitored fermentation process, during which the coffee may acquire sour flavors. The drying is often done on the roadside or on the ground, which increases the amount of contamination by foreign matter. Primary cooperatives pool resources to buy better (manual) pulping machines and drying stands, and the transport of larger volumes allows them to finance more professional forms of transport that are less likely to affect the quality of the washed coffee.

29 The anecdotal evidence of individual training programs published by donors and NGOs generally illustrates locally confined outcomes, while some organizations have analyzed the structural constraints to the development of more effective training systems. However, few tracer studies exist and there are no figures on the total number and reach of training programs. Thus, there is a serious lack of data on the quantity and quality of non-formal training in the country.

30 Growers, but also representatives of the Ministry of Agriculture as well as donors, confirmed that none of the farmer field schools in the fieldwork area was providing regular services.

31 As indicated above, much of the data are anecdotal, and there is a lack of comparable time series data sets.

32 NGO representatives pointed out that one reason for this is that NGOs rarely compete successfully for public contracts for the provision of rural training programs

within Uganda's exceedingly corrupt outsourcing system, because their dependency on foreign funding is associated with high pressure to ensure transparency. However, because outsourcing to private providers has been cut back radically following the government's move towards tightening state control over rural development processes, this applies to a small and decreasing part of NGO-provided training (Joughin & Kjaer 2010).

33 The project has been implemented in selected districts of Eastern, Southern, Western, and North-West Uganda and was in the process of being expanded during the time of the fieldwork for this study. The training is also used for generating gender-sensitive household data. The project is partly funded by the Danish government.

34 In addition to semi standardized interviews with employers' representatives, the survey in the hotel and construction sectors indicated a lack of transferable skills among workers, as perceived by employers.

35 However, individual aspects of different discourses may well be compatible, as is shown by Duveskog *et al.* (2011) in their analysis of FFSs in Kenya, which noted that training participants perceived the ideals of FFSs and those preached by the church as mutually reinforcing, because both encourage hard work as a way to improve one's living standards. This example illustrates how training programs may contribute to the reproduction of larger discourses, although the latter possibly promote contradictory values.

36 Based on participant observation in villages and towns, as well as unstructured interviews with growers who regularly attend church sermons, these contradictions became apparent. They were also pointed out by one of Gumutindo's advisers.

37 Training was frequently noted as the most important benefit after access to better prices. For more detail, *see* part two of this chapter.

38 Uganda's central bank, the Bank of Uganda, commissioned an audit report of the Cooperative Bank from Ernst & Young in 1998, which found the bank insolvent. When the government failed to inject new capital, the Cooperative Bank was closed and parts of its fixed assets and deposits were bought by two commercial banks (Bossa 2003). In agreement with the overall objectives of liberalization reforms in Uganda, the closure amounted to a significant cutback in public sector support to the provision of financial services in rural areas.

39 A commonly cited benefit was a more effective division of labor between wife and husband and within the wider community. Many respondents stressed that joint work plans and the exchange of knowledge increases output and contributes to improved social relations within and between households.

40 However, men were more likely to use the terminology of 'division', while women tended to emphasize the creation of new opportunities in cooperatives since the liberalization of the agricultural sector.

41 Throughout the fieldwork area, informal self-help groups get together on market days to drink a locally brewed spirit.

42 *Busera* is the Lugisu word for a locally brewed spirit made from millet or maize, which is also called *kamalwa*, from the Lugandan word *malwa*.

43 The view that cooperatives successfully combine business enterprises with concerns of communal welfare is widespread. For an overview, *see*, for example, Develtere *et al.* (2008).

44 The Government of Uganda continues to support small producers through the National Agricultural Advisory Services (NAADS), but NAADS increasingly focuses on the distribution of agricultural inputs and has radically cut back its training and advisory services (interviews with NAADS regional advisors). This contributes to a current shift away from structural assistance provided to poor rural population sections towards a more singular and controlled support of individual households or groups.

45 These objectives include better access to markets, higher prices through bulk selling, value addition through primary processing, and access to good-quality training and advisory services to improve the quantity and quality of output.

46 Many small producers have unrealistic perceptions of the profit margins made by TNCs who buy and export, but do not roast coffee, while there seems to be little or no awareness of the government's considerable role in shaping the conditions for both TNCs and small producers within the domestic value chain.

47 However, extension workers of all four cooperatives, as well as skilled workers at coffee-processing stations, bemoaned the lack of public investments in the rural infrastructure.

48 During the time of the fieldwork, two field officers were cautioned following irregularities reported by members.

49 For the sake of clarity and simplicity, the secondary level personnel of cooperatives, who provide training, advisory and marketing services to primary cooperatives, are called 'extension workers' throughout this study. As a matter of fact, a range of terms are employed by different organizations, including "business managers" (NUCAFE) and "field officer" (UCA).

50 ACEs provide marketing and training services to members and raise awareness of cross-cutting issues, such as gender equality, the sustainable use of natural resources, and HIV/AIDS prevention. They are superior organizational units that comprise up to twenty primary cooperatives or around 500 members.

51 One likely reason for this is that many extension workers neither own land nor are able to buy any to start their own farm, so they tend to emphasis their considerable social and economic success as distinct from that of rural elites.

52 In Kapchorwa district, as opposed to the rest of Eastern Uganda, coffee was sold through the SECU. At the time of the fieldwork, SECU was not buying coffee and all its primary cooperatives were dormant, while only few primary cooperatives were selling to BCU.

53 Theoretically, this was also an option before liberalization, but given that the monopolistic cooperative was the only trader authorized to sell to the national marketing board, any sales outside the cooperative were associated with higher costs and a considerable risk of fines.

54 The general chairman's experience outside the local community is a potential source of power and social status, because many cooperative members, and local community members more generally, associate an individual's so-called "exposure" to the wider world with the ability to access organizations and institutions beyond the local level that can provide resources, services and improved economic security. Returnees from Mbale or Kampala, such as the general chairman, therefore exert considerable power as social and economic leaders, because they can potentially create new opportunities for local people.

55 The quality of living standards was estimated on the basis of the housing, clothing, and education levels of children. The cooperative leaders, who were considered to be relatively well-off, all lived in fortified houses with roofs made of corrugated iron, they wore shoes rather than going barefoot, and their children generally went to secondary school. None of the above applied to any of the cooperative's members.

56 Given that UOCG's internal organizational relations of power and hierarchy closely reflect existing inequalities within the relevant villages, it is ultimately not certain that all members joined the organization voluntarily. Anecdotal evidence indicates that a significant amount of social pressure was exerted by members of the local elites on poorer households to join, but a definitive statement in this regard would overstretch the available evidence.

57 Extension workers occasionally take part in primary cooperative meetings and they frequently visit the coffee plant nurseries or make informal visits to members.

58 Relevant government institutions include the cooperative officers attached to the local government as well as the department of cooperative development in the Ministry of Trade, Tourism and Industry (MTTI). Throughout the fieldwork area, none of the five district-wide posts of cooperative officer were filled at the time of fieldwork, seriously limiting the ability of the MTTI to promote the development of cooperatives at the district or local level.

59 Migrants in the Mt. Elgon region are mostly from South Sudan, Kenya, and Rwanda, as well as from Northern and North-Eastern Uganda. They are typically landless. As casual wageworkers, they have commonalities with asset-poor small producers; however, for the sake of comparability, they were not included in the coffee sector survey sample.

60 The Ugandan land reform laws legally recognized customary land ownership, allowed local courts to settle land disputes, and outlawed the discrimination of customary rules of land ownership (Tripp 2004). The effects of clan-based, customary laws on women's land rights have since been discussed controversially: while policy makers and some NGOs argue that customary laws are relatively neutral or even grant land rights to women, some scholars and women's rights activists emphasize the patriarchal structures that dominate customary law practice (*see* Tripp 2004; Razavi 2007; Women's Land Link Africa 2010). Without doubt, severe discrimination against women continues since the decentralization of land laws. As Razavi (2007, p. 1490) suggests, increasing competition over scarce resources may be intensifying the patriarchal tendencies of the lineage system. Gender equality in land acquisition and ownership is granted by Uganda's 1995 constitution and women's control of family land was strengthened in the 2004 Land Act amendment, but the relevant laws remain largely unenforced.

61 Throughout the fieldwork area, women move to their husbands' villages after marriage. In some cases, the spouses start a new home, but this is seldom economically independent of the husband's paternal household. Among the Sabin people in Kapchorwa, women are frequently given a new name upon arrival in their husband's villages, a ritual to signify not only their new social affiliation, but also their status as a "guest" or newcomer.

62 Within the fieldwork area, the members of two women's primary cooperatives were interviewed. Others exist throughout the fieldwork area, but their degree of formalization remains unclear. Those that were visited were less formalized and effectively depended on a "regular" primary cooperative for selling their coffee.

63 Harvesting generally demands both male and female labor from households.

64 Since its temporary collapse in 2002, BCU has only bought small amounts of coffee, and most of its primary cooperatives are dormant or have dissolved. Thus, little information was available at the time of the fieldwork in 2009 about the prevalence of gender-based inequalities today. However, female respondents indicated that they expected recent changes within primary cooperatives to continue if they should sell to BCU again in the future.

65 Throughout the fieldwork area, cases where men have pulled their wives out of meetings by force were reiterated by women, and some emphasized that they abstained from meetings out of fear. This reflects the barriers to organization that have been observed for women in India, who fear to lose their livelihoods if they organize against the will of their husbands, employers, or the wider community (Sinha 2006).

66 This female cooperative leader had graduated from primary school and participated in several skills trainings, including NUCAFE's gender equity training, but also technical and entrepreneurial trainings provided by NGOs.

67 The exploitation of women's labor within household-based export crop production tends to be hidden by notions of joint production in "family farms." Instead, women in Eastern Uganda generally make their own money from the production

of cash crops for local markets, such as bananas and maize, while men control the marketing of export crops.

## References


ADAMS, A. V. 2010, 'The Role of Skills Development in Overcoming Social Disadvantage', Technical Note to Inform UNESCO's *2012 Global Monitoring Report on Education*.

ANAND, S. 2007, 'Departures from everyday resistance and flexible strategies of domination: the making and unmaking of a poor peasant mobilisation in Bangladesh', *Journal of Agrarian Change*, 7(2), 183–224.

ANDERSON, J. R., FEDER, G. & GANGULY, S. 2006, 'The rise and fall of training and visit (T&V) system: An Asian mini-drama with an African Epilogue', *World Bank Policy Research Working Paper 3928*, The World Bank, Washington D.C.

BANERJEE, T. 2009, 'Economic impact of self-help groups—a case study', *Journal of Rural Development (Hyderabad)*, 28, 451–467.

BERIK, G., RODGERS, Y. V. D. M. & ZAMMIT, A. 2009, 'Engendering Development Strategies and Macroeconomic Policies: What's Sound and Sensible?', *Social justice and gender equality: rethinking development strategies and macroeconomic policies*, Routledge, New York.

BETCHERMAN, G., GODFREY, M., PUERTO, S., ROTHER, F. & STAVRESKA, A. 2007, 'A review of interventions to support young workers: Findings of the youth employment inventory', *World Bank Social Protection Discussion Paper*, 715.

BOESEN, J. & MIIRO, R. 2004, 'Basis for poverty reduction? A rich civil society, farmer innovation and agricultural service provision in Kabale, Uganda', DIIS Working Paper, Faculty of Agriculture, Makerere University, Kampala, Copenhagen.

BOSSA, J. F. 2003, 'Dealing with Banks in Distress: The Uganda Experience', Paper presented at the regional seminar on comparative experiences in confronting banking sector problems in the sub-Saharan African region, Bank of Uganda, Cape Town, South Africa.

BRASS, T. 2007, 'How agrarian cooperatives fail: Lessons from 1970s Peru', *Journal of Peasant Studies*, 34(2), 240–287.

BUNKER, S. G. 1987, 'Peasants against the state: the politics of market control in Bugisu, Uganda, 1900–1983', University of Illinois Press, Urbana.

BUNKER, S. G. 1983, 'Dependency, Inequality, and Development Policy: A Case from Bugisu, Uganda', *The British journal of sociology*, 34, 182–207.

CHANT, S. 2008, "The feminization of poverty' and the 'feminization' of anti-poverty programmes: room for revision?', *Journal of Development Studies*, 44, 165–197.

CHAPMAN, D. W., BURTON, L. & WERNER, J. 2010, 'Universal secondary education in Uganda: The head teachers' dilemma', *International Journal of Educational Development*, 30, 77–82.

CHEN, M., VANEK, J., LUND, F., HEINTZ, J., JHABVALA, R. & BONNER, C. 2005, *Progress of the world's women 2005: women, work, and poverty*, UNIFEM, New York.

CRAMER, C. 1999, 'Can Africa Industrialise by Processing Primary Commodities? The Case of Mozambican Cashew Nuts', *World Development*, 27, 1247–1266.

CRAMER, C. 2003, 'Should developing country industrialisation policies encourage processing of primary commodities?', *The Courier: the magazine of ACP-EU development cooperation*, 196, 30–32.

DAVIS, K., NKONYA, E., KATO, E., MEKONNEN, D. A., ODENDO, M., MIIRO, R. & NKUBA, J. 2010, 'Impact of Farmer Field Schools on Agricultural Productivity and Poverty in East Africa', International Food Policy Research Institute (IFPRI).

DEININGER, K. 1993, 'Cooperatives and the Breakup of Large Mechanised Farms: Theoretical Perspectives and Empirical Evidence', World Bank, Washington D.C.

DEVELTERE, P., POLLET, I. & WANYAMA, F. O. 2008, *Cooperating out of Poverty: the renaissance of the African cooperative movement*, ILO and the World Bank, Geneva.

DUVESKOG, D., FRIIS-HANSEN, E. & TAYLOR, E. W. 2011, 'Farmer Field Schools in Rural Kenya: A Transformative Learning Experience', *Journal of Development Studies*, 47, 1529–1544.

DUVESKOG, D. 2006, 'Theoretical perspectives of the learning process in Farmer Field Schools, with reference to East African experiences', Swedish University of Agricultural Sciences, Uppsala.

ELSON, D. & CAGATAY, N. 2000, 'The Social Content of Macroeconomic Policies', *World Development*, 28, 1347–1364.

FAIRTRADE FOUNDATION 2007, 'Gumutindo Coffee Cooperative Enterprise Ltd. Uganda Profile', Unpublished Document.

GOODWIN-GROEN, R., BRUETT, T. & LATORTUE, A. 2004, 'Uganda Microfinance Sector Effectiveness Review', The Consultative Group to Assist the Poor (CGAP) and World Bank, Washington D.C.

GUERIN, I. & PALIER, J. 2005, *Microfinance challenges: empowerment or disempowerment of the poor*, French Institute of Pondichery, Pondichery.

GUMUTINDO 2009, 'Growers' Lists', Unpublished Document, Gumutindo Cooperative Enterprise Ltd.

GUMUTINDO 2016, 'Growers' Lists', Unpublished Document, Gumutindo Cooperative Enterprise Ltd.

HIRSCHMAN, A. O. 1970, *Exit, Voice and Loyalty: Responses to Decline in Firms*, Harvard University Press, Cambridge, Mass.

HUSSI, P., MURPHY, J., LINDBERG, O. & BRENNEMAN, L. 1993, *Agricultural Workers and Their Contribution to Sustainable Agriculture and Rural Development*, World Bank, Washington D.C.

ICO 2011 and 2017, International Coffee Organisation, Available from: <http://www.ico.org/trade_statistics.asp>. [September 2011 and 2017].

ISHENGOMA, E. K. & KAPPEL, R. 2008, 'Business Constraints and Growth Potential of Micro and Small Manufacturing Enterprises in Uganda', Leibniz-Institut fur Globale und Regionale Studien.

JOUGHIN, J. & KJAER, A. M. 2010, 'The Politics of Agricultural Policy Reform: The Case of Uganda', *Forum for Development Studies*, 37, 61–78.

KABEER, N. 2008, 'Gender, Labour Markets and Poverty. An Overview', *Poverty in Focus: Special Issue on Gender Equality*, 13, 3–5.

KABEER, N. 2003, 'Gender inequality in educational outcomes: a household perspective', *Background paper prepared for the Education for All Global Monitoring Report 2003/4 Gender and Education for All: The Leap to Equality*, UNESCO, Paris.

KABEER, N. 1999, 'Resources, Agency, Achievements: Reflections on the Measurement of Women's Empowerment', *Development and Change*, 30, 435–464.

KAGUNDU, P. & PAVLOVA, O. 2007, 'Gender wage differentials in Uganda: Evidence from the Uganda National Household Survey', Andrew Young School of Policy, Atlanta.

KAPIRIRI, M. 2008, 'Baseline Study of the Status of the Cooperative Movement in Uganda, Dar es Salaam', International Labour Organization, Coop Africa, Dar es Salaam.

KATUNZE, M., KUTEESA, A., MIJUMBI, T. & MAHEBE, D. 2016, 'Uganda Warehousing Receipt System: Improving Market Performance and Productivity', *African Development Review*, 29, 135–146.

KYAMULESIRE, A. R. 1988, *A History of the Uganda Cooperative Movement 1913–1988*, Uganda Cooperative Alliance Ltd., Kampala.

KYAZZE, L. M. 2010, 'Cooperatives: The sleeping economic and social giants in Uganda', International Labour Office, Dar es Salaam.

LADEFOGED, P., GLICK, R. & CRIPER, C. 1972, *Language in Uganda*, Oxford University Press, London and New York.

LA FONTAINE, J. S. 1962, 'Gisu marriage and affinal relations', In: FORTES, M. (ed.) *Marriage in Tribal Societies*, Cambridge University Press, Cambridge.

LEONARD, M. 2012, 'Perspectives for cooperatives in Eastern Africa: the case of Uganda', Uganda Cooperative Alliance (UCA), Regional Conference "Perspectives for cooperatives in Eastern Africa, October 2012, Kampala, Uganda. Available from: <www.fes-uganda.org>. [9 May 2017].

LEE, S. E. 2010, 'The Ties Made in the Harvest: Nicaraguan Farm-worker Networks in Costa Rica's Agricultural Exports', *Journal of Agrarian Change*, 10, 510–536.

LEWIS, M. P., SIMONS, G. F. & FENNIG, C. D. 2009, *Ethnologue: Languages of the World*, SIL International, Dallas, TX.

MCELROY, M. B. 1990, 'The empirical content of Nash-bargained household behaviour', *Journal of Human Resources*, 24, 559–583.

NANNYONJO, J. 2013, 'Enabling agricultural cooperatives through public policy and the State: The case of Uganda', In a draft paper prepared for the UNRISD Conference. Available from: <http://www.unrisd.org/sse-nannyonjo>. [8 May 2017].

NUCAFE 2016, 'Farmers' Lists Eastern Uganda', National Union of Coffee Agribusinesses and Farm Enterprises. Unpublished document.

NUCAFE 2015, 'About NUCAFE', Available from: <www.nucafe.org>. [10 October 2015].

NUCAFE 2009a, 'The Farmer Ownership Model', National Union of Coffee Agribusinesses and Farm Enterprises, Kampala.

NUCAFE 2009b, 'Farmers' Lists Eastern Uganda', National Union of Coffee Agribusinesses and Farm Enterprises, Unpublished document.

NUCAFE 2009c, 'NUCAFE Training Materials Gender Equity for Coffee Farming Households', National Union of Coffee Agribusinesses and Farm Enterprises, Unpublished document.

OFFICE OF THE PRIME MINISTER 2009, 'Gender and Productivity Survey: Analytical Report', Republic of Uganda, Kampala.

OKELLO, L., & AHIKIRE, J. 2013, 'The cooperative movement and the challenge of development: a search for alternative wealth creation and citizen vitality approaches in Uganda', ActionAid, Centre for Basica Research, and The Uhuru Institute.

OWENS, T. & WOOD, A. 1997, 'Export-Oriented Industrialisation Through Primary Processing?', *World Development*, 25, 1453–1470.

PATTENDEN, J. 2010, 'A neoliberalisation of civil society? Self-help groups and the labouring class poor in rural South India', *Journal of Peasant Studies*, 37, 485–512.

PEOPLES, K. L. 2006, 'A Review of Current and Potential Practices for Warehouse Receipts in Uganda', USAID, Washington D.C.

POLLET, I. 2009, 'Cooperatives in Africa: The age of reconstruction - synthesis of a survey in nine African countries', *Series on the status of cooperative development in Africa*, Cooperative Facility for Africa, International Labour Organization, Geneva.

PONTE, S. 2002, 'Brewing a Bitter Cup: the Restructuring of Coffee Marketing in East Africa', *Journal of Agrarian Change*, 2, 248–272.

PONTE, S. & KAWUMA, F. 2003, 'Coffee Certification in Uganda: Feasibility Study (Final Report)', IS/EAFCA.

PORVALL, H. 1993, 'The Development of Co-operatives', World Bank, Washington D.C.

PURCELL, D. L. & ANDERSON, J. R. 1997, *Agricultural Extension and Research: Achievements and Problems in National Systems,* World Bank, Washington D.C.

RAZAVI, S. 2007, 'Liberalisation and the Debates on Women's Access to Land', *Third World Quarterly*, 28, 1479–1500.

RIBBINK, G., NYABUNTU, P. & KUMAR, S. 2005, 'Successful Supply Chains in Uganda: A study of three successful chains in the coffee, dried fruit and fresh vegetables sectors', DFID; ILO, Geneva and London.

SAUL, J. S. 1976, 'The Unsteady State: Uganda, Obote, and General Amin', *Review of African Political Economy*, 5, 12–38.

SEBAGGALA, R. 2007, 'Wage Determination and Gender: Wage Discrimination in Uganda', Economic Policy Research Centre (EPRC), Kampala, Uganda.

SEGUINO, S. & GROWN, C. 2006, 'Gender Equity and Globalization: Macroeconomic Policy for Developing Countries', *Journal of International Development*, 18, 1081–1104.

SEN, A. 1990, 'Gender and Co-operative Conflicts', In: TINKER, I. (ed.) *Persistent inequalities*, Oxford University Press, Oxford.

SINHA, S. 2006, *Building Visibility and Voice. Documenting Lesson and Learnings in Organising Home-based Workers*, United National Development Programme, New Delhi.

TILLY, C. 1998, *Durable inequality*, University of California Press, Ltd., Berkeley and Los Angeles, California.

TRIPP, A. M. 2004, 'Women's Movements, Customary Law, and Land Rights in Africa: The Case of Uganda', *African Studies Quarterly*, 7.

TRIPP, A. M. 2001, 'The Politics of Autonomy and Cooptation in Africa: The Case of the Ugandan Women's Movement', *The Journal of Modern African Studies*, 39, 101–128.

TRIPP, A. M. & KWESIGA, J. C. 2002, *The Women's Movement in Uganda: History, Challenges and Prospects*, Fountain Publishers Ltd. and African Books Collective Ltd., Kampala and Oxford.

UBOS 2010, 'Uganda National Household Survey 2009/10', Socio-economic module, Uganda National Bureau of Statistics, Kampala, Republic of Uganda.

UCA 2017, 'Uganda Cooperative Alliance Petitions', Available from: <www.parliament.co.ug>. [30 May 2017].

UCA 2016, 'Growers' Lists Eastern Region', Uganda Cooperative Alliance Eastern Regional Office, Unpublished Document.

UCA 2015, 'Annual Report for the year 2014/15', Uganda Cooperative Alliance, Available from: <www.uca.co.ug>. [8 May 2017].

UCA 2009a, 'Growers' Lists Eastern Region', Uganda Cooperative Alliance Eastern Regional Office, Unpublished Document.

UCA 2009b, 'UCA Draft Training Materials', Uganda Cooperative Alliance Eastern Regional Office, Unpublished Document.

UCDA 2009 and 2017, 'Annual and Monthly Reports, 1995–2017', Available from: <www.ugandacoffee.go.ug>, Uganda Coffee Development Authority, Kampala, Uganda.

UDRY, C. & CONLEY, T. G. 2004, 'Social networks in Ghana', Economic Growth Center, Yale University, New Haven, CT.

UOCG 2007, 'United Organic Coffee Growers Bylaws', United Organic Coffee Growers Ltd., Unpublished document.

WANYAMA, F. O., DEVELTERE, P. & POLLET, I. 2009, *Encountering the Evidence: Co-operatives and Poverty Reduction in Africa.*

WHITEHEAD, A. 2001, 'Trade, Trade Liberalization and Rural Poverty in Low-Income Africa: A Gendered Account', UNCTAD, Geneva.

WOMEN'S Land LINK AFRICA 2010, 'The Impact of National Land Policy and Land Reform on Women in Uganda', WLLA network.

YOUNG, M. C. 1976, *The Politics of Cultural Pluralism*, University of Wisconsin Press, Madison.

# 6 Corporate power in Uganda's coffee sector

Cooperatives that seek to achieve functional upgrading by moving into processing (milling and grading) and export face intense competition from the transnational buyers, processors, and exporters that dominate Uganda's coffee market, but so far, this fundamental difficulty for locally-owned value addition, which applies to much of Africa's export agriculture, has received limited attention by policy makers and international donors. Given the enormous asymmetry in access to capital, technology, knowledge, and markets between transnational corporations (TNCs) and cooperatives, small farmers are unlikely to seriously infringe upon corporate market power without benefiting from targeted state support and increased public investments into the processing infrastructure that is available to local producers. Notwithstanding the obvious asymmetry in economic power, government and donor support to cooperatives seems to rely on the notion that the ability of cooperatives to significantly improve their members' living standards depends primarily on ensuring better access to skills, markets, and financial services, while inequalities in asset ownership, access to production infrastructure, and political lobbying capacities seem to matter less. Thus, cooperative development programs generally advance a vision of inclusive rural development that is almost exclusively based on small farmers' improved production and marketing capacities, while external political-economic barriers to small farmers upgrading into higher value-added activities is deemphasized.

A brief introduction to the current market structure in Uganda's coffee sector shows that small farmers' pursuits to expand into processing and export face formidable barriers due to the high concentration of corporate power in processing and export. The micro-level data on the relations between TNCs and small farmers, which is presented and discussed in the remainder of this chapter, further indicates that TNCs use their significant market power to incentivize small farmers to improve their productive capacities and remain focused on production. Fostering pragmatically progressive relationships with small farmers, some transnational buyers offer transparent pricing and limited benefits, such as advice on production and harvesting techniques, as well as free crop transport for small farmers who are willing to commit to selling

*Figure 6.1* Kyagalanyi washing station in Gibuzale, Sironko District

unprocessed crops in regular quantities. Especially for farmers who are "too poor to organize" (*see* Chapter 5), such relationships are frequently the best option, because they cannot afford the delayed payments that often characterize bulk selling agreements with cooperatives. Small farmers' share of the ensuing "win-win" situation is small indeed: the benefits that arise from selling to TNCs narrowly surpass those from selling to local traders, who – albeit paying very low prices – often give advances and generally purchase cherries or parchment at any level of quality, but opportunities for functional upgrading are foregone.

So far, there is little data about the strategies of TNCs vis-à-vis cooperatives in African export agriculture. Using the example of Uganda's coffee sector, this chapter provides previously unavailable insights into the complex and asymmetric relations between TNCs and small farmers in a region and sector that is characterized by strong and economically viable cooperatives. Any comprehensive assessment of these relations needs to reflect the contested terrain that arises from the limited options available to asset-poor small farmers, the economic challenges of agricultural cooperatives that operate in buyer-driven value chains in which few TNCs have substantial market control, the relatively higher profit margins in processing and export as compared to production, and the focus of many African governments on improving the investment climate for transnational processors and exports, which (even if possibly unintendedly) reduces the chances for expanding locally-owned value addition. Out of this conflictual situation arises a picture of economic organization under adverse conditions: cooperatives face an uphill battle against first, the short-term solution offered to small farmers by TNCs (i.e. selling un- or semi-processed crops at relatively favorable conditions while forgoing the opportunity for functional upgrading), and second, a state that advances an agenda of FDI-based agricultural modernization that seemingly fails to balance much-needed investment promotion with strategic support to locally-owned value addition and domestic industrialization processes.

Across Africa, there is a lack of robust data on the strategies of transnational commodity buyers, processors and exporters vis-à-vis small farmers, and more research is needed to better understand the relations between TNCs and farmers and the prospective for social and economic change in Africa's export agricultural markets, which could potentially arise from this arena of conflictual yet interdependent interests. TNCs offer limited and carefully controlled information about their relations with small farmers[1]. The available narratives, generally told as PR stories that are directed primarily at consumers in importing countries, tend to paint a harmonious and de-politicized picture of a win-win situation that is created through the corporation's support to smallholder production. According to these strategically placed stories, the farmers benefit from training, advisory services, and sometimes improved access to inputs, thereby achieving higher prices for their produce. The corporation, based on its investments in improving smallholder productivity and quality, benefits from its first buying rights of increased volumes of higher-quality un- or primary-processed agricultural commodities. Some TNCs also invest into CSR projects that support local environmental or social projects, which generally benefit the communities of small farmers that have entered into stable sales relations with the corporation. In addition, contract farming (CF) schemes can ensure modestly higher prices for un- or primary-processed commodities, if they include support for farmers to improve quality and increase output.

The scholarly debate on large-scale land deals in countries and regions with a predominantly smallholder-based agricultural sector provides a growing wealth of analysis of corporate power in export agriculture, largely but not exclusively in Africa, and it tells a different story about the relations between TNCs and small producers. This literature is focused on the nature, scale, geography, and drivers of land deals and it offers insights into the political-economic dynamics of small farmers' displacements for the realization of large-scale, mostly agricultural projects by TNCs or other, usually foreign investors (*see*, for example Amanor 2012; Cotula 2012; Doss et al. 2014; Woodhouse 2012). Studies on the effects of large-scale agricultural and fisheries projects in terms of land and water grabs, associated human rights violations, and the lack of access to the expected economic benefits by farmers or fishers illuminate how a focus on capital-intensive economic transformation projects can lead to an increased concentration of corporate power while offering questionable solutions to pressing social-ecological problems (*see*, for example, Wedig 2018).

Land deals tend to force small farmers to transition from farming (and land ownership) to (overwhelmingly casual and agricultural) wage work, thereby impacting agrarian change processes. However, their contribution to the expansion of rural economic organization through the increase in the numbers of landless wage workers has so far been very limited at best. Trade unions or other forms of politicized economic organization among workers or farmers-cum-wageworkers (with the exception of cooperatives) remain virtually non-existent. Furthermore, a large-scale transition of small farmers to year-round agro-processing factory jobs – rather than limited post-harvest engagements – has so far not taken place in Africa. Due to the often extremely poor working conditions and the lack of prospects for significant higher-skilled job creation in agricultural processing, the positive socioeconomic effects that some governments and donors seem to expect from large-scale agricultural land deals are questionably (*see*, for example, Li 2011). The data from Uganda's coffee sector that were discussed in Chapter 2 confirm such doubts by illuminating the highly insecure working conditions in agricultural processing and the complex socioeconomic structures of informal (rural) labor markets that impede improvements in the position of labor.

Contract farming (CF) is arguably a more development-oriented way of engagement between large exporting companies (mainly TNCs) and small farmers than any corporate take-over of locally-owned land (with or without reimbursements to farmers). CF is largely promoted as an instrument for inclusive rural development – a 'partnership for growth' – by African governments and donors (*see*, for example, various World Bank and FAO supported agricultural development programs), because it can improve the participating farmers' access to agricultural inputs, extension services, and credit[2], and it can thus lead to significantly higher incomes of contract farmers compared to other farmers (da Silva 2005; Glover 1990; Eaton and

Shepherd 2001; Zimny 2009). The win-win notion underlying CF schemes is based on the idea of higher supply standards that help farmers achieve higher prices and processors/exporters to secure higher and more stable volumes of increased-quality commodities.

However, various studies on CF schemes have pointed to the creation and reinforcement of structural inequalities between farmers and contractors, despite the possibility of realizing higher incomes for participating farmers (Glover and Kusterer 1990; Grosh 1994; Little and Watts 1994; Oya 2012; Reardon and Barrett 2000). For example, contractors have multiple opportunities to default on the contract if they determine the quality supplied by the farmer to be insufficient. The contracting company is not responsible for the production process and while it stands to lose if farmers divert credits to other uses and thereby reduce the quantity and/or quality of the yields that the company was expecting to buy, the farmers generally have a strong incentive not to do so. However, if the harvest fails or production quality is lower than expected despite the farmers having taken out loans to pay for inputs, advisory services, and technology, it is solely the farmer who carries the costs. As opposed to the contracting company, these costs are generally serious and potentially life-threatening to the businesses and in many cases the livelihoods of small farmers and their dependents.

The limited benefits for farmers in CF reflect the primary function of such schemes: a vertical integration strategy of large buyers that helps to ensure access to increased volumes of crops at higher quality while minimizing production, asset, and labor risks – including the possibility of conflicts with a unionized agricultural labor force. (Oya 2012). At the same time, the contracted farmers loose authority about production decisions to the processor (*ibid.*), which creates a structural change within the value chain that intensify and reinforce existing inequalities. CF schemes *de facto* increase the concentration of corporate power in agricultural export markets, because TNCs fill a gap that was created by neoliberal reforms: The provision of inputs, advisory services, and new technologies, now paid for by farmers through loans, contributes to increased production and improved quality and can open up new markets for small producers. State-run marketing boards were meant to provide such services as part of their mandate to protect farmers' interests. They often failed to do so effectively or at all, but they were, at least in principle, accountable to the population. Private companies with significant market control may exploit their near-monopolistic power and fail to honor contractual obligations without any higher-ranking mechanisms in place that could effectively enforce such contracts.

There may also be a bias against smallholders in contract farming schemes, because it is more difficult for them to meet buyer requirements as compared to medium or large-scale farmers (Fold 2008). CF is thus unlikely to be a superior instrument for *inclusive* rural development; instead, it may create a new form of stratification between farmers who can and those who cannot match the land, personnel, and technical requirements of contracting companies. It should be noted here that cooperatives are only open to farmers who own land *and* can afford the financial costs of membership, (mainly registration fees, but sometimes also minimum payments to saving groups). Also, cooperative members must have the ability to bridge the time between harvest and bulk sales if the cooperative is unable to offer advance payments. However, as Chapter 5 showed, farmers can expect to receive significant and relatively fast material and immaterial support from membership in cooperatives, which can help to overcome initially barriers to entry. A key difference between CF and cooperatives – apart from the obvious discrepancy between economic goals – is the emphasis of cooperatives on the pooling of resources and the creation of political lobbying activities to strengthen members' structural bargaining position vis-à-vis stronger economic actors and the state.

Based on his review of the available case studies and quantitative data, Oya (2012) suggests that CF only accounts for a small share of agricultural production in African export agriculture[3]. Surely, the globalization of agribusiness has shifted much of the potential for value-addition into processing, packing, trading, transport, branding, and distribution, which has made any investments in raw commodity production less attractive (Gibbon and Ponte 2005). Regarding the coffee sector, it is also noteworthy that the nature of coffee production can in some geographical contexts provide incentives for TNCs to buy from small farmers, instead of establishing CF schemes. First, Arabica coffee[4] only grows well within monocropping systems if sun-resistant hybrids are used, because monocropping exposes the trees to the sun, which is not the case in traditional shrub cultivation. While sun-resistant hybrids are widely available and apparently do not reduce product quality, sun cultivation has significant negative effects on soil quality, watering needs, and local biodiversity, which may increase production-related costs even if the longer-term costs of environmental degradation are not (yet) internalized. Thus, mechanization in coffee production is associated with greater costs than in other crops, such as cereals. Second, it takes several years for coffee trees to mature, which can be an incentive to buy from existing small farms, and third, many of the regions where Arabica coffee grows well are not easily suitable for plantations due to mountainous terrain.

Despite the relatively small role played by CF in African export agriculture, especially in the coffee sector, the brief discussion of the major goals and effects of such schemes helped to illuminate two essential aspects of the economic framework conditions under which cooperatives operate. First, there is a huge power asymmetry between small producers and large, mainly transnational buyers and processors, even in arrangements that are deemed to be "partnerships for growth" by international donors and some African governments, and there are no legal frameworks that effectively balance this asymmetry. Second, current relations between small farmers and large commodity trading companies are likely to 'lock' farmers in a position at the bottom of the value chain, because they provide services for producers to improve their production processes *in direct exchange* for a commitment to sell their produce in an un- or primary-processed state. Thus, the win-win notion underlying CF depends on disregarding the cooperative option: large processors/traders gain control over production decisions without carrying the costs in case of production failures, while producers gain access to more reliable markets, inputs, and credits in exchange for remaining focused on the production of un- or primary-processed commodities.

The data presented in the next section includes an outline of the concentration of corporate power in Uganda's coffee sector as well as fresh evidence about TNCs' relations with small farmers. The data were collected through participatory observation and unstructured interviews in coffee processing plants in Eastern Uganda's coffee sector, semi-structured interviews with operational managers in the local subsidiaries of transnational commodity buyers and processors, as well as semi-structured interviews with local processors, and an analysis of the largest recent TNC "engagement project", which is implemented by Neumann Kaffee Gruppe (NKG), one of Uganda's leading transnational coffee exporters. The project builds direct relations with small farmers by creating cooperative-like organizational structures. While the discussion below can only provide first insights into a complex subject that is evolving dynamically under the current drive by donors and African governments to mobilize private investment for agro-industrial development[5], I hope that it will reinvigorate a debate about political and economic power asymmetries at a time when the concentration of global corporate power is consolidating and inequality is intensifying.

## 6.1 The concentration of corporate power

The extent of market control over downstream activities by a small number of TNCs in Uganda's coffee sector has been high since the mid-1990s, when neoliberal reforms opened the country's agricultural markets to international competition and ended the trading monopoly of state-subsidized cooperatives. The figures on market shares by the largest exporting companies since the mid-1990s indicate substantial and by now consolidated corporate power in Uganda's coffee export market (*see* Table 6.1). A CR4 (the market share of the top four companies) that exceeds 40 percent is generally considered an oligopoly, which is associated with declining competitiveness and increasing spreads between what consumers pay and what producers make from their produce. In more than two decades, the CR4 in Uganda's coffee market was continuously above 40 percent, mostly remained above 45 percent, and sometimes rose to over 60 percent (UCDA annual and monthly reports, 1995–2017). The early 2010s saw a slight downward trend that brought the CR4 to 40.91 in 2013/14, but by 2017, it had risen again to 51.14 percent (*see* Table 6.1). For the earlier years of

*Table 6.1* Market share by exporting company in Uganda's coffee sector

| *Year* | *Top four coffee exporting companies (fifth added in parentheses)* | *CR4* | *Share of top 5 exporters* |
|---|---|---|---|
| Dec. 2017 | Ugacof (U) Ltd; Kyagalanyi Coffee Ltd (TNC, part of Volcafe); Ideal Quality Commodities (U) Ltd; Ibero (U) Ltd (TNC - Neuman Kaffee Gruppe); (Olam (U) Ltd) (TNC) | **51.14** | 58.26 |
| 2015/16 | Ugacof (U) Ltd; Kyagalanyi Coffee Ltd; Olam (U) Ltd; Ideal Quality Commodities (U); (Ibero (U) Ltd) | **47.73** | 54.57 |
| 2014/15 | Ugacof (U) Ltd; Kyagalanyi Coffee Ltd; Kawacom (U) Ltd; Olam (U) Ltd; (Ibero (U) Ltd) | **45.25** | 52.37 |
| 2013/14 | Ugacof (U) Ltd; Kyagalanyi Cofee Ltd; Olam (U) Ltd; Export Trading Company; (Kawacom (U) Ltd) (TNC - ECOM) | **40.91** | 47.13 |
| 2010/11 | Ugacof (U) Ltd; Kyagalanyi Coffee Ltd; Kawacom (U) Ltd; Olam (U) Ltd; (Savannah Commodities) | **45.58** | 52.72 |
| 2004/5 | Kawacom (U) Ltd; Ugacof (U) Ltd; Olam (U) Ltd; Kyagalanyi Coffee Ltd; (Great Lakes Ltd) | **61.14** | 68.02 |

Sources: UCDA (2018; 2016; 2015; 2011; 2008; 2005; 2001) and Daviron & Ponte (2005).

1996/7 to 2001/2, Daviron & Ponte (2005, p. 206) note a similar concentration of corporate power, with market shares of the top five companies between 46.1 and 54.7 percent.

Furthermore, the composition of the CR4 reveals that a small number of TNCs started to dominate processing and export shortly after the liberalization of agricultural markets, and that this group of firms has remained essentially unchanged since. Thus, the majority of the top coffee exporters in Uganda have been TNCs since the mid-1990s, with a TNC share of total coffee exports that has stayed roughly between 35 and 45 percent and few signs of a turnaround in favor of (larger) local or regional firms (*see* Table 6.1 and Daviron & Ponte 2005; UCDA annual and monthly reports, 1995–2017). Cooperatives, despite the official rhetoric by donors, which promotes them as a 'win-win' instrument of rural development and the even more ambitious government rhetoric that describe them as a key driver of national prosperity and unity, only control a negligibly small percentage of total coffee exports. Gumutindo, the Eastern Ugandan coffee cooperatives discussed in Chapter 5 is the only cooperative that regularly appears in the available market data (which cover the first 10 to 15 largest exporters) and its market share has never risen above 0.3 percent (UCDA annual and monthly reports, 1997–2017).

Coffee production remains dominated by small farmers in Uganda, as it does across Africa. Indeed, around 80 percent of production worldwide comes from small farms (Zimny 2009, p.26). The market power of TNCs concentrates on downstream activities, from primary- and secondary-processing and exporting to roasting, and to retail. Value-adding activities that take place inside producer countries are generally limited to primary-processing (washing and pulping or drying) and secondary-processing (milling and grading). Roasting, as well as retail, still almost exclusively takes place in importing countries. The largest profits within the value chain are probably made within the roasting industry, which provides insufficient information to create figures, but the available data indicate that profits are higher than in production, processing, and trading (Daviron & Ponte 2005; interviews with producers and exporters).

The high revenues achieved by roasters are worth mentioning here, because they provide information about the distribution of profits within the entire coffee value chain, thereby drawing attention to economic opportunities for producers beyond secondary-processing and export. Large processors/exporters who operate within producer countries, many of them TNCs, are major competitors for producers who seek to expand into downstream activities. The processors/traders purchase wet or dry cherries (unprocessed coffee) or primary-processed beans (parchment) and process these into green beans for export. They buy either from local traders, cooperatives, or directly at the farm gate. Improving the production processes of small farmers is in their interest, because they rely on the supply of large and stable volumes of high-quality coffee. Functional upgrading by small farmers, however, cannot reasonably be in their interest and some TNCs seem to pursue aggressive strategies vis-à-vis cooperatives that seek to enter secondary-processing and export.

Broadening the focus onto the distribution of profits in the entire, global value chain is also important to address a somewhat misleading rhetoric by some government officials and TNCs' representatives, which points to the higher profits for small farmers as compared to traders, processors, and exporters. An example is a recent statement by Edmond Kananura, director of the Uganda Coffee Development Authority (UCDA) that 'Nearly 80 percent of all the value/money in coffee is taken by the farmer. The traders, middle men, the processors, and other involved, fight for the 20 per cent' (Uganda Electronic Single Window 2018). The potentially implicit notion that processors/exporters scramble for survival while small producers can live comfortably off their farms if they produce and sell high-quality unprocessed commodities creates a highly misleading picture of farmers' living standards and ignores the transformative power of an agricultural development strategy that envisions local producers entering higher value-added activities.

It also implicitly communicates that large processors and traders make a significant contribution to the country's comparative advantage in coffee, and that their profit margins are therefore worthy of state protection, even in the face of large numbers of struggling small farmers. However, TNCs' investments in processing facilities and supporting infrastructure, such as feeder roads, have so far not significantly benefited producers. Across Africa, the high concentration of transnational corporate power in value chains of agricultural commodities has led to increased discrepancies between world and domestic prices, and reduced benefits for producer countries (Zimny 2009). As Zimny (p. 30–31) notes: 'The share of revenues of major coffee producing countries in the retail price at destination declined from one third in the early 1990s to 10 percent in 2002, while the sales of coffee doubled'. The level of inequality in the distribution of profits has not been reversed since the early 2000s, and there are no indications that this is about to change.

The emphasis, in official rhetoric, on the tight profit margins of processors and traders can also be used to legitimize a policy focus on improved investment conditions for large and mainly transnational investors without a simultaneous transformative agenda that supports and protects the large-scale entry of farmers and local firms into secondary-processing and export. For example, Uganda's National Development Plan (NDP) II and the Agricultural Strategic Sector Plan (ASSP) 2015/16–2019/20 both formulate clear goals for increasing value addition for cooperatives, but these are almost entirely limited to primary-processing and stop short of promoting the integration of cooperatives into higher value-added processing and export as well as roasting and retail in domestic markets (GoU 2015; MAAIF 2016). Thus, public support to cooperatives focuses on improving production, postharvest handling and quality control, bulking and marketing, as well as corporate governance and business management, but there seems to be no clear strategy in these policies to link agricultural cooperatives to cooperatives in other economic sectors or to support agricultural cooperatives' move into higher value-added activities.

## 6.2 Corporate strategies vis-à-vis small producers

This section provides fresh evidence about TNCs' relations with small farmers in Uganda's coffee sector. The discussion is based on qualitative data that were collected through participatory observation and unstructured interviews in coffee processing plants in Eastern Uganda, as well as semi-structured interviews with operational managers in the Ugandan subsidiaries of transnational commodity buyers, and with local processors and exporters. The results illuminate how TNCs seek to ensure a stable supply of primary-processed coffee from small farms by creating organizational structures that seem to emulate those of cooperatives, but neither provide comparable services nor pursue structural changes in the relations between producers and processors/exporters. Such strategies, similar to contract farming schemes, seek to protect the status quo of a highly unequal distribution of risks, but are promoted as a 'triple win', with benefits for small farmers (productivity increases, access to markets), transnational processors/exporters (higher-quality and more stable supply) and the country at large (increased competitiveness of the country's coffee production).

The losses for small farmers (no functional upgrading into higher value-added activities) and the country (large share of profits from coffee exports repatriated to shareholders abroad) are concealed.

In a similar vein, an analysis of the largest recent TNC project to support small coffee farmers in Uganda, implemented by the *Hans R. Neumann Stiftung* or foundation of Neumann Kaffee Gruppe (NKG), illuminates strategies of co-option that provide direct, and in this case substantial, benefits for participating farmers, while also reshaping the cooperative ideal into a de-politicized vision of economic organization. While the promotion of economically viable social enterprises is welcome from an inclusive rural development perspective, it is questionable what developmental outcomes are to be expected from the (almost entirely donor-financed) creation of cooperative structures that seem to replicate existing, locally-grown cooperatives, but fail to build any capacities for political advocacy to represent farmers' interests vis-à-vis stronger economic actors and the state. The proven effects of the project's activities center on the achievement of increased production output and improved quality, including more extensive primary-processing by small farmers, and these effects undoubtedly benefit small farmers directly. However, the project entirely ignores the history and current revival of Uganda's long and politically influential cooperative movement and makes no attempt to connect its activities in the creation of new organizations with existing cooperative structures. Instead, the creation of a parallel apex organization seems to introduce and promote business-like competition between small farmers' organizations, despite utilizing a rhetoric that heavily borrows from the realms of the social and solidarity economy.

### *Corporate farmers' groups*

As discussed in Chapter 5, many small producers in Uganda's coffee sector today are too poor to organize. Persistently high poverty rates due to small and decreasing on-average land holdings, a still severely limited access to capital and insufficient access to technology and training, low wages in agricultural employment and poor working conditions in other survivalist economic activities, as well as a lack of social security mean that the small investments that are required to become a cooperative member present a serious entry barrier to economic organization among farmers. Such small investments include registration fees for primary cooperatives, contributions to credit and saving groups, and the ability to bridge the time between harvest and bulk sales in cases when a cooperative cannot offer advances. The immediate and generally reliable payments by TNCs are, therefore, an incentive for growers to sell unprocessed cherries or primary-processed beans and forego opportunities for further value addition.

In Eastern Uganda, Kyagalanyi, a company that belongs to the Volcafe division of EDF&MAN, has been one of the largest exporters of Ugandan coffee since the liberalization of the country's agricultural markets in 1990.[6]

The company has continuously expanded its competitive advantage by taking control of increasing shares of the existing processing infrastructure. During the first phase of data collection for this book, in 2009, Kyagalanyi had bought or rented most larger primary-processing stations (so-called washing stations) in the Arabica-growing area on the slopes of Mt. Elgon, which stretches across five Ugandan districts (*see* Chapter 5 for a description of the area). All of these processing stations had previously been owned by cooperatives and were thus perceived as semi-public, community-owned infrastructure. The company had also rented a large coffee processing factory in Mbale municipality from the formerly monopolistic Buganda Cooperative Union (BCU), which for years had been unable to operate it due to a lack of capital. Lastly, the corporation was in the process of building new primary-processing stations in the area. The purchase and rental of most of the assets that were formerly owned by cooperatives was widely seen as controversial by farmers.

Like other exporters, Kyagalanyi sometimes struggles to secure a regular supply of sufficient volumes of high-quality cherries or parchment to enable it to fulfill longer-term contracts with roasters. Given the costs and risks associated with a heavy reliance on local traders, the corporation has established pragmatically progressive relations with small producers, which allows it to improve its supply without taking on responsibility for production and labor processes. As part of these relations, the corporation supports productivity increases and quality improvement by providing short trainings and advisory sessions on cultivation and harvesting techniques. According to farmers, these services are offered once or twice a year, usually in one-day field visits by officers from the Kyagalanyi headquarters in Mbale municipality. The company also offers free transport of parchment or cherries from some of the more accessible villages to its primary-processing field stations. During the harvest period, farmers from other, more remote villages can frequently be seen carrying their cherries or parchment in large bags on their heads through the rugged terrain of the Mt. Elgon area.

Despite these moderate benefits, small farmers in Eastern Uganda, as elsewhere, are unlikely to secure even a modest standard of living for themselves and their dependents on the basis of selling un- or primary-processed commodities. Throughout the Mt. Elgon area, producers who sell to Kyagalanyi emphasize that they have inadequate access to cash to cover basic household needs prior and during the harvesting season and are therefore not able to cope with the delay in payments caused by bulk sales through a cooperative, even though they recognize the benefits of economic organization. As Bernard Nandege, a non-organized farmer from Bukigai village, explained, many farmers who join cooperatives clearly know that they cannot afford to do so, but hope to secure access to training or agricultural tools such as hand pulping machines, before they are forced to leave because they are unable to contribute to bulk sales. For such farmers, selling to Kyagalanyi or other TNCs is less a choice than a last resort. While many non-organized farmers voice critique of cooperatives, interviews frequently unveiled that the decision to sell raw coffee to a company was taken only after a failed attempt to participate in bulk-selling arrangements through a cooperative.

Among those farmers who sell to Kyagalanyi, many note their appreciation of the corporation's transparent price policies and contrast this with their past experiences of payment delays within BCU, the formerly monopolistic coffee cooperative union in Eastern Uganda. At the beginning of the harvesting season, Kyagalanyi publishes its buying price at its storage facilities and primary-processing field stations throughout the area, visible for everyone. On this basis, growers are able to calculate their expected incomes, which is hardly possible when selling to local traders who negotiate their buying price on a daily basis and often depress prices within a particular locality by targeting farmers at times when they need immediate access to cash. This may, for example, include the need to pay school fees or cover medical, wedding, or burial expenses; something that is made possible by the intimate knowledge that local traders have of the farms they buy from. The unethical business strategies of local traders (for a detailed analysis, *see* Wiegratz 2016) frequently lead to the sale of wet cherries or coffee flowers. Given the uncertainty about the quality and in the case of flowers the additional risk of harvest failure, the price thus achieved by farmers is very low. Kyagalanyi, as well as other TNCs, generally do not seem to be involved in such practices, although many TNCs regularly buy from local traders.

Despite Kyagalanyi's pragmatically progressive relationship with small farmers, the company has faced widespread criticism by farmers for its takeover of the local and formally farmer-owned processing infrastructure in Eastern Uganda. Purchases through local traders who are known for unethical business practices, and the relatively low, albeit not rock-bottom prices paid for un- or primary-processed produce added to farmers frustration, voiced during interviews and informal gatherings, about the company's lack of investment in local development. The company responded by starting to actively promote the notion of cooperation and partnership with farmers through the establishment of so-called "farmers' groups" that resemble cooperatives in many ways. The groups, organized with the goal to establish new and maintain existing relations with producers who supply raw or primary-processed coffee, have 25 to 30 producers, as do primary cooperative societies. The company's fieldworkers promote membership in these groups in a language that is reminiscent of that used by cooperative leaders, using a terminology of strength through unity and cooperation, local development through partnership, and pride in high-quality products.

Unsurprisingly, Kyagalanyi's farmers' groups have none of the organizational functions of a cooperative union. They promote no changes to the existing relations between producers and buyers, but rephrase these in a language of cooperation and formalize them through the registration of groups, while setting the conditions for this formalization without consultation from farmers. Access to extension services for group members is free, but provision is limited to occasional technical trainings for tree pruning and harvesting. Group membership also facilitates access to free transport of produce. Most farmers were unsure whether the groups have any additional purpose, and there were some who seemed to be unclear about the exact differences between primary cooperatives and Kyagalanyi's farmers' groups. The decision of many farmers to enter these groups was overwhelmingly economic. In contrast, the data presented in Chapter 5 pointed to the relatively significant role played by non-material benefits for farmers' positive attitudes towards cooperatives.

In sum, farmers who sell to Kyagalanyi or any other TNC that buys coffee in Eastern Uganda are not supported to improve their processing or business skills, nor do they benefit from access to financial services. In the case of Kyagalanyi, relations between the company and growers, as experienced by both sides, are generally friendly, but just as in any other sales agreements for unprocessed coffee, small farmers are effectively locked at the bottom of the value chain, selling their product when its value is lowest. This is a serious limitation to opportunities for functional upgrading, which certainly exist in Eastern Uganda's coffee growing area (*see*, for example, Ribbink et al. 2005; Gowa 2001).

The creation of farmers' groups by large processing companies is in many ways comparable to a 'light' form of CF schemes. The company, although not a contractor in the strict sense, provides services to farmers in exchange for exclusive buying rights for their un- or primary-processed produce and without assuming responsibility in case of harvest failure. Fieldworkers from the company, who provide services to the group, described their role as a supervisory one, trying to ensure that the expected output volumes were produced and sold to the company. The group members frequently talked of 'pressure' to stick to the arrangement they entered with the company, although in the absence of credit services for the groups, there was in fact little the company could do in case of default by a farmer[7].

Overall, few farmers explained the often problematic reputation of large processors/exporters with the latter's strategies to incentivize sales of un- or primary-processed coffee. One reason for the problematic reputation of transnational or other non-African corporations in Uganda is the country's tension-laden historical relationship with foreign (largely South Asian) investors, but some TNCs, like Kyagalanyi, reduce the likelihood of adverse attitudes on these grounds by creating the impression of being a domestic company. This is achieved, for example, by choosing a local name and promoting a founding narrative that excludes any mention of the TNC that the company belongs to. Another well-known reason for the problematic reputation of large foreign investors is the still-heavy reliance of TNCs on local traders, who are known for their unethical business practices (Wiegratz 2016). However, the data on cooperatives' training services, discussed in the

Chapter 5, also points to a growing awareness of TNCs' position and role in the global coffee value chain, which may contribute to distrust. In particular Gumutindo, but to some extent also UCA, provide trainings that go well beyond the technical and business skills and explicitly deal with the distribution of profits and the barriers for small farmers to enter higher value-added activities.

### *Corporate creation of cooperative enterprises*

Throughout rural Africa, different TNCs are engaged in CSR projects that are on the one hand described as instruments of inclusive rural and agricultural development by the companies that design and/or implement them, and are on the other hand criticized by NGOs and some scholars as fig leaves or strategies of co-option vis-a-vis farmers' attempts to establish a social and solidarity economy. The recent project 'Building Coffee Farmers' Alliances in Uganda', designed and implemented by the *Hanns R. Neumann Stiftung* (HRNS), the foundation of the TNC Neumann Kaffee Gruppe (NKG), is a fitting example.[8] Its explicit focus on building a large, two-tiered farmers' organization – the Coffee Farmers Alliance Uganda (CFAU) – and a national apex organization for coffee farmers is particularly noteworthy, because it exposes a corporate strategy of engagement with small farmers that promotes economic organization as an instrument of *limited* redistribution, but blatantly ignores the country's own growing, politically influential, and often economically viable cooperative movement. The farmers' organizations that are built by this project are an exact equivalent of existing, locally-developed structures of economic organization, except for the remarkable difference that they do not engage in political advocacy to represent the interests of small producers.

The project consists of two initiatives that offer direct support for the development of farmers' organizations during four years (from 2009 to 2014 and from 2012 to 2016), first in a Robusta coffee growing area, then in an Arabica coffee growing area.[9] Funding, which seems to extend beyond the initial 4-year phase for organizational development, is provided by different international donors, including bi- and multilateral organizations and private foundations, as well as private companies, mainly roasters and retailers from coffee-importing countries.[10] In-kind support is provided from the Uganda Coffee Development Authority (UCDA). An extensive pilot project was implemented as a test case: The Kaweri Coffee Farmers' Support Project (KCFSP), which included setting up the 2,500-ha large Kaweri Coffee Plantation Ltd. in Mubende District to produce Robusta. The EU-funded, $10 million project aimed at facilitating the organization of up to 20,000 farmers into independent production and processing units that would sell sustainably-sourced specialty coffee to exporters (Greenhalgh & Kitching, 2005).

The Coffee Farmers Alliance Uganda (CFAU) project aims to increase small farmers' returns by increasing coffee production, improving quality, and expanding value addition up to the hulling stage and opening access to new markets. (Note that the project documents refer to 'farmers' improved access to export markets', meaning higher rates of direct sales of un- or primary-processed coffee to processors/exporters, but not the ability of farmers to export secondary-processed coffee themselves.) Additional, interlinked project objectives include improvements in living standards (livelihood) and greater gender equality. The key strategy of the project is organizational development: the farmers' organizations that were created, with an apex body called the Uganda Coffee Farmers' Alliance (UCFA) as an umbrella, form the basis and institutional framework for all project activities, and the sustainability of the project, once donor funding has ended, depends on the economic viability and organizational functionality of the farmers' organizations and the UCFA (Techel & Wanda 2014).

The project's activities concentrate on the following main themes: i) technical advice/extension services, ii) value addition and marketing, iii) market linkages to buyers, iv) access to finance and farm inputs, and v) linkages with other service providers. Technical advice and extension services are delivered through farmer field schools with demonstration plots where farmers can learn techniques (based on the Good Agricultural Practices approach) to increase the quantity and improve the quality of their coffee yields. Increased value addition, marketing, and market linkages to buyers are supported through capacity-building trainings for decision-making and management skills of individual farmers. The two-tiered farmers' organization, consisting of clusters of Producer Organizations (POs) at the village level and Depot Committee (DC) companies at the sub-regional level, facilitate the delivery of services to lower the production and marketing costs of farmers and increase their capacities for bulk selling. Access to finance and farm inputs and linkages with other service providers are promoted through the apex body UCFA.

The organizational structure created by the HRNS foundation mirrors that of Uganda's cooperative movement, except for the key difference in the design of the apex body UCFA, which has no objective or capacities for political advocacy. The UCFA is exclusively focused on strengthening farmers' marketing capacities by establishing partnerships with external service providers, such as mobile payment facilities, banks, and software developers for e-services in storage, marketing, and sales. At the local (first) and sub-regional (second) organizational level, functions are almost identical. The POs form the first level for the bulking of coffee and the platform for training on agricultural practices for individual farmers. Several POs form a cluster, which are served by one Farmer Field School for trainings and advisory sessions. A collection of 20–30 POs form a so-called DC company and all DC companies are under the umbrella of the UCFA. The DCs form the aggregate level for bulking, primary-processing, and marketing to exporters. Each DC company has a board that is supported by a legal, a financial, and a marketing committee, as well as a manager, an extension officer, and several Farmer Field School facilitators.

In 2017, the HRNS foundation stated that the overall CFAU project reached 53,000 farmers who are organized in 1,668 farmer groups. The major benefits for these farmers were agricultural skills trainings that are facilitated by Farmer Field Schools, improved transport, storage, and marketing capacities, and better access to credit (HRNS 2017). The detailed benefits of UCFA membership, as reported by UCFA itself, by media articles and by donors, include a mobile money service, a financial service provider, and a software developer to lower farmer transaction costs and improve the transparency of sales.

At the output level, the foundation reports the widespread adoption of mainly low-cost good agricultural practices among participating farmers, substantial yield increases, (measured by the average amount of dry cherry per tree and year), improved quality due to better harvesting and post-harvesting practices, greater efficiency in transport and storage through the pooling of resources, lower administrative costs through the introduction of electronic registration, payment, and tracking services, and an increase, albeit small, in the coffee marketed by the DC companies as FAQ (hulled beans at 'Fair Average Quality') to exporters (*ibid.*; Techel & Wanda 2014). As a result, the foundation reports price increase achieved by farmers of up to 8 percent and improved living stands, estimated on the basis of assets acquired by households since the project start – although it notes that it cannot distinguish the effects of its own project on living standards with those of other rural poverty reduction programs that are active in the same areas (HRNS 2017).

There is little doubt that the project is having positive effects on yield growth and the quality of unprocessed coffee by participating farmers, despite several points of caution with regard to the results claimed by the foundation. These include the timing of the baseline study (Loisa 2011), the selection of participating farmers, the low objectives for living standards improvements, and the apparent lack of consultation with existing cooperative organizations in Uganda's coffee sector. First, the baseline study for at least one of the two project areas was conducted during a drought, meaning that the income levels and other "quality of life" metrics[11] defined as the baseline are likely to be below-average. Second, none of the participating farmers were previously organized in cooperatives (*ibid.*), thus allowing for near-guaranteed success in achieving basic value addition targets. Third, the objectives for improvements in living standards are low in comparison to other export agriculture projects that are funded by international donors, with farmers' ability to rise above the international poverty line after 8 years noted as a key objective. Furthermore, the term 'livelihood improvements' that is used in project documents (rather than the more tangible living standards) remains poorly defined, with some unclarity about the reasons for measured changes in asset ownership (higher earnings, improved access to credit, selection bias, other projects, etc.).

Finally, the reported increases in farmer incomes are mostly due to increased production, but not value addition. The DC companies originally aimed to process the coffee delivered by POs to FAQ and also grade the coffee to produce ready-for-export green beans. However, at the time of writing, none of the DC companies is able to meet the standards of exporters for grading (Techel & Wanda 2014; HRNS 2017) and due to competition with local traders who buy any-quality cherries at the farm gate, the quantities received that meet the companies' standards for hulling remain low. As a result, the main tasks of DC companies had become bulking and limited quality control of primary-processed coffee.

The key constraints of the project, however, concern its effects on the broader potential for the achievement of structural changes, as envisioned by cooperatives, in Ugandan export agriculture. These effects are impossible to measure precisely, but some of the key characteristics of the farmers' organization and apex body that were created by the TNCs' foundation allow observations about how such projects can reshape the cooperative movement that this book has discussed.

Thus, the UCFA, although called an apex body, is a marketing organization without the social motivations and political advocacy capacities of the UCA or the Uganda National Farmers' Federation (UCFA 2017). Furthermore, the democratic structures that are part of secondary- and primary-level cooperative societies only partially apply to the farmer organization created by the HRNS foundation. In a cooperative, members (or member-appointed committees) vote to establish the balance between member returns and working capital to grow the cooperative. In the CFAU's design, however, DC companies appear to be able to make the choice unilaterally and there have already been complaints of self-serving behavior and corruption against DC management.

It is also noteworthy that the terminology used by the project emulates that of social and political movements with transformative goals. Regarding the goal to develop its own farmer organizations, the foundation notes: "To access key services and be able to compete in markets, farmers have to move toward collective action in the form of farmer organizations. The problem is that these farmers, in particular women, usually lack the skills and resources to develop strong farmer organizations that can provide the services required by their members." (HRNS 2017). The CFAU project therefore aims to build "the technical and management capacities of individual farmers and also the leadership of farmer organizations", because "As members of these organizations, farmers can free themselves from dependencies and are no longer held captive to commercial relationships." (*ibid.*) It remains unclear in how far small farmers become independent of commercial relationships, and why that is a good thing, by organizing and selling through the foundation's limited liability companies.

Finally, the evaluation of the CFAU project notes that the UCFA is heavily donor dependent, with 75 percent of resources coming from external sources. It is estimated that the UCFA would need to more than double its trade volume (from 1,600 tons to 4,000 tons) to become financially sustainable (Techel & Wanda 2014). In their evaluation, Techel & Wanda (2014, p. 51) also suggest that DC companies, in order to become more competitive, must gain farmers' trust, and "pay substantially higher prices", which requires increased operating efficiency and an expansion of value addition. In this context, it is noteworthy that the UCFA seems to suffer from similar shortcomings than other cooperatives that were established by farmers without extensive external guidance and funding. The evaluation concludes that the functionality of Depot Committees, which were described as the "keystone" of the project's sustainability, is hindered by poor governance, a lack of a financial strategy, a lack of managerial capacity, inefficient bulking processes, and poor communication between UCFA and POs (Techel & Wanda 2014). Thus, there is little indication that limited liability companies are necessarily better managed than member-based (one-member-one-vote) cooperative enterprises.

Transnational exporters have significant market control, but they also have tight profit margins, and in the context of global value chains, a direct involvement in production has become less and less attractive for them (Daviron and Ponte 2005; Greenhalgh & Kitching 2005). Thus, TNCs increasingly depend on steady and good-quality supply of raw or primary-processed coffee from local producers and traders. Rural development projects such as the one discussed above are therefore a reminder that CSR has initiatives are not isolated from the corporation's core business interests; instead, they tend to be highly-integrated, long-term investments based on shared value creation (company and local community), which helps to build and protect an ethical reputation that may be needed to remain profitable in the future.

Thus, initiatives such as the "Building Coffee Farmers Alliances in Uganda" project should be understood as part of the core business strategies of the world's largest green coffee trader. The overlap between TNCs' interests and those of small farmers is limited and refers to relatively short-term economic interests. Any transformative goals of cooperatives towards the creation of a social and solidarity economy that is guided by local community and societal interests is not easily compatible with the interests of highly mobile big capital. The co-option of the former by the latter needs to be understood and communicated to allow a sober evaluation of the benefits – in form of limited improvements of living standards – and risks to the cooperative goals of structural transformation.

## Notes

1 See, for example the websites of Volcafe (which owns Kyagalanyi Ltd. and is itself part of E.D.&F. MAN) and the Interamerican Coffee Company (owned by Neumann Kaffee Gruppe). Volcafe says it provides "social and economic support" and references "group origin companies" as a means by which they promote sustainable

production. The Interamerican Coffee Company states that part of their mission is to "build, support and foster sustainable relationships with [...] suppliers, customers and communities and the environment."

2 In some cases, TNCs were able to fill the financing gap left by the collapse of cooperative banks and the disinterest of commercial banks to provide loans to small farmers. The TNC Olam, for example, offers interest-free financing for cacao farmers in Côte d'Ivoire, which allows the TNC to compete with local traders that offer cash advances. However, all of the thus-supplied financial services are limited to the production of un- or primary-processed commodities.

3 However, in Uganda both the National Development Plan (NDP) II and the Agricultural Strategic Sector Plan (ASSP) include support for contract farming schemes and support for large-scale agro-processors.

4 Arabica makes up 75–80 percent of the world's coffee production, while the lower-quality Robusta beans account for only 20–25 percent.

5 See, for example, the G20 initiative Compact with Africa, which seeks to mobilize corporate and institutional investment for industrialization, which in many participating countries will be heavily dependent on an expansion of agro-processing.

6 Kyagalanyi is part of Volcafe, a privately-owned transnational commodity trading company that was taken over by the E.D.&F. MAN Group to create the world's largest coffee trading group.

7 However, the psychological pressure seemed to be significant, judging from interviews and focus group discussions with group farmers.

8 For information provided by the foundation itself, see https://www.hrnstiftung.org/uganda.

9 The present analysis focuses on the first initiative, due to the more complete evaluations that were available for this part of the project at the time of writing.

10 Funds are provided by the European Union, the Bill & Melinda Gates Foundation, the AgriBusiness Initiative Trust (mainly DANIDA funded), USAID programs, FAO, the Jacobs Foundation, the Douwe Egberts Foundation, and the "International Coffee Partners" (http://www.coffee-partners.org).

11 Quality of Life Metrics: "Assets, transport, waste disposal, nutrition, house type, source of water, savings, school enrolment rates" (Loisa 2011, p. 16).

## References


AMANOR, K.S. 2012, 'Global resource grabs, agribusiness concentration and the smallholder: two West African case studies', *The Journal of Peasant Studies*, 39(3–4), 731–749.

COTULA, L. 2012, 'The international political economy of the global land rush: A critical appraisal of trends, scale, geography, and drivers', *The Journal of Peasant Studies*, 39, 649–680.

DAVIRON, B. and PONTE, S. 2005, *The coffee paradox: Global markets, commodity trade and the elusive promise of development*, Zed books.

DA SILVA, C. 2005, 'The Growing Role of Contract Farming in Agri-Food Systems Development: Drivers, Theory and Practice,'Food and Agriculture Organization of the United Nations (FAO).

DOSS, C., MEINZEN-DICK, R. & BOMUHANGI, A. 2014, 'Who Owns the Land? Perspectives from Rural Ugandans and Implications for Large-Scale Land Acquisitions', *Feminist Economics*, 20.

EATON, C. & SHEPHERD, A. 2001, 'Contract Farming: Partnerships for Growth, Numéro 145', Food and Agriculture Organization of the United Nations (FAO), 166Pages.

FOLD, N. 2008, 'Transnational sourcing practices in Ghana's perennial crop sectors. Journal of Agrarian Change', 8(1), 94–122.

GIBBON, P. & S.Ponte. 2005, *Trading Down: Africa, Value Chains, and the Global Economy*, Temple University Press.

GLOVER, D. & KUSTERER, K. 1990, *Small Farmers, Big Business: Contract Farming and Rural Development*, International Political Economy Series, Palgrave McMillan, 170 pages.

GLOVER, D. 1990, 'Contract farming and Outgrower Schemes in East and Southern Africa', *Journal of Agricultural Economics*, 41(3), 303–315.

GOU 2015, 'Second National Development Plan (NDPII): 2015/16–2019/20', Kampala, Uganda.

GOWA, A. 2001, 'The Path Forward in Uganda's Coffee Sector', Prepared for the Presidential Conference on Export Competitiveness, February 2002, Kampala, Uganda.

GREENHALGH, P., & KITCHING, S. 2005, 'Commodity Warehouse Receipts and the Uganda Coffee Sector', *Report for CFC UNOPS WRS Project.*

GROSH, B. 1994, 'Contract Farming in Africa: An Application of the New Institutional Economics', *Journal of African Economies* 3(2), 231–261.

HRNS 2017, 'Hanns R. Neumann Stiftung', Available from: <https://www.hrnstiftung.org/uganda>. [17 November 2017].

LI, T.M. 2011, 'Centering labor in the land grab debate', *Journal of Peasant Studies*, 38(2), 281–298.

LITTLE, P.D. & Watts, M.J. 1994, *Living Under Contract* (Eds.), University of Wisconsin Press, Madison.

LOISA, K. 2011, 'Building coffee farms alliances in Uganda', *CFAU project: baseline study report.* Hanns R. Neumann Stiftung. Nairobi, Kenya.

MAAIF 2016, 'Agriculture Sector Strategic Plan: 2015/16–2019/20', Republic of Uganda, Entebbe.

OYA, C. 2012, 'Contract farming in sub-Saharan Africa: a survey of approaches, debates and issues', *Journal of Agrarian Change*, 12(1), pp. 1–33.

REARDON, T. & BARRETT, C.B. 2000, 'Agroindustrialization, globalization, and international development: an overview of issues, patterns, and determinants', *Agricultural Economics*, 23(3), 195–205.

RIBBINK, G., NYABUNTU, P. & KUMAR, S. 2005, 'Successful Supply Chains in Uganda: A study of three successful chains in the coffee, dried fruit and fresh vegetables sectors', ILO, Geneva and DFID, London.

TECHEL, G., & WANDA, K. 2014, 'Building coffee farmers' alliances in Uganda: project evaluation', *Final Report*, Unique Forestry and Land Use GmbH, Kampala, Uganda.

UCDA 1995–2017, 'Annual and Monthly Reports', Available from: <www.ugandacoffee.go.ug>.Uganda Coffee Development Authority, Kampala, Uganda.

UCFA 2017, 'Roles', Uganda Coffee Farmers Alliance., Available from: <http://www.ucfa.or.ug>. [17 November 2017].

UGANDA ELECTRONIC SINGLE WINDOW 2018, Available from: <www.trademarkea.com>. [15 January 2018].

WEDIG, K. 2018, 'Water grabbing or sustainable development? Effects of aquaculture growth in neoliberal Uganda', In: WIEGRATZ, J., MARTINIELLO, G. & GRECO, E. (eds.) *Uganda: The dynamics of neoliberal transformation*, Zed Books, London.

WIEGRATZ, J., 2016, *Neoliberal Moral Economy: Capitalism, Socio-Cultural Change and Fraud in Uganda*, Rowman & Littlefield International, London.

WOODHOUSE, P. 2012, 'New investment, old challenges. Land deals and the water constraint in African agriculture', *The Journal of Peasant Studies*, 39:3–4, pp. 777–794.

ZIMNY, Z. 2009, 'FDI and TNCs in Agriculture of Developing Countries', Background paper for the UNCTAD 2009 World Investment Report "Transnational Corporations, Agricultural Production and Development', UNCTAD, Geneva.

# 7 Conclusion

## Economic organization under adverse conditions

Based on previously unavailable ethnographic and survey-based evidence from Uganda's coffee sector, this book has examined the development of cooperatives in Africa's agricultural export markets. The discussion has illuminated the political and economic conditions and the internal organizational characteristics that allow agricultural cooperatives to improve the economic prospects of their farmer-members and engender institutional changes, at the national level, that strengthen the interests of small farmers vis-à-vis stronger economic actors and the state. In this book, I have argued that member-based, democratically organized cooperatives that pursue a transformative agenda of social and economic change, including a redistribution of resources, face adverse conditions in African export agriculture, because of narrowly-defined public sector support and sometimes antagonistic state-cooperative relations, as well as significant power asymmetries in favor of transnational corporations.

In the late 2000s, about two decades after neoliberal reforms led to the dismantling of the often poorly-functioning state institutions that had controlled agricultural exports, the Government of Uganda, alongside other African governments and international donors, once again started to support producer organizations – this time as a civil society driven solution to rural poverty and inequality. Governments and donors are investing in the creation of cooperative policies, the reintroduction of dedicated state institutions, and support programs that strengthen the capacities of small farmers' organizations. However, state support to cooperatives remains limited, despite an official rhetoric that hails cooperatives as a triple-win instrument for rural development, helping to i) improve the economic prospects of small farmers, ii) stabilize supply for international buyers and processors, and iii) increase the country's expert earnings. A review of Uganda's cooperative policies and institutions has illuminated a top-down state engagement with cooperatives, which undermines the autonomy and democracy principles of cooperatives. Many regulations pertaining to small farmers' organizations remain vague with regard to the transformative goals that the cooperative movement pursues: they are either deficient in their enforceability or

*Figure 7.1* Small producer in Maguze Village, Sironko District

directly fail to tackle the main barriers for a cooperative-friendly economic and political environment.

Furthermore, the success of cooperatives in achieving their transformative goals is under attack by the expanding and increasingly sophisticated CSR-like support programs of some large buyers and processors. These programs focus on creating limited economic benefits for small farmers, while advancing a de-politicized version of cooperatives that largely accommodate the existing power asymmetries in agricultural value chains. The relevant TNCs have significant market power in Africa's export agriculture and given that profit opportunities in production have become less interesting, their focus lies on the ability to secure greater volumes of crops for processing. Their limited shared interests with small producers include productivity growth and improved quality of raw or semi-processed agricultural commodities. This book has provided new ethnographic evidence of TNCs' relations with small farmers and has examined one larger donor-funded corporate support program for small farmers, showing how the latter actively advances the co-option of the existing cooperative movement by creating parallel organizational structures that promote a narrowly-defined business cooperative model. In case of a large-scale rollout of such programs, the existing homegrown cooperative movement, which aims at strengthening small farmers' legal, economic, and social capacities to defend their interests vis-à-vis more powerful economic actors and the state, is under threat.

## The potential of cooperatives as an instrument for change

The analysis of agricultural and non-agricultural employment relations as well as agricultural production and marketing conditions in Uganda clearly shows that economic organization among small producers and wage workers is essential to advance equality in the context of weakly regulated labor markets and buyer-driven agricultural value chains. The labor market data presented in this book demonstrate the discriminatory nature of informally regulated labor relations. At the same time, wage work has steadily become more important for small farmers – who have been described as *farmers-cum-wageworkers* in an attempt to capture their dependence on multiple and precarious income sources. Given the almost complete lack of formal labor organization in rural Africa, cooperatives emerge as a key instrument for advancing a redistribution agenda that can provide the basis for inclusive rural development processes. As the most prevalent form of permanent economic organization in rural Africa, agricultural cooperatives can improve the economic prospects of farmers-cum-wageworkers through better access to financial services, training, and market linkages. Importantly, cooperatives are the only widespread type of formal economic organization that strengthens the capacities of large numbers of rural people to engender institutional change processes that aim at improving precarious conditions of reproduction for an economically marginalized majority.

An ethnographic and survey-based investigation of the development and functioning of different types of cooperatives in Uganda's coffee sector has also illuminated how cooperatives may contribute to the reproduction of local relations of inequality. The micro-level data presented in this book highlights that cooperatives can be economically viable, at least in the short term, while excluding some, often the poorest, members from the benefits of price premiums that are achieved through bulk-selling agreements. In the longer term, however, maintaining economic viability becomes more closely related to an organization's ability to *reduce* inequalities, because cooperatives depend on attracting and keeping growing numbers of productive farmer-members. In sum, cooperatives are more likely to remain economically viable and continue to grow, if they are able to reach large numbers of farmers with tangible economic benefits and also contribute to greater equality in the distribution of these benefits among members.

Under the pressures of neoliberal reforms and in the absence of any significant social protection by the state, large numbers of small producers are unable to commit to the medium-term economic strategies of cooperatives. These sections of the rural population become "too poor to organize", but some cooperatives have developed supportive institutional mechanisms that reduce entry barriers to cooperative membership and ensure a minimum safety net that reduces the defection rates of the poorest members. In-depth case studies of medium-sized and larger cooperatives in Uganda have illuminated the ability of such organizations to develop and maintain functional democratic structures of representation for their members. This ability stands in stark contrast to the insights gained from a case study of a small, community-based organization, which is characterized by undemocratic internal organizational structures that allow numerous footholds for an elite capture of resources at the local level. Overall, the book has highlighted the ability of larger member-based organizations, which entail local, regional, and national organizational structures, to allow disadvantaged groups to disrupt elite capture of resources at the local level and to initiate and advance broader social change processes in distributional patterns.

## Formal versus informal economic organization

The evidence from Uganda's agricultural and non-agricultural labor markets has highlighted the limited ability of informal labor organizations to end exploitative labor relations in large and small enterprises, and within families or clans. For the coffee sector, it was shown that informal labor organization, including labor gangs and sporadic labor action, plays an important role in regulating access to jobs, negotiating wages and pushing for minor improvements in working conditions. However, it can also lead to the creation of new inequalities, for example if local labor gang leaders exploit their broker position between employers and workers. Furthermore, informal labor organization emerged as a weak instrument for the generation of structural changes in the regulation of labor market transactions: while it is likely to strengthen organizational capacities among workers, it fails to offer opportunities for improving the representation of workers' interests beyond the individual employer. Negotiation processes based on informal labor organization generally remain confined to the local level or, in most cases, to the individual work place, so that the concessions that workers extract from employers will apply only to the workforce of that employer, often only temporarily, and not to the sector in general. Informal labor organization may still contribute to improved economic prospects for marginalized and disadvantaged people, but its shortcomings indicate that it may not necessarily contribute to greater economic equality or even substantial transformative change.

The data presented from small, community-based cooperatives in Uganda confirms this by showing how these organizations allow for the reproduction of existing inequalities among their members, while also having weak socio-economic effects in general. Informal and small-scale forms of organization, therefore, seem to be no substitute for larger organizational structures that allow for the representation of subaltern interests in political negotiation processes and at higher levels of administration. Such larger organizational frameworks entail problems of their own, most notably the tendency to a closing of ranks between local elites and different management levels, which frustrates the development of democratic structures within an organization (and possibly does so without reducing its economic viability in the short term). However, the nature and development of medium-sized and larger cooperatives in Uganda's coffee sector highlights how greater equality in socio-economic outcomes for members may directly contribute to the achievement of economic viability. The ability of these organizations to ensure the sustained increase of rates of growth and productivity – and thus contribute to greater economic equality – depends on the ability of all members to share in the benefits. If the poorest members are not able to participate on equal terms in the organization's activities, defection rates are likely to increase, thereby threatening the organization's economic viability. Thus, a positive causal link between the improvement of aggregate welfare levels and the reduction of inequalities emerges in the context of these organizations.

Finally, yet importantly, the possible spillover effects from dynamically developing cooperatives to the expansion of rural labor organizations are noteworthy. The similarities of the internal organizational characteristics of larger cooperatives and trade unions, but also the multiple survival strategies of farmers-cum-wageworkers may strengthen the potential for such spillover effects. Thus, a strong base of active members and well-functioning representational structures at different organizational levels are crucial for the ability of both trade unions and cooperatives to improve their members' economic prospects and defend their rights vis-à-vis stronger economic actors and the state. The establishment of relatively flexible, transparent, and democratic structures in some cooperatives can provide important lessons for the expansion of trade and agricultural labor unions in rural Uganda. As the discussion of informal labor organization in the coffee sector has shown, labor gangs and sporadic labor action is unlikely to contribute to an improved representation of workers beyond individual work places.

Overall, the data from Uganda indicate that cooperatives may, at least in the short term, contribute to improved economic prospects for most of their members without addressing existing inequalities in heterogeneous rural societies. However, they can, under certain conditions, contribute to greater economic equality through the advancement of progressive institutional change and a redistribution agenda in favor of small producers. While these conditions are historically specific, some factors were singled out that could occur across countries, thereby according the Ugandan case a wider relevance.

First, the conditions for wider social change, at least at the local level, need to be favorable. This might be the case when external factors, such as the collapse of the monopolistic cooperative system or political change processes lead to disruptions in existing power relations and a weakening of local elites. Against this background, the realization of social agency by disadvantaged groups to achieve more equality in socio-economic outcomes at the local level becomes more likely. Second, a supportive economic and political environment is essential for the success of cooperatives and other member-based organizations. This includes the existence of effective state institutions that ensure the provision of an appropriate infrastructure for locally-owned agricultural production and marketing, and a regulation of foreign direct investment that balances the need for capital with the necessity to nurture the development of locally-owned processing capacities. Third, cooperatives need to be able to function independently of the state to reduce the likelihood of political capture. In the past, managers of cooperatives have turned member-based organizations into instruments for accessing political and economic power in the state, thereby abusing democratic organizational structures and frequently and significantly reducing the economic viability of the affected cooperatives. Fourth, cooperatives need to provide access to larger organizational frameworks to allow members to bypass local elites if necessary, while ensuring the influx of new ideas and concepts at the local level. This strengthens the capacities of disadvantaged groups to influence organizational development and institutional change, either through participation in decision-making processes, or through the promotion of changes in the dominant social norms and practices that legitimate existing distributional patterns.

To conclude, this book has argued that cooperatives, under certain conditions, can contribute to greater economic equality and the transformation of societies on the basis of economic solidarity and democracy. Against the background of increasing numbers of farmers-cum-wageworkers, and the persistence of poor economic prospects for the majority of the working population, the dynamic development of cooperatives provides an essential starting point for a wider discussion of organizational approaches to improve living standards in low-income countries. The social and economic effects of cooperatives and labor organizations are closely linked to and to some extent dependent on the institutional framework in which such organizations operate. To allow democratic, member-based organizations to function effectively, the design and implementation of institutional rules to ensure the development of relevant infrastructure and to mitigate existing inequalities in distributional patterns is essential. Furthermore, these organizations themselves need to provide access to a wider institutional framework to allow disadvantaged groups to protect their rights in the face of local structures of organization that are dominated by elites.

# Index

Entries in *italic* refer to figures and those in **bold** denote tables.